DATE DUE

DE 2102			
DE 7 05			

THE NEW RIGHT IN CHILE, 1973–97

ST ANTONY'S SERIES
General Editor: Eugene Rogan (1997–), Fellow of St Antony's College, Oxford

Titles include:

St Antony's Series
Series Standing Order ISBN 0–333–71109–2
(*outside North America only*)

You can receive future titles in this series as they are published by placing a standing order.
Please contact your bookseller or, in case of difficulty, write to us at the address below with
your name and address, the title of the series and the ISBN quoted above.

Customer Services Department, Macmillan Distribution Ltd
Houndmills, Basingstoke, Hampshire RG21 6XS, England

The New Right in Chile 1973–97

Marcelo Pollack
Research Associate
Institute for European–Latin American Relations
Madrid

First published in Great Britain 1999 by
MACMILLAN PRESS LTD
Houndmills, Basingstoke, Hampshire RG21 6XS and London
Companies and representatives throughout the world

A catalogue record for this book is available from the British Library.

ISBN 0–333–72473–9

First published in the United States of America 1999 by

10

ication Data

elo Pollack.

index.

ISBN 0-312-22278-3 (cloth)

1. Conservatism—Chile—History—20th century.   2. Chile—Politics
and government—1973–   I. Title.   II. Series.
JC573.2.C5P64   1999
320.983'09049—dc21   99–21776
                                                                CIP

This book is printed on paper suitable for recycling and made from fully managed and
sustained forest sources.

10   9   8   7   6   5   4   3   2   1
08   07   06   05   04   03   02   01   00   99

Printed and bound in Great Britain by
Antony Rowe Ltd, Chippenham, Wiltshire

To Kate Joyce and Alan Angell
for their invaluable help and moral support

Contents

Introduction

Chile has throughout its history been a country at the centre of international interest, partly the result of its rich mineral resources and relatively stable political system. The left-wing *Unidad Popular* government (1970–3), led by President Salvador Allende, attracted particular worldwide attention, given that its radical reform programme, and the viability of democratic socialism itself, posed a question of universal importance for the left: could there be a peaceful transition to socialism in a pluralistic and democratic society? Yet the right-wing military coup of 11 September 1973, the ferocity of which caused shock waves around the world, shattered not only the country's long democratic tradition, but facilitated the implementation of the earliest and most radical neo-liberal economic liberalization programme. Although the armed forces, led by General Augusto Pinochet, finally relinquished power on 11 March 1990, the military still retains considerable authority and autonomy, while the civilian governments are severely restrained by the military-imposed 1980 constitution.

Although much attention has focused on the reaction of the left, both domestic and international, to the events surrounding the 1973 coup and its aftermath, this study will focus on the question of how the Chilean right, politically and economically dominant during the authoritarian Pinochet regime, has adapted both to functioning within a democratic framework and as a loyal opposition force.[1] While it is still, in many cases, too early to assess adequately whether the right has been successful in becoming a fully democratic opposition, it is nevertheless instructive to analyse what steps have been taken so far by the right in inserting itself into the democratic process, and from this to hypothesize on future developments.

In the last two decades, the Latin American right has expanded its level of influence. Its ideas and policies appear hegemonic within as well as beyond the region. Even traditionally hostile anti-marketeers such as the Peronists in Argentina and the *Partido Revolucionario Institucional* (PRI) in Mexico have become converts to neo-liberal dogma, some for pragmatic reasons, others through ideological conviction. In Brazil, the centrality of the state was accepted by liberals, conservatives and the left. Yet today, virtually every party has expressed the need to restructure it. The right, while

1

not being extensively represented in parliament, was highly influential in the presidential elections and in the policy-making process. Brazilian President Fernando Henrique Cardoso has reformed the constitution to allow private sector participation in state companies such as Petrobras and Telebras (the oil and telecommunications state monopolies), which were previously the 'sacred cows' of Brazilian industry. In Peru too, the new right has been expanding since the 1980s. It is now not only a vigorous political force but is gradually emerging as an important reference point in Peru's political spectrum. While Mario Vargas Llosa's neo-liberal *Fredemo* coalition had been expected to win the 1990 general election, the eventual winner, the populist Alberto Fujimori, introduced similar economic shock policies. His re-election in 1995 represented further evidence of the electoral capital to be gained from pursuing strict neo-liberal policies in the fight against inflation. In Chile, despite losing the 1989 and 1993 presidential elections and the 1997 mid-term congressional elections, the right was still able to poll over 30 per cent.[2]

Studies of the right are also critical in advancing our understanding of groups that have played an important part in the democratic transition process. When examining the left, we are, for the most part, dealing with a philosophy of the dispossessed, the marginal and the weak. In contrast, the right, as representatives of the privileged and the powerful, occupy an influential and pivotal position. The armed forces, the media, the economic conglomerates and the business sector, all have the capacity to determine, in one way or another, the course of the democratization process. The often informal and personal interconnectedness of the right means that these groups have been closely linked to power in a manner that is most problematic for institutionalizing democratic regimes. Democracy, after all, requires institutions which are capable of ensuring that group demands are transmitted fairly and accurately, and that groups are subject to accountability. It is problematic, and often very difficult to assess, to what extent the personal, bureaucratic and clientelistic ties traditionally linking the right to state power have evolved into institutionalized, accountable and responsible representation.

While comprehensive studies of the right in Europe and the United States are abundant, there is a paucity of literature relating to the Latin American context. Of course, studies have been undertaken, but these have tended to concentrate on specific groups, such as economic conglomerates, entrepreneurs and theorists. Very little attempt has been made to bring all of these interconnected elements together.

Furthermore, studies have tended to focus on the left to the exclusion of the right. The left being viewed as ever-changing, heterogeneous and reactive, while the right, in contrast, has been categorized as homogeneous and static. As this examination of the Latin American right will show, however, such assumptions are misleading.[3]

But why is the Chilean right of particular interest? First, it was unique in its ability to develop and carry out, without any democratic constraints, a global project based on ideals marginal to the country's political and cultural traditions. Indeed, unlike Ernesto Zedillo in Mexico, Carlos Menem in Argentina, Alberto Fujimori in Peru and Fernando Henrique Cardoso in Brazil, Pinochet and his team faced few opponents in their quest to implement painful economic policies.

Second, the Chilean right was successful in combining a monetarist economic policy with a social and political theory, the function of which became to strengthen and legitimize the intended model. For most of Latin America, neo-liberalism was applied and became articulated in a more restricted 'economic' sense. For example, many see the introduction of neo-liberalism in Brazil as an improvised reaction following the collapse of the country's developmentalist model, while in Peru, the creation of the new right could be seen as more the result of backlash politics precipitated by the 1987 nationalization of the banking system. Only in Chile was the neo-liberal model applied in tandem with a committed social and political project.

Third, the Chilean new right, unlike its counterparts elsewhere in Latin America, was successful in transforming itself into a party political force. This was largely due to Chile's long tradition of party politics. Although Pinochet was successful in repressing all forms of political expression, one thing he was unable to break, and eventually forced reluctantly to accept, was Chile's dominant party system. In Brazil, the right is one of the least institutionalized in terms of political parties. Most of the entrepreneurs and right-wing intellectual associations are not yet integrated into the party system. There are parties associated with neo-liberalism, but they lack socio-political grounding and have little, if no, political representation. While the Mexican *Partido Acción Nacional* (PAN) does represent neo-liberal interests, its dominant ideology remains Catholic social doctrine. Its liberalism is only evident when business groups resort to the PAN as a vehicle for electoral politics. The PRI's conversion to the free market bandwagon extinguished what little fire the PAN possessed, although as a consequence of the PRI's current political difficulties, the party is enjoying a resurgence in support. Meanwhile, the

Argentine UCeDE remains small. After all, what influence can it possibly hope to exercise with the presence of a dominant revisionist Peronist movement?

Fourth, Chile was used as a laboratory in which foreign theories, programmes and strategies were implemented without any of the constraints normally associated with western liberal democracies. The Chilean neo-liberal experiment was the first of its kind in the developing world, as well as in the industrialized economies. When Chile began to reorient its economy in 1975 most other countries were still grappling with developmentalist and Keynesian models. Budding neo-liberals from other countries looked to Chile for inspiration and education. Chile's experiment has also been applied longer than anywhere else, and remains in operation to this day.

Fifth, most Latin American businessmen do not adhere to a strict neo-liberal model.[4] The debate over free markets versus protectionism is still raging. And while most businessmen may approve of the descriptive neo-liberal analysis, many disapprove of its prescriptive tendencies. In Chile the situation is very different, having experienced over 24 years of 'rolling back the state'. As a consequence, most now favour a strict neo-liberal approach.[5]

Chapter 1 will advance a theoretical framework for the study of the Chilean new right. What exactly do we mean when we refer to the right? Several interpretations have emerged including: the economistic Marxist approach in which the right is viewed merely as a mechanism for the defence of private property, the essentialist definition which claims there exists a common set of principles which in themselves reflect accurately the nature of the right; and also the more organic view of the right as a dynamic philosophical and movementalist phenomenon. This chapter also examines the diverse strands of liberal and conservative thought, their implicit regional variations, and how these are relevant to a study of the Chilean right.

Chapter 2 analyses the historical and ideological roots of the Chilean new right, which evolved out of previously marginal ideologies: the Catholic ultra-conservative *gremialista* movement and the Chicago-trained monetarist economists. A philosophical explanation of this pre-coup right is accompanied by a political and historical analysis of the changes which took place within the various movements prior to 1973. Of particular importance is the question as to how the *gremialistas* and the Chicago Boys, both based at the prestigious Catholic University in Santiago, succeeded in becoming the vanguard in the political campaign against the left-wing *Unidad*

Popular government. This chapter also examines how the traditional actors of the right, the *Partido Nacional* (PN) and the entrepreneurial sector, readily accepted the insurrectional aspirations of the *gremialistas* and the Chicago economists, which culminated in the 1973 military coup.

Chapter 3 explores the right's reaction to Pinochet's military insurrection and how it chose to abandon its political responsibilities in favour of the armed forces. This unleashed an ideological battle among those previously marginal right-wing sectors, including not only the *gremialistas* and Chicago economists, but an amalgam of nationalist groups, in an attempt to influence the military regime. The chapter also explores how the nationalists and other marginal tendencies were finally excluded to the benefit of the *gremialistas* and the Chicago Boys, who now began a process of ideological amalgamation in an attempt to maximize their influence within the military.

Chapter 4 examines the right's institutional and political legacy: the so-called *siete modernizaciones* and the 1980 constitution. The modernizations, inspired by the Chicago Boys economist team, infused market forces into the country's social relations network. In contrast, the 1980 constitution was written virtually singlehanded by the founder of *gremialismo*, Jaime Guzmán, and sought legally to bind the military's economic, social and political model in order to secure its survival.

Chapter 5 examines the political consequences of the economic crisis which plunged Chile into recession in 1981–3. The ensuing political crisis led the right to re-examine what was until then its dominant political position. The right recognized that if its hegemonic position was now likely to be undermined, and that consequently a transition to democracy would become inevitable, it would have to examine the best way of confronting this challenge. The parties on the centre and the left, although much reduced as a result of the repressive measures adopted by the military regime, re-emerged as the principal opposition to a government in economic and political crisis. The right had no option but to organize itself along similar party political lines. Two principal tendencies emerged by the mid-1980s: the *Unión Demócrata Independiente* (UDI), which grouped together the principal supporters of the military regime, the *gremialistas* and the Chicago economists; and *Renovación Nacional* (RN), which sought to rekindle, albeit in modern form, the representatives of the traditional pre-1973 party right. The chapter also examines the right's response to the 1988 plebiscite which led to the downfall of the military regime. The debates which surrounded this electoral contest, in which the only candidate was Pinochet himself, set the scene for the internecine warfare, which has since afflicted these two parties.

Chapter 6 examines the nature of RN and UDI and how their constituent parts differed from those existent before the coup. While RN has attempted to promote a strategy involving the reinsertion of the parties into the democratic process and has sought to distance itself from the legacy of the military regime, UDI has evolved as the political and civilian voice for the Pinochet administration and its political, economic and social legacy.

Chapter 7 moves on to explore in more detail RN and UDI's internal organization and financing, as well as the social sectors which both have sought to attract. The argument advanced is that the internal makeup of these parties has been shaped by the groups that they have targeted, beyond their natural base of support. UDI has succeeded in penetrating sectors normally alien to the right, the marginalized urban popular classes, while RN has expanded into those middle-class, politically moderate sectors which represent the traditional electoral fodder of the *Partido Demócrata Cristiano* (PDC), Chile's most powerful political party since the mid-1960s.

Chapter 8 explores the parties' policy agenda and political strategy, which have also been shaped by the new electoral constituencies. RN and UDI's differences are partly ideological, but also reflect their different styles and strategic options. While RN aspires to become a mass-based, media-oriented, western-style democratic centre-right party, UDI has developed into an elite-based, ideologically rigorous, morally conservative and economically hardline semi-authoritarian movement. These differences, as well as certain ideological affinities, have meant that RN and UDI find themselves in the impossible position of not knowing whether they should cooperate or compete with each other.

Chapter 9 assesses the electoral consequences of this reality. Electoral results show that the right performed well in the 1989 and 1993 presidential elections and the 1997 mid-term congressional elections. Its electoral support may even have been boosted by the existence of two very different right-wing organizations. However, an inability to adhere faithfully to the rules of the democratic game, for reasons outlined in the chapter, means that the right's electoral effectiveness has been damaged. Unless the right develops a viable, and alternative, programmatic identity, as well as a mature and fully democratic approach to politics, and a strong, national organization, its prospects for improved performance in future elections are uncertain. And while the left may welcome such a prospect, this outcome may have damaging repercussions for Chile's democratic consolidation process.

Part I
The Right in Authoritarianism

1 Theories of the Right

Before examining the particulars of this case-study we must first ask ourselves whether it is possible to produce an acceptable definition of the right. Are we alluding to a single, static ideology, or to a series of disparate, dynamic philosophical doctrines? Can we examine the right only in terms of tangible political movements, or should we simply define it as a loose amalgam of diverse and sometimes incompatible interest groups? The right must surely be understood in terms of all three: as ideology, movement and coalition of interests. The inadequacy of existing definitions lies in the fact that, on the whole, they ignore or misunderstand the complex and evolving nature of the right. Political scientists have tended to concentrate on a specific property, be it the right as political movement or ideology. Very rarely have they approached the question with an adequate holistic understanding of the issues involved. Walter Theimer, for example, in the *Encyclopedia of World Politics*, limits his definition to a purely physical and somewhat tautological interpretation of right-wing political parties. In his view, conservative parties are those whose representatives in parliament sit on the right-hand side when viewed from the president's chair.[1] Of course, this spatial representation of left and right stems from the seating arrangement in the post-1789 French National Assembly in which the nobility and clergy sat on the right and the third estate on the left. The ideological components revolved around three set of issues. Politically, the right was associated with defending the concept of absolute monarchism, the left with universal suffrage. Economically, the right defended the feudal state while the left espoused the virtues of the free market. Socially, the right represented the aspirations of the Catholic Church while the left leaned towards secularism.[2] While this definition is appropriate for a specific examination of the post-revolutionary French right it does not satisfy the requirements of a more global (post-Eurocentric) and less historically specific analysis of the right. Clearly, while the French right were defenders of absolute monarchy, their English counterparts tended to accept the parliamentary model. Also, religion was a key component of the French conservatives, whereas elsewhere a more class-based polarization often emerged. The picture was further complicated in the last quarter of the nineteenth century. With the rise of economic *laissez-faire* ideas in both

Europe and North America the whole political spectrum moved left-wards. As such, many of those who had previously been on the left now found themselves defending the status quo. The conflict no longer involved the landed aristocracy and the bourgeoisie, but both the emerging business and working classes.

The political models developed in the 1950s by North American social scientists such as Seymour Lipset attempted to create a more acceptable typology of left and right. In *Political Man*, Lipset established three categories for right-wing movements. A *centre* consisting of the classic fascist movements, a corporatist and nationalist *left* and a conservative *right*. While Lipset's broad categories solve the problem of differentiation, they also reflect a central preoccupation of the social science literature of the period: that is, regime type and political movements. A preoccupation which resulted in the exclusion of such fundamental concerns as ideology.

A third approach stems from orthodox Marxist analysis which sees ideology as 'superstructural' and the state as an instrument of the ruling class. In these terms, the right is perceived as a cluster of ideas whose sole function is to reinforce the false consciousness of the masses and to defend private property and the capitalist state.[3] This definition would locate the *Partido Demócrata Cristiano* (PDC) and the *Partido Socialista de Chile* (PSCh) on the right. As such, the approach is excessively reductionist, obscuring any meaningful distinctions between (left- and right-wing) political parties. Orthodox Marxists would argue that such distinctions are meaningless and that the pursuit of logical consistency in an ideological model is misleading. The end, not the means, gives meaning to an ideology. All ideas are thus intrinsically linked to the dynamics of class struggle.[4] The economistic approach also fails to find an acceptable classification for issues which escape orthodox Marxist categories, such as abortion, divorce and crime.

A fourth approach attempts to produce an essentialist definition. This would recognize that differences do exist between the myriad of right-wing ideologies, but holds that there remains a common core. An approach of this form was employed by Robert Nisbet in his seminal work, *The Sociological Tradition*. In dealing with the history of philosophical doctrines, Nisbet breaks up the various components into 'unit-ideas': community (religion, work, family), authority (the structure of an association and its given legitimacy), status (the hierarchy of prestige and influence), the sacred (non-rational and religious modes of behaviour) and alienation (the view of man as estranged and rootless when cut off from the community). Each idea being located within a conceptual polarity, thus community–society, authority–power, status–class, sacred–secular, alienation–progress.[5] This schema might be perceived as the historic conflict between tradition and modernism, between right and left.

Roger Scruton is more specific and provides a definition of right-wing ideology which includes: doctrines of social obligation framed in terms of obedience, legitimacy and piety, rather than contract, consent and justice; a resistance to liberalizing reforms in the law; cultural conservatism; respect for the hereditary principle and prescriptive rights; belief in private property, not as a natural right, but as an indispensable part of the condition of society; belief in elementary freedoms and in the irreplaceable value of the individual as against the collective; a belief in free enterprise and a capitalist economy as the only mode of production compatible with human freedom; and varying degrees of belief in human imperfectibility and original sin.[6]

Definitions such as these pose a variety of problems. First, key terms are poorly explicated and often vague. For example, what exactly does Scruton mean by 'elementary freedom'? Is it the freedom not to starve, to be in possession of employment, or does it refer to freedom of speech and/or movement?[7] Second, some aspects of the definition appear contradictory. For example, there seems to a theoretical tension between the commitment to authority and tradition on the one hand, and the belief in individualism and the free market on the other. Third, while these attempts to establish some kind of coherent set of values are in themselves useful, they tend to be both static and Eurocentric. This, of course, does not undermine the value of the approach but does illustrate its limitations. Both Nisbet's and Scruton's definitions are adequate in the sense of accurately reflecting the ideology of a specific group at a specific point in time and in a particular place. However, while providing a useful 'snapshot', such approaches fail to be more generally applicable.

The inadequacies of the above approaches opens the way for a fifth, which emerges as the most appropriate for dealing with the Chilean right. This method does not see the term *right* as referring to an ideology in the sense of delineating a coherent set of values. Instead, it is understood simply as a spatial reference point which links various styles of thoughts which have emerged as responses to the left.[8] As such there is no requirement for consistency between the various strands of right-wing ideology. This framework, for example, enables us to view the eighteenth-century reactionary and moderate right in Europe as a response to the Enlightenment, and the radical and extreme right of the late nineteenth and early twentieth centuries as a reaction to the rise of socialism. This method thus circumvents the myopia of more traditional approaches which claim universality but simply provide a static and Eurocentric picture of the right. This is a framework, therefore, that takes into account national idiosyncrasies and categorizes the right not as static but as a dynamic and evolutionary force.

THE TRADITIONAL RIGHT: LIBERALS AND CONSERVATIVES

Liberalism appeared in Europe at the end of the eighteenth century and established itself as a political force in the nineteenth. Its central tenet was devotion to the individual and his political, civil and social rights. What tradition was to the conservative, individual autonomy was to the liberal. It stood for individualism against hierarchy, free trade as opposed to intervention and freedom of thought in contrast to the confessional state. Norman Barry highlights some of the basic tenets of classical liberalism.[9] These include the individual as the source of his own moral values; trade and exchange between individuals as the most efficient and freedom-enhancing process of relations; the market as a spontaneous tool for the allocation of resources; and exchange between nations as the most efficient way of maximizing wealth and reducing international conflict.[10]

Conservatism is an offspring of the Industrial and French Revolutions. What the two revolutions engendered – democracy, technology and secularism – the conservatives attacked. If the central ethos of liberalism was individual freedom, the ethos of conservatism was tradition; with emphasis on community, kinship, hierarchy, authority and religion.[11] Norman Barry summarizes the basic tenets of conservative thinking: a view of human nature which stresses ignorance (because the future cannot be known, it cannot be planned for, except negatively); espousal of a pessimistic view of human nature because of a belief in the corruptibility of man; and a belief in the rule of law, which is in turn supported either by an appeal to natural law or to the law of God. Moreover, while conservatives stress the responsibility of the individual for his own actions, this can only be understood within a socially organic context.[12] Conservatives were defenders of tradition, justified on the grounds that 'established practices embodied the accumulated practical wisdom of the past'.[13] Only the emergence of nationalism and imperialism in the nineteenth century swung conservatives behind the liberal vision of a nation-state. They gradually accepted the concept of democratic politics with the purpose of containing, coopting and dividing their liberal and socialist enemies. What both liberals and conservatives had in common, however, was their distrust of political philosophies, condemning them as abstract and ideological. Any such schema was unacceptable to the traditional right because it would claim to provide a science of society which could be used to redesign the world.

THE EMERGENCE OF THE NEW RIGHT

The new right is an ambiguous and complex political term. Several interpretations have evolved, none of which is erroneous, although their relevance to the Chilean case is doubtful. The term 'new right' was first coined in the 1960s for the extreme right-wing French *Groupement de Récherche et d'Études pour la Civilisation Européene* (GRECE), but its impact has far wider implications. Specifically, it has been used to describe both the American populist neo-conservatives of the 1970s and 1980s and the French *Nouvelle Droite,* whose inspiration lies with the far-right cultural theorist, Alain de Benoist. In the context of the present study both of the above interpretations are irrelevant. A more general definition is needed to incorporate those previously marginal ideologies and movements which developed in Chile in the 1960s and 1970s.

The term 'new right' is best expressed by Stephen Davies, who describes it as a 'portmanteau label for the many anti-socialist movements in politics and philosophy which have become poignant in recent years'.[14] The new right is simply the entire collection of neo-conservative and neo-liberal movements which have developed since the 1960s. This categorization is more meaningful in so far as the varied components of the new right have cooperated on the basis of a shared, albeit largely negative, agenda based only on their general hostility to socialism. This single factor has brought together a diverse set of intellectuals, ranging from libertarian thinkers to defenders of reactionary values. Another linking strand is that the ideas of the new right embody a critique of both left-wing philosophies and the experience of left-wing governments.[15]

The new right phenomenon arose as a direct result of dramatic political and economic changes which occurred in the postwar international order: the breakdown of the post-1945 Keynesian social democratic consensus. Capitalist society's political and economic structures increasingly came into conflict as rising demands on the state could not be met without pushing up inflation and thereby risking the profitability of capitalist enterprises.[16] Many commentators believed that this conflict would destroy the fragile base of liberal democracy's dominant ideology which had cemented the postwar consensus. In the 1960s, there was a certainty that the welfare state and social democracy, as the ideological pillars of the post-1945 welfare-state consensus, would function as an efficient system underpinned by postwar economic recovery and expansion. The welfare state would intervene along Keynesian lines to maintain full employment and ensure economic growth. Daniel Bell even proclaimed the end of history as pragmatism in the field of social reform became the catchphrase. However, in the late 1960s and early 1970s, the civil rights movement in the United States and the European student protests emerged on the political scene. From then on, the development and multiplicity of the antagonism created by the interventionist state, together with the concurrent economic recession, led to an excess of demands. Political parties began to promise everything to win votes. The only solution was to reduce both expectancy levels and mass political participation. The economic gospel, that high inflation and high unemployment would not occur simultaneously, was questioned and the party system was accused of placing excessive demands on the political system to provide goods and services it no longer had the resources to finance.[17]

This pattern of state development and crisis had similar repercussions in Chile. The *Estado de Compromiso*, developed in the 1930s and consolidated in the 1940s, involved the creation of a highly advanced welfare machinery, the legalization of powerful trade unions and state participation in economic activity.[18] This process contributed to the integration of the masses into the political arena and entailed the implementation of Import-Substituting Industrialization (ISI), which replaced the previous dominant model of export-led development. This pattern collapsed in the 1970s when the ISI strategy, as well as extremely unfavourable international constraints, led to developmental bottlenecks, creating serious and chronic balance of payment problems. This resulted in complex sectoral conflicts and political crises. Lower rates of growth, high inflation and unemployment weakened the social base of the Keynesian model. As a result, conservatives abandoned the Keynesian compromise and the middle sectors broke off their relationship with the working class.[19] With the associated problems of international market competition and the need for large-scale investment, the traditional right began to face an ideological crisis. While classical nineteenth-century liberalism could equate the national cause with economic *laissez-faireism*, the development of the state, together with the continuous problems of crisis and poor performance in the international market, which appeared to necessitate centralized action by all nation-states, forced a reappraisal of the role of government by many on the right.[20] In Chile, as in the industrialized world, new conservative coalitions began to demand a return to a more market-based economy. These new *laissez-faire* arguments were tied in with ungovernability theories, which asserted that mass democracy imposed demands that exceeded the capacity of governments to respond. The solution to this apparent crisis was to expand the marketplace so as to shelter the state from these claims. This approach became the bedrock in which a revitalized new right found theoretical support.

The new right differs from the traditional right in one fundamental way. The latter distrusted political philosophies as abstract, unfeeling, ideological and rationalist, while the new right aspires to be philosophically and theoretically sophisticated. It has sought to develop a rigorous analysis of the reasons behind the collapse of classical liberalism and conservatism in the face of political ideals propped up by the welfare state. Nöel O'Sullivan locates this process within the principal conflict of modern western politics: the struggle between the ideals of civil association and social politics.[21] In the post-1945 period the social mode of interaction dominated the civil under the guise of a compromise: social democracy. What the new right represents is the re-stating of the classical tradition of civil philosophy. This is distinctive, not in the sense of the development of new ideas (few of the ideas associated with the new right are innovative), but that its situation is new. Unlike the traditional right, the new right developed within the context of social politics. Therefore, the old and once familiar ideas have acquired a new significance. In this context, the new right provided theoretical support to the general disillusionment which followed decades of postwar optimism.[22]

One link, therefore, between its various tendencies has been that its ideas arose not only as a consequence of the emergence of left-wing ideologies but out of the very experience of left-wing governments. In the case of the United States, where it became most influential, the new right emerged as a response to the liberal coalition supporting McGovern's attempt to revive the ideas of Roosevelt's New Deal. It is within this context that we must consider the role and development of the new right, not only in the industrialized world, but in Chile itself. As such, the rise of the welfare state in Chile must be viewed as intrinsically linked to that of the new right.

Essentially, the new right can be divided into two umbrella groups: liberal and conservative. I have chosen this typology because it best represents the historical and ideological traditions which spawned them, and also more accurately reflects the development of the new right in Chile. Other tendencies do exist, such as the mythical wing, typified by groups such as the French *Nouvelle Droite* and other far right organizations. This tendency is more concerned with securing support for the right through ideas such as race and nation. It has had very little influence in Chile and is strictly European in its makeup. Although the nationalist right in Chile did participate in the pre- and post-coup power struggles it cannot accurately be described as a mythical movement or even as truly belonging to the new right.[23]

The Liberal Tradition

Although various strands can be identified, such as libertarianism and anarcho-capitalism, by far the most influential branch is represented by the neo-liberals. The term originated from the desire to separate this ideology from 'pseudo-liberalism', defined as a social democratic liberalism corrupted by the welfare state, and to revive and develop classical liberal ideas such as the importance of the individual, the limited role of the state and the value of the free market. The neo-liberals were first identified as a group in 1947, when Friedrich Hayek brought together, in Mont Pélèrin, Switzerland, a group of mainly European and American intellectuals, including Carl Popper and Milton Friedman, who represented the academic critical response to the rise of postwar communism. Their objective was to organize the intellectual defenders of the new version of liberalism, and more specifically to develop a methodology which was anchored in the concepts of economic science: benefit, demand and competition. This methodology would break with the intellectual tradition of social and political theory, grounded in organizing concepts such as power, conflict, class and structure. A departure which was not simply coincidental, therefore, but instead reflected a conscious and systematic rejection of the social democratic consensus of society.

Neo-liberalism perceives man as an individual in constant search of maximum benefit for the lowest possible cost. Society is the sum of individuals, with different interests, who act within it for their individual interest. Liberty is defined as the absence of coercion, enabling the market to operate without interference. In this way everyone is free to choose in the market. Economic freedom is given predominance and is the first and most fundamental among the liberties, upon which political freedom is conditional and thereby subservient. The state is the natural enemy of individual liberty when it intervenes in the market, distorting its natural process and breaking the social optimum that only the market can provide. For neo-liberals equality is a value inferior to that of liberty, since the pursuit of individual freedom which seeks personal gain produces inequality: there will always be winners and losers. Central to the free society is the dominance of the market. Democracy, therefore, has to be functional to it. It is a mechanism at the service of a free society, which as such should be depoliticized thus reducing pressure on the state to concede certain demands.[24] Three strands of neo-liberalism are most readily identifiable: the Chicago School, Public Choice and the Austrian School.

The Chicago School

The Chicago School is not a monolithic institution, but simply the name used to identify a set of influential economists associated with the University of Chicago. These have sought to explain government failure by pointing to the inability of the public sector to satisfy consumers. In contrast, the market, through incentives such as profit, is deemed superior in this respect. The model taught at Chicago has adopted a *global* vision of the world which claims to be applicable to all aspects of national and international life. Its main source of inspiration came from Adam Smith whose three principles, economic freedom, the necessity of private property and a dominant role for the market, became the basis for economic liberalism. Milton Friedman, in *Free to Choose*, expanded these ideas with a critique of state intervention in the markets and a defence of free individual initiative. Within the field of economic theory, Friedman is most associated with monetarism: the view that strict control of the money supply is the key to controlling inflation. Consequently, the fiscal deficit and public expenditure must be reduced as they are the main causes of inflation. Such views became popular against the backdrop of 1970s stagflation, as did his belief in the need to curb the power of the trade unions, since Friedman believed that unemployment was in part the consequence of unions pricing labour out of the market.[25] In concrete terms, the application of these ideas have led, economically, to a reduction in the size of the state, the privatization and decentralization of economic activity and a predominant role for the market free from 'distortion' and 'interference'. Socially, they have entailed the breaking-up of social organizations in order to prevent pressure group action on the state 'distorting the actions of the market'.

Public Choice

Public Choice is a distinctive methodology in political science. Its main exponents have been Gordon Tullock and James Buchanan. Known as the 'economics of politics' it refers to the application of economic assumptions to the analysis of political behaviour. Public Choice explains and predicts political behaviour on the assumption that political actors are rational 'utility maximizers', seeking to promote their own self-interest. Their central contention is that the absence of market mechanisms from the political arena is responsible for the growth of government. Thus politicians are viewed as rational actors whose primary objective is to maximize their votes, while bureaucrats permanently seek to increase their budgets and personal prestige. The conclusion of most Public Choice theorists is that government is much larger than people desire because the preferences of politicians and bureaucrats are satisfied instead.

The Austrian School

The Austrian School, referred to as the economic 'ideology' of conservative and classical liberal thinkers, explains government failure by pointing to the lack of knowledge available to political decision-makers and the much richer but widely dispersed knowledge in the market which is conveyed through prices. Its major twentieth-century exponents were Ludwig von Mises and Friedrich Hayek. The latter, in his book, *The Road to Serfdom*, developed the notion of 'negative freedom' which he defined as the absence of coercion of the will of one person by another.[26] However, it is important to stress that Hayek's views were not libertarian. They were more concerned with reversing the 'ratchet effect' whereby in the postwar world the state continued to grow regardless of the political complexion of respective governments. Hayek, for example, developed an important distinction between the provision of a generous but limited welfare scheme, and more extensive ones in which welfare was seen as part of the quest for greater equality. The neo-liberals thus became the economic role models for the emergent new right in Chile. Friedrich Hayek, Milton Friedman and their disciples, Arnold Harberger, James Buchanan and Gordon Tullock, played an active and vital part in the dissemination of neoliberalism in Chile.

The Conservative Tradition

As a political force, the new right not only represents a restatement of liberal values but also certain social and moral conservative positions, including those advocated by social authoritarians concerned with the decline of state power and moralists wishing to rejuvenate religious values. Conservatism, however, is secondary to liberalism within the new right because it arises primarily in response to the atomic consequences of liberal economic policies. Neo-conservatism is the term used to describe this revival of conservatism in recent years, but a distinction must be made between the British and American versions.

British Neo-Conservatism

British neo-conservatism represents the revival of traditionalist conservatism which distinguishes itself from both the interventionism of postwar conservatism and the liberal conservatism of Thatcherism. Roger Scruton and the Salisbury School are the main exponents of this ideological current. The British neo-conservatives believe that order, as opposed to freedom, is the principal organizing principle. They reject interventionist conservatism because of its tendency to compromise with the left, and liberal conservatism because of its excessive concern with liberty at the expense of order. The liberal believes that the burden of proof is on those wishing to defend the status quo. Scruton and the neo-conservatives reverse this position by claiming that the burden of proof is on those wishing to disturb the status quo. This emphasizes that individuals are the consequence of social organization not the premises of it. Liberals, such as the libertarian Robert Nozick, construct a model of society based on what individuals would have wanted had they had the chance to start again. Scruton agrees with this notion of moral individualism, but only in a particular way. Although individualism reflects a strand of the western moral tradition, Scruton believes it does so in a misleading manner: individualism must be understood as the product of, and only sustainable by, a certain kind of society, namely a conservative one.

Alan Ryan highlights a series of fundamental propositions in relation to conservatism. Most importantly, there are no natural rights. The existence of rights and the rule of law is a social achievement, which depends on maintaining certain institutions. The state may do absolutely anything and no individual holds any ultimate right against it. People need private property because they need privacy. People come into the world as indiosyncratic individuals. Without private property, this idiosyncracy is compromised as is the stability of family life. This is not, however, a defence of *laissez-faire* thought. Since there are no natural rights, the state can do anything it wishes: it can tinker with the property rules as much as it likes. This argument holds that something close to *laissez-faire* is likely to be desirable. It defends a kind of moderate capitalism, and it certainly says that the attempt to enforce social justice, or to interfere too far, will result in greater evils than are suppressed.

However, it does not defend capitalism in a Nozickian way. For conservatism, society must offer people the kind of work which will allow them some sense of identity in the world, not of course the political identity that Marx presupposed in his concept of 'alienated labour', but rather a measure of self-achievement in the world. There is no right to private moral views. Society sets moral standards by tradition, and must rely on a degree of control which would be deplored by liberal thinkers. The Nozickian view is best summed up in this respect as *since my body is mine, I can do what I like*. However, society has to develop people who can work in that society; its standards have to be anchored within the environment such that anyone failing to meet the requirements is ruled out of the social 'game'. This allows, therefore, individuals the right to exclude others from sharing their existence, for without such exclusionary rights it is impossible to maintain an environment in which parents are able to train their children in the appropriate ways. Some degree of xenophobia or racism is regarded as inevitable in this view. After all, no attempts should be made to force people into an accommodation of other people's strangeness or divergent ways. Indeed, individuals will be less xenophobic if free from coercion. In essence, therefore, politics is not about achieving ideals, but rather about preserving society as it essentially exists.[27] European neo-conservatism has been of considerable influence within sectors of the Chilean new right, particularly the

Catholic *gremialista* movement, which provided the political and social backbone of the military regime.[28]

American Neo-Conservatism

The American neo-conservatives are a particular group of former left-liberal intellectuals who converted to conservatism in response to the new left of the 1960s. Its principal exponents are Daniel Bell and Irving Kristol. The American neo-conservatives were influenced by the burgeoning drug problem and the perceived breakdown of law and order in the United States. Decadence has thus become a key word in their vocabulary. Such problems are seen to reflect a permissiveness which has allowed 'subversives', referred to as the 'new class', to undermine social stability. This *new class* consists of a left-wing elite who, in the eyes of the neo-conservatives, are bent on a programme of 'social engineering'.

This branch of neo-conservative thinking has been a formative influence in US–Latin American relations. During both the Reagan and Bush administrations, neo-conservative pressure groups and individuals were given an important voice in public policy-making. For example, the concept of the United States' 'lost hegemony', and the quest to recapture it, was at the forefront of US foreign policy during the last two Republican administrations, and is still evident to some extent under the Democratic Clinton presidency. This is demonstrated by IMF structural adjustment programmes, which are primarily determined by a country well used to exporting its vision of the world as the only just and correct one. The same consideration is present in the ideas of liberating the markets from state intervention, adopting a *laissez-faire* attitude towards the transnationals and the pragmatic consideration that governments reserve the right to carry out whatever corrective measures are necessary until the end result is achieved: universal economic liberalism.[29] The neo-conservative critique has precise methods to achieve this goal: any measure useful in defeating the 'counter-culture' is by definition an alliance with that sector and as such is a return to a form of rigid bipolarism. In sum, the neo-conservatives see the United States as the only 'moral reserve' of the western world in the face of a decadent Europe. For this reason, hegemony cannot be shared, and to be effective it must be exercised.

The contradiction between neo-liberalism and neo-conservatism is striking, yet an accommodation has taken place with the synthesis of new right ideology as the definitive corollary. This was clearly evident in the development of the new right in Chile where neo-liberals and neo-conservatives joined in an 'unholy alliance' to revolutionize the country's political, economic and social structures. Their similarities seemed more important than their fundamental differences. They shared an antagonism towards socialist developments in postwar capitalist countries. Both neo-liberals and the neo-conservatives feared the expansion of citizenship rights; the former because of an increased role of government and the consequent limits upon individual liberty; the latter because an extension of rights to wider groups limits traditional hierarchical and authority relationships. Moreover, the two groups needed each other. The Chilean neo-liberals did not really have a notion of the state, while the neo-conservatives, represented by the *gremialistas*, provided a theory of statehood with its organic conception of the state, society and individual obligations. The neo-liberals, on the other hand, were the source of the new right's economic policies. However, it remains clear that liberalism represents the core element of new right rhetoric. Conservatism has simply provided a set of residual claims to cover the consequences of pursuing liberal policies.[30]

2 The Origins of the Chilean New Right

The political and ideological development of the Chilean right was shaped by the specific nature of the state. The post-1930 Chilean political system, symbolized by the *Estado de Compromiso*, was characterized by political bargaining between the parties, a process of industrialization, a slow but progressive consolidation of political democracy, increased state involvement in the economy, and the establishment of a relatively open system of negotiation between organized workers and the entrepreneurial sector.[1] Since the nineteenth century and until the mid-1960s, the right was represented by the historical parties of Chile's dominant classes, the conservatives and liberals. Until the late 1930s, both parties dominated the presidential election process. Between 1938 and 1948 however, the right was unable to win any presidential contest.[2] Despite these setbacks, liberals and conservatives still obtained significant representation at the parliamentary level through the mobilization of local client networks and control of political resources, including economic power and vote-rigging.

Following dramatic increases in electoral suffrage from the 1960s onwards, the right's twin strategy of clientelism and electoral manipulation began to falter, since it lacked the will and the means to appeal to a broader electorate.[3] According to Pilar Vergara, both conservatives and liberals were unable to develop a 'global' project because the central ideological traits of the right in this political system were the absence of a developed theoretical position or doctrine and a distinctly pragmatic and defensive attitude towards politics.[4] This weakness was the direct result of the right's gradual secularization, caused by the progressive marginalization of traditional conservative Catholic thinking and the corresponding strengthening of Social Christianity. This development weakened the ethical component of the political thinking of the elites. The right thus eventually lost its capacity to use conservative Catholicism as the matrix for a global theory. With the loss of these ideological concepts, it developed into both a pragmatic and defensive force, adopting a strategy of *mal menor*. It became increasingly difficult to represent the interests of the country's elites and to assume the defence of capitalism in universal terms.

25

The tactic of seeking parliamentary rather than presidential support, and the lack of an adequate programme and strategy, created a paradox. The right's defensive approach of forcing compromises in parliament eliminated the need for urban entrepreneurs and rural landowners to find alternative sources of representation. Instead, the political and economic elites chose to express themselves as a class-based group (representing their own very narrow interests) rather than as a multi-party, alliance-building organization. It was, then, also these very interests represented by the right which engendered its politically limited characteristics, through its incapacity to espouse programmes of modernization which would have led to the loss of rural domination and, thereby, an important base of electoral support.[5]

The spectacular growth of the Christian Democrats in the late 1950s led to the dramatic collapse of the right. The still nascent *Partido Demócrata Cristiano* (PDC) succeeded in attracting both large sections of the rapidly growing electorate and a considerable part of the right's clientele. The reasons for this were threefold. First, the 1938 departure of the Conservative's Social-Christian tendency (which subsequently formed part of the PDC). Second, the succession of Pope John XXIII, who in 1961 adopted a structuralist approach to developmental issues. Third, President John F. Kennedy's 'Alliance for Progress', which sought to promote the ideals and institutions of social moderates in Latin America in an attempt to stem the growth of radical left-wing ideologies. Right-wing parties were thus abandoned, to the benefit of more 'moderate' left-wing alternatives such as the PDC. The right, therefore, became increasingly marginalized from its Catholic electorate. The final blow came in the 1964 presidential elections when the Catholic Church, through the pulpit, advised its constituents to abandon the *Partido Conservador* for the newly established PDC. In the 1965 Congressional elections, the right polled just 12.5 per cent of the vote and won only nine out of 180 seats in the lower house. The time was ripe for a change.

THE *PARTIDO NACIONAL*: FROM OLD RIGHT TO NEW RIGHT

After its cataclysmic 1964 presidential performance, the Chilean party right abandoned its traditionally pragmatic approach to electoral politics. In 1966, the *Partido Conservador* and the *Partido Liberal*, whose ideological differences had virtually disappeared, merged to create the *Partido Nacional* (PN).[6] The new party also included previously marginal nationalist elements whose aggressively entryist strategy prevailed within the new movement. The substitution of the traditional leaders by new ones, less tied to the politics of the old right, changed the very nature of Chilean elite politics. Following the inspiration and leadership of those nationalist groups, the new party abandoned the upper-class image of the traditional right to assume the role of a dynamic and efficient middle-class party. Their immediate objective became to regain the electoral terrain lost to the PDC. An examination of the 1966 seminal PN document, the *Declaración de Principios del Partido Nacional*, reveals the extent to which traditional right-wing doctrines had been displaced by those of Chilean nationalism.[7] The document denounced the post-1891 parliamentary state for 'accelerating the process of political and moral decadence which had created the deep divisions prevalent in Chilean society'. This terminal crisis would be surmounted by adopting the *criollo* concept of *portalianismo* which would restore Chile's longgone Golden Age. The logical assumption was that only an authoritarian system of government would have the strength of conviction to carry through such a radical transformation.

There was also a marked change in the right's traditional conception of the nation. Perceived as a corollary of history, the nation was understood in terms of a historical process, as 'past history made in the present'. The constitution of the Nation resides in a memory of an idyllic past; tradition thus became the synthesis of this past. The concept of government was that of 'national government' in which the executive became the servant of the whole nation and not the slave of sectarian interests. The PN viewed all post-1891 governments (with the exception of Carlos Ibáñez's first administration and part of Arturo Alessandri's) as vassals in the service of sectarian party political interests. The PN thus became a party critical of parties.

Moreover, the Chilean right not only set out to create a new party organization, but assumed a new style of behaviour, developed in response to changing political circumstances. President Eduardo Frei's (1960–4) radical Christian Democrat political and economic reform programme had become increasingly hostile to the right's vested interests and, in consequence, felt it could no longer sustain a defensive political stance.

The new party was also shaped by the nature of its political opponents, the Marxist left and the reformist centre. During the Frei administration it was the right's clashes with the Christian Democrats which determined the political image of the PN; they crystallized into an anti-reformist conservative force. These conflicts made impossible a repetition of the right's previously defensive electoral position. In 1964, the intransigence of the centre had been counterbalanced by a subdued right prepared to renounce its presidential candidate in order to prevent a left-wing victory.[8] Yet by 1970 their mutual hostility created an intransigent right, dashing any hopes for a single candidate or a centre-right alliance. The right had clearly abandoned the historical strategy of *mal menor*. This new and pronouncedly aggressive attitude was also the result of the nationalist takeover of right-wing party politics. As the traditional leaders of the movement found it increasingly difficult to come to terms with the rapid changes taking place within the country they were incapable of developing alternative and appealing strategies. The more populist tendencies inherent in the Chilean nationalists thus perceived the PN as an organization lacking both an effective leadership and a global theory. As a former member of the PN wrote:

> We would have questioned the incorporation of the nationalists if instead of being in opposition we would have been in government, because the majority of National Party members had democratic credentials, while the ... [nationalists] ... were, what you might call 'democratic revisionists'.[9]

The infusion of nationalist discourse into an already pugnacious ideology is critical to understanding the development of the right in subsequent years. For the first time, it began to formulate a national project. Its language adopted the concepts of order versus chaos, of promoting the technical rather than the political, of defending private initiative in the face of what they perceived as growing state interference, and of a preference for political authoritarianism. By 1970, the right had dramatically altered its historic tendencies and began to adopt the principal characteristics of previously marginal ideologies. These were to play a key role in the political and economic strategy of the military regime. The right had become very disillusioned with a political and electoral process and a state-based political economy which had for so long denied it an active role in successive administrations. From a rearguard position the right thus developed into an aggressive and authoritarian tendency unable to tolerate the frustration of exclusion any longer. This new perspective was consolidated during the *Unidad Popular* government of President Salvador Allende (1970–3).

While the victory of the left-wing coalition in 1970 marked the low point in the electoral failures of the right, its *rupturista* policy was not yet sufficiently explicit. Andrés Benavente puts forward three reasons as to why this was so. First, sectors of the traditional right continued to be loyal to the ideals of liberal democracy; second, the nationalist sector had yet to propose a total rupture from the system, and third, the very nature of the pre-1973 period was unfavourable to demands for a radical change in the rules of the democratic game.[10] This situation changed as the democratic elements of the right were silenced in the face of an increasingly hostile nationalist element and as the Allende administration began to lose legitimacy in the eyes of the Chilean electorate. Yet until 1971, the right was apparently still committed to the existing political system and attempted to remove Allende by constitutional means.[11] This strategy was based both on an evaluation of the legitimacy of the system and on the apparent impossibility of mobilizing the necessary militant sectors to remove Allende from office by force.

The turning point occurred in July 1972 with the break of talks between the PDC and the Popular Unity government.[12] This provided the right with the opportunity to organize the national stoppage of October 1972 which immobilized the country for nearly a month, the aim being to create a mass movement forcing the centre into adopting either a pro or anti position towards the government. The right recognized that the PDC would have no option but accept the latter for fear of losing the initiative and the majority of an already rightward moving electorate. The PDC did indeed clarify its position *vis-à-vis* the government and, despite adopting a more explicit oppositional stance, still lost the leadership mantle. It was willingly accepted by an increasingly truculent right which, unlike the PDC, was possessed with a purpose: the overthrow of the *Unidad Popular* government.

In the post-March 1973 period, the right's discourse became overwhelmingly insurrectional; yet it was extremely careful in the type of rhetoric it employed. The cultural strength of democratic values in Chile was strong enough to demand extra delicacy in broaching insurrectional intentions. As such, the right expressed its position in terms of *restauración*, emphasizing the defence of democracy and the need to re-establish the indispensable conditions essential for the functioning of the political system. It was presented as an anti-left rather than an anti-system stance, a return to order and authentic democratic values. Indeed, at no time did the concept of a *revolución capitalista*, the dominant ideology in post-coup Chile, surface as a rationale for military intervention. Such an approach would have failed to yield the necessary electoral support. Instead, concepts such as *restauración* and *continuidad* enabled the right to gain the essential popular support needed to carry out the insurrection. And this *código comunicativo* concealed the right's true ideological and political intentions: the system had become an obstacle in its strive for power, for private initiative and to safeguard property. Unequivocal support for the 1973 coup signalled the right's final and categorical rejection of the country's political and electoral system.[13] Understanding these transformations within the right enables us more clearly to comprehend its development during the military years.

NEW RIGHT POLITICAL ORGANIZATIONS

To understand properly the complexities of the Chilean new right we must not only examine its theoretical influences but evaluate its political and historical development in the period prior to the 1973 military coup. These previously marginal ideological currents were to exert considerable and in some cases decisive influence on the political, cultural and economic development of the Pinochet regime. While the most important of these were undoubtedly the ultra-conservative *gremialistas* and the neo-liberal Chicago Boys, other sectors, such as authoritarian-nationalists, entrepreneurial associations and multi-sectoral economic conglomerates (*grupos económicos*), played a vital role in the regime's ideological makeup. The particular nature of these once peripheral tendencies and their interrelationships is of paramount importance.

The Non-Party Right: *Gremialistas* and Authoritarian Nationalists

The articulation of Chilean conservative thought was initiated at the turn of the twentieth century and was expressed through two doctrinarian strands. The first, nationalist-conservatism, as later represented by the PN and the extremist *Patria y Libertad*, was political in character and favoured an authoritarian and highly centralized system of government. This strand corresponded to Dubos's eighteenth-century *Thèse Royale* which favoured a strong and centralized monarchy.[14] The dictatorship of Carlos Ibáñez (1927–31) represented the triumph and quick defeat of this ideal. The second, corporatist-conservatism, as later represented by the *gremialista* movement, surged precisely at the moment of Ibáñez's fall from power. Its character was social in nature and stressed a corporatist-professional order which would partly replace the functions of the state. This corresponded to Boulainvilliers's *Thèse Nobiliaire,* which sought to reinforce the power of the nobility and a gamut of intermediary organizations which would conserve aspects of its feudal nature.

The Gremialista Movement

Unlike the historical elements of the PN, *gremialismo,* a corporatist and ultra-conservative tendency, virulently anti-Marxist and inspired by the traditional elements of Catholic social theory, played a decisive role in the political and social development of the post-1973 military regime. Its origins lie in the most integrationist versions of social Catholic thought, in particular the French and Spanish traditionalists of the nineteenth century, whose main exponents were Vásquez de Mella and Donoso Cortez in Spain and De Maistre and De Bonald in France. Its principal *criollo* source of ideological inspiration came from the Chilean philosopher and historian Jaime Eyzaguirre, considered one of the most important intellectual representatives of mid-twentieth-century conservative thought in Chile. The three fundamental elements of Eyzaguirre's ideology, which became the central tenets of the *gremialista* movement, were the concepts of Catholic traditionalism, corporatism and Hispanism.

Jaime Eyzaguirre embraced a traditionalist interpretation of Catholic social doctrine as expressed by the papal encyclicals of Leo XIII and Pius XI. In his work, he stressed the cataclysmic and decadent nature of Chilean political and social life. According to Eyzaguirre, two principal factors underlay this crisis: capitalism's destruction of feudal social relations which despite imperfections had constituted a positive construct of community life, essentially Christian, and embedded in an intimate articulation of human nature and the supernatural; and social and cultural disintegration caused by the market economy, and leading to the development of revolutionary processes, principally communism and socialism, each anathema to Eyzaguirre's traditionalism. To challenge these processes, Eyzaguirre proposed the enactment of Church doctrine, especially that of Pius XI and his 1931 encyclical, *Quadragesimo Anno.*[15]

Eyzaguirre believed in the state as the regulator of economic life because it possessed the means and the independence to act as the arbiter of individual interests. This did not entail a rejection of private economic activity, but a recognition that the state was an essential supervisory mechanism which would direct and replace the private sector's role when necessary. Eyzaguirre also stressed that although the state was the supreme authority in 'temporal' matters, a series of 'natural communities' existed between the state and the individual. These so-called 'intermediary organizations', such as the family, the municipality and the corporation, had their own defined objectives, and their autonomous development was intrinsically linked with the common good of the whole of society. This is undoubtedly a schema similar to the fascist organizational project of corporatist regimes such as Antonio Salazar's Portugal and Francisco Franco's Spain. Such a corporatist model is characterized both by its virulent opposition to all forms of liberal and democratic participation and by the notion of subsidiarity. This explicitly corporatist notion endows specific 'natural' organizations, as outlined above, with a certain degree of political autonomy *vis-à-vis* the state. It is through this project that Eyzaguirre attempted to delineate an alternative pattern of political activity – an authoritarian and anti-democratic response to Chile's presumed oligarchical crisis.

Despite supporting the notion of private property, Eyzaguirre defined limits on its use. He asserted that the state had a right to impose restrictions if by so doing a nation can achieve a more equitable distribution of land. His criticism of liberal democracy arose from a belief that it was inherently corrupt and 'unnatural'. Emphasis on a competing party system, according to Eyzaguirre, ignored the 'natural', organic, vertical division of society. Instead, promoting class struggle which was both 'inorganic' and obsessed with distributing rights and privileges to those who would best ensure its survival as a power elite. The corporatists thus insisted that society must be 'naturally' ordered and 'naturally' hierarchical, with the intermediary organizations acting as protectors. These organisms, also characterized as 'natural', would become the vehicles through which traditional forms of domination could better operate. It was a vision aimed primarily at the middle sectors; the professions and the entrepreneurial guilds (known as *gremios*). For the popular sectors it promised little more than the disintegration of their autonomous organizations. As was the case with the European fascist regimes, the corporatist project was intrinsically linked with a desire to articulate an alliance between monopolistic capital, the large rural landowners and the middle sectors, alarmed, as they were, at the rise of popular and working-class movements. The corporatist order thus implied the restoration of traditional oligarchical power: freedom for the large entrepreneurial groups, agrarian associations and the upper-class guilds, in conjunction with a strengthening of state authority and control over rank-and-file popular organizations. The role of the latter being superseded by single, vertical unions or by an authoritarian state bureaucracy.[16] Eyzaguirre also elaborated a vision of Chile's history by re-evaluating sixteenth- and seventeenth-century Hispanic cultural values which '*dio estimulo a la mezcla fraternal de las razas ... y llevada de un real anhelo de justicia, se enforzó por ajustar a severas normas de derecho sus actitudes en el campo de trabajo y de la vida internacional.*'[17] Eyzaguirre believed that Latin America had lost the essential anti-liberalism and Catholicism of Spanish culture and blamed the pro-liberal independence leaders, US-structured pan-Americanism and Marxism/socialism for the failure of this culture to take hold in post-independence Latin America.

The failure of the nationalist-conservative-inspired Ibáñez dictatorship meant that the corporatist model became a viable option. However, the victory of the Chilean Popular Front in 1938 together with a new international situation, World War II, and the great divisions which the war produced within the industrialized capitalist world, quickly put an end to corporatist-conservative aspirations.[18]

The corporatist-conservative model, in the guise of the *gremialista* movement, resurfaced in the 1960s and manifested itself most clearly among students in the university sector, who felt unrepresented in the PN. According to Jaime Guzmán, *gremialismo*'s spiritual, ideological and political leader, the movement was born out of a desire to promote and encourage a wide-ranging process of university reform and to channel such reforms through non-political student federations in accordance with the corporatist thesis of depoliticized intermediary organizations.[19] This corporatist initiative was motivated by Guzmán's preoccupation that the universities had become '*cajas de resonancia de los partidos políticos*'.[20] In reality the *gremialistas* re-emerged as a response to the radical university reforms proposed by Eduardo Frei's Christian Democrat government (1964–70), which were supported by the left, and sought to open up Chile's system of higher education. The *gremialistas* hoped to maintain its elitism and managed to group together a large part of the traditional right which had been weakened by the success of Christian Democrat ideology.

The *gremialista* movement originated in the Catholic University's Law School during the turbulent years of the mid-1960s.[21] The increasing levels of ideological radicalization, which emerged with the Frei administration, were also reflected in the universities.[22] The rise of the *gremialistas* must, therefore, be seen within this more global context. The *Movimiento Gremial de la Cátolica* became an official entity in March 1967 with the publication of its Declaration of Principles. The document stressed that the universities were alien to any ideological or political conceptions of society and possessed distinctive objectives which were both universal and permanent. They thus rejected any socialist, Christian Democrat and even national notion of the university. In essence, the movement sought to depoliticize higher education and promote the notion that its mission was to foster the integral development of man.[23]

While professing to be a university movement inspired simply by a student-oriented ideology, the *gremialista* doctrine went far beyond these purely parochial concerns. Jaime Guzmán, in strict adherence to Eyzaguirre's corporatism, had developed a 'modern' interpretation of archaic corporatist dogma. His principal premise stemmed from a view of man as a dignified and transcendental entity whose nature was superior to that of society's. According to Guzmán, this ontological superiority resides in the temporality of societies: while temporal societies come and go, man lives on. Therefore, society is at the service of man and not vice versa. Recognition of man as the axis of all societal action and the 'common good' led Guzmán to conclude that the multiple societies, which man creates between the family and the state (to secure his full spiritual and material development), should be respected as a sign of the 'sociable' nature of man and his right to create various associations with the objectives as outlined above.[24] Although the family is the basic unit of society, it does not satisfy all the requirements of man's sociability. The groupings which tie individuals for reasons of proximity and work, emerge owing to their functions in terms of complementarity and variety. Because they are larger than the family and smaller than the state, they are termed 'intermediary organizations'. These organisms have their specific goals which can be determined pragmatically, without recourse to any political ideology.[25] Guzmán believed that social autonomy was the basic principle of a free society. Each intermediary organization has the ability to achieve its own specific objectives and so should be given the autonomy to do so. As the concept of 'governance' entails the attempt by a community to achieve its specific goals, this autonomy extends only to a group's precise aims and objectives. The concept of social autonomy is better known as 'subsidiarity'. Guzmán argued that if all intermediary organizations were to benefit from this autonomy, it was improper for a superior society, such as the state, to assume the functions of a lower-scale organization. The state exists to administer those areas which individuals cannot adequately perform for themselves, such as foreign affairs and defence. Guzmán rejected the politicization of these non-political intermediary organizations on the grounds that this denaturalized their objectives. The politicization of the universities, the *gremios*, or any other entity whose objective is not implicitly political, limits their autonomy, thereby weakening one of the fundamental pillars of a free society.[26] *Gremialismo* is also profoundly religious, in an integrationist sense, differing from nationalism, which does not identify itself with a particular religious position. Its conservatism does not imply the defence of existing institutions or a given social order, but rather the struggle against the structures of the political regime and the predominant political mentality of Chilean society itself.

A distaste for liberal democracy is expressed through a critique of universal suffrage. Jaime Guzmán accused this system of creating artificial equality among all citizens, failing to represent all 'shades' of opinion, being subject to 'mass' distortions, causing a state of permanent struggle, and allowing for the penetration of totalitarian ideas. Corporatism, for Guzmán, is the true expression of the people through their natural organizations: the family, the municipality, the *gremio* and the trade union. This would strengthen the ties of social unity, replacing the struggle with political parties, which are seen as an artificial grouping. These natural organizations would constitute the parliament, where the real needs of the citizen would be represented.[27]

The August 1967 student occupation of the Catholic University marked the single most important turning point for the *gremialista* movement during this period. The Christian Democrat-dominated student federation, the *Federación Estudiantil de la Universidad Católica* (FEUC), organized the occupation in protest at the university's 'reactionary' position *vis-à-vis* the Frei government's higher education reform proposals. The *gremialistas* made their mark as the most vociferous opponents of the FEUC position. Their forceful campaign against the occupation, together with their populist anti-party line, enabled them to win the FEUC presidency for the first time in October 1968.[28] This was an important step forward for the movement, mobilizing campus-wide support, and thus extending its web of influence far beyond the myopic and privileged ivory towers of the law faculty. In the years that followed, the *gremialistas* took control of a number of student unions around the country.

The election of the Salvador Allende-led Popular Unity government in 1970 coincided with the election of a new *gremialista* FEUC directorate. Their oppositional activities during the 1970–3 period ensured a realm of influence far exceeding their origins as a student-based movement.[29] As Guzmán himself said, '*gremialismo* became the civic vanguard in the struggle against the Popular Unity'.[30] The FEUC, headed in 1973 by the *gremialista* Javier Leturia, transformed the Catholic University into the symbol and bastion of right-wing opposition to the Salvador Allende government. In an attempt to qualify their overtly political opposition to the administration, the *gremialistas* strove to situate their position within a specific student context by claiming that '*nuestra posición frente al Gobierno fue clara y categórica desde el primer instante, no fue de oposición política, ya que eso no nos correspondía por no constituir la FEUC o el gremialismo un partido político o una organización similar*'.[31] Yet their support for striking miners, particularly the provision of safe houses within the university campus, and their mobilization of the first national demonstration against the government, revealed how far they were prepared to go in ensuring its defeat. In June 1973, Leturia published an open letter in the right-wing establishment newspaper *El Mercurio* demanding Allende's resignation.[32] By the time of the 1972 insurrectional strike, the *gremialistas* had become the country's principal mass organizer, mobilizing the middle and various popular sectors in opposition to the government.

The Nationalist Sector

Nationalism had also existed on the margins of Chilean political and cultural life. Nevertheless, with the founding of the PN in 1966, it began to acquire substantial influence among important sectors of the right. The nationalists had until then refused to link themselves organically with the traditional parties of the right and had attempted to become a viable alternative in their own right. This strategy failed and forced the sector to participate in electoral politics despite their historical objections to liberal democracy. Chilean nationalism's most important postwar leader was Jorge Prat, who masterminded Ibáñez's victory in the 1952 presidential elections, served as finance minister in his administration and edited the influential nationalist journal *Estanquero*. Prat represented the most nationalist, authoritarian and radically anti-party and anti-communist tendencies of Chilean conservatism.[33]

The fundamental concepts of Chilean nationalism were strong authority and 'national unity'. Partisan splits and ideological dogmatism were seen as the basis of a nation's disintegration. As such, the liberal democratic and parliamentary systems were seen as incapable of mobilizing around the essential values of the nation.[34] Nationalists believed in the right of individuals to create a nation based on four elements – people, territory, sovereignty and tradition – and to defend it, internally and externally, through all means necessary. They held the conviction that all nations possess historical continuity as expressed by certain styles, customs, ideas and attitudes which subsist and are projected through time. Nationalists claimed that as a consequence of this process of historical continuity, the study of a nation's problems must be understood in terms of its historical evolution. Nationalism thus claimed to have discovered a new method of analysis – historical realism – which rejected ideological interpretations alien to the intimate nature of each nation.

Linked to the above, nationalists maintained that the reality and problems of a nation differed from that of other nations and so defied comparison. From this they deduced that each nation must confront its specific reality and problems with its own material, spiritual and human resources. Thus nationalists claimed to reject all forms of 'ideological imperialism', including capitalism and socialism.[35] They were, in essence, pursuing a notion of the nation as autonomous in nature. Yet Chilean nationalists were defenders of individual free enterprise and private property and critical of excessive state intervention in the economy. They believed the state was not an end in itself, but simply an instrument of general progress which should be at the service of the common good rather than at the command of political parties, ideologies or pressure groups.

This rather surprising economic position was incorporated by the nationalists when the PN was created as a compromise between corporatist-leaning nationalists and the traditional right.[36] Nationalism had been critical of the traditional right's political style which it saw as opportunistic and oligarchical. It also criticized the democratic politics of compromise, which it saw as a *mezquina* fight of private or party interests *'en la cual la constitución del interés público era pensada según el principio de mayoría y no de acuerdo a definiciones objetivas de carácter transcendental'.*[37] Instead, the nationalists proposed a 'national' system of politics. The liberal democratic notion of majority politics and the subordination of state policies to the will of a single party would be replaced by a strong authoritarian government capable of fulfilling the general interest. This authoritarian government would be given considerable autonomy *vis-à-vis* organized interest groups, thus dispensing with the need for representative politics.

These overtly authoritarian tendencies were toned down when the nationalists fused with the PN. The same could not be said, however, for the more extreme elements of Chilean nationalism as represented by Pablo Rodríguez's movement *Patria y Libertad*. Following the Popular Unity electoral victory, Rodríguez called on all Chileans 'not contaminated nor committed to the liberal party system' to mobilize in favour of the creation of a nationalist state, thus replacing the 'anachronistic liberal political system and preventing the establishment of a Marxist state'.[38] *Patria y Libertad* was overtly terroristic in its political activities. During the Popular Unity it was active in the bombing of left-wing party offices and again in the June 1973 attempted military coup. As a result, Pablo Rodríguez went into exile in Ecuador due to his involvement in the failed insurrection. Together with the *gremialistas*, the group was responsible for organizing the first anti-Marxist demonstration shortly after the 1970 elections.[39] It also infiltrated the armed forces and various mass organizations. According to Julio Faúndez, the views held by *Patria y Libertad* were not at all different from those held by certain leaders of the PN who, in their youth, had been members of the Nazi *Movimiento Nacional Socialista*. It seems likely that many of the PN membership was closely involved in the insurrectional activity of the more extreme nationalist movements.[40] Like the PN, *Patria y Libertad* dissolved itself following the 1973 coup. Despite offering full support to the military, the radical nationalist movement became highly critical of its neo-liberal tendencies and as a result became marginalized from the regime.

The Economic Right: Technocrats, Businessmen and Conglomerates

Unlike the right-wing political ideologues of the PN, the economic right had little influence in the pre-1973 period. The overriding role of the state meant that the economic elite lacked the political power to influence government policy. The problem faced by the intellectual representatives of the more ideologically minded economic conglomerates was further confounded by an entrepreneurial sector which was both unorganized and non-political. Despite these handicaps, the neo-liberal economists, together with the economic conglomerates and their media empire, launched an ideological attack to change the nature of Chile's economic right.

The Chicago Boys

In the economic sphere, the historically marginalized and curiously named Chicago Boys became the dominant expression of the Chilean ruling class in the post-1973 period. Their origin is directly linked to the debate which took place in the late 1950s and 1960s between structuralists and monetarists on the causes and solutions of the developmental problems facing Latin America.[41] According to the structuralist approach, Latin American governments needed to play an active role in promoting economic development by adopting a planned policy to generate Import-Substituting Industrialization (ISI). This policy had to be accompanied by protectionist regulations for domestic industry, such as high tariffs for the import of consumer goods, the manipulation of exchange rates and the adoption of a series of fiscal measures designed to expand the internal market. The structuralist approach also stressed the need for land reform and the redistribution of income to stimulate demand. The United Nations Economic Commission for Latin America and the Caribbean (known by its Spanish acronym Cepal), led by the Argentine economist Raúl Prebisch, was the most important bastion of structuralist thought in the region. From its headquarters in Santiago, Cepal successfully diffused its theories on economic development throughout the continent, obtaining a clear intellectual hegemony in the early 1960s among economists and technocrats.

The monetarists, on the other hand, considered state intervention as the crux of Latin America's economic and political problems. They stressed the need to adopt free market policies in which private initiative would lead the process of development according to principles of economic profit and government non-interference. During the 1950s and 1960s, monetarist views in Latin America were sustained by only a small group of economists operating within an adverse ideological climate. Consequently, in the 1950s the Department of Economics at the University of Chicago initiated a strong counter-attack against the spread of Keynesianism in the field of economic development. In 1955, Professor Theodore W. Shultz, president of the department of economics at the University of Chicago, made an official visit to the faculty of economics at the Catholic University in order to sign an agreement of academic cooperation. Under this arrangement select groups of Chilean students were given the opportunity to pursue postgraduate courses in economics in the United States. The programme consisted of three parts. First, the selection of young Chileans to be sent to Chicago to perfect their studies. Second, the creation of an economics research centre, the *Centro de Investigaciones Económicas*, to be based at the Catholic University, and third, a research programme on Chile's economic problems to be carried out by academics from Chicago.[42] Between 1955 and 1963 a total of 30 young economists from the Catholic University took advantage of the Chicago grants. Having completed their postgraduate studies in the United States, these Chilean economists returned as lecturers and began to disseminate the idea of free markets. Friedman's *Capital and Freedom* became their new bible, despite the fact that its political viability at that time was small. Soon, Sergio de Castro, intellectual leader of the group, became dean of the economics faculty at the Catholic University. Many of them became well-known academics, industrialists and leading figures of the Pinochet regime's neo-liberal model.[43]

The model taught at Chicago shaped the *criollo* Chicago Boys, whose mission became to guarantee the permanence of liberal capitalism, to improve the flexibility and adaptiveness of the national economy, and to create indissoluble links with the major sources of capital in the developed world.[44] They criticized the course of Chilean history over the previous 40 years. For the country to succeed, they claimed, it would have to break with its political habits of 'economic paternalism and feudalism'. Politics was seen as inefficient and corrupt, as a direct result of the state-oriented nation. Authoritarianism became for this tendency a vital element in the neo-liberal revolution. For real personal freedom could only be guaranteed by such a government. The principle which claimed that personal freedom and economic freedom were synonymous became the dominant ideological concept of the military regime: without economic freedom and the power to enforce it there could be no political freedom. The market thus became the economic manifestation of freedom. The Chicago model theorists perceived the market as a neutral, technical mechanism, with no ideological connotations.[45] Economic measures were not guided by their own decisions or by those of the government, but were determined by science and thus dictated by nature. There is, then, an explicit desire to replace the concept of politics with one of technology and politicians with economists. To accomplish this they not only had to cloak their language with technological jargon but it also became necessary to initiate a restructuring of society in order to remove from politics its base of support. However, the Chicago School constituted an alien ideology, which did not encompass the right's conception of Chilean history.

The model was simply the legacy of a group of economists who had shared the same university education. But as a result of the increasing *Cepalista* threat to the right, and the increasing interest shown by the powerful entrepreneur and owner of *El Mercurio*, Agustín Edwards, this current of economic thinking began to gain influence in right-wing circles.

The 1967 student occupation of the Catholic University also became the political catalyst for the Chicago Boys. It convinced them of the need to leave the university and penetrate the political field, bringing them closer to another group defeated by the university reforms, the *gremialistas*.[46] The fight the economists were waging against the dominant developmentalist project thus moved beyond the academy to the media, where ideological argument was easier. While the diffusion of the purely economic thought of the group took place in *El Mercurio*, it was *Política, Economía y Cultura* (PEC), a right-wing magazine tied to very small groups of young ideologues, which served as the vehicle for the most free and least academic arguments in favour of a market economy. The ties of personal solidarity which developed during that time between these two groups and the influence of *gremialismo* over a conservative and anti-political economics department, facilitated a process of reciprocal influence.

The first signs of this mutual ideological insemination became more apparent during the Popular Unity when the *gremialistas* took the political lead in the insurrectional struggle against the Allende administration. Their defence of the *poder social* and the autonomy of the intermediary organizations was picked up by *El Mercurio* and the neo-liberals, who believed it would infuse an ideologically malign entrepreneurial movement with the necessary global discourse. The Chicago Boys soon absorbed the non-liberal notion of the 'subsidiary state', just as denunciations of statism and the belief in the market as the guarantor of a free society were seized by the *gremialistas,* who had no qualms about adopting 'the invisible hand of the market' to execute the 'common good'. The most important aspect of this association was the bond which the liberal technocrats forged with an ideological group who rejected liberal democracy and supported an authoritarian political model on doctrinarian grounds.[47]

In the mid-1960s, the influential *El Mercurio* newspaper invited several Chicago-trained economists to become editorial writers and to establish an economics section, *Página Económica*. Thus the process of validating the new revolutionary economic model began to take root with the entrepreneurial and journalistic sectors. This ideological dissemination was deepened with the creation of a right-wing think-tank, the *Centro de Estudios Socio-Económicos* (CESEC), which sought to develop and publicize the new economic gospel. During the Popular Unity, CESEC economists participated in a series of initiatives designed to undermine the government. Together with the *gremialistas*, it published the virulently anti-Marxist *Qué Pasa* magazine. Yet its main activity involved the preparation of an alternative economic plan with the proviso that Allende would resign or be ousted.[48] In the last year of the Popular Unity, when tensions were at their highest, the Chicago Boys and their backers maintained extensive clandestine contacts with influential military sectors, principally the navy, to ensure that their economic dream would come to fruition in the not too distant future.[49]

The Entrepreneurial Sector

The domestic entrepreneurial sector was to be an integral source of support for the military and played a decisive role in the process which ended in 1973 with the fall of the Popular Unity coalition government. Two main business sectors could be identified at the time: the small and medium-sized entrepreneurs and the large economic conglomerates, each possessing distinctive ideologies and objectives.

The small and medium-sized entrepreneur.   Traditionally, this sector was not linked to particular political processes, since its creative activity was maintained on the margins of political life, intervening only when its individual interests were threatened. As a result, its experience was one of defensive struggle without a common project, of individualism and division. The larger more historic *gremios* such as the *Sociedad Nacional de Agricultura* (established in 1838) and the *Sociedad de Fomento Fabríl* (established in 1883), tied to the more powerful entrepreneurs, were gradually confronted by smaller organizations which emerged during the 1940s. They were characterized by their anti-statism, but still demanded protection for their activities. This reflected their economic dependency *vis-à-vis* the state. In general, the entrepreneurs attempted to justify their position by differentiating between positive and negative state intervention. The former included state protection on tariffs, public investment in industrial infrastructure and subsidized credit. Simultaneously, they rejected the concept of an entrepreneurial state which controlled prices, determined wages and which sought to redress the problem of social inequality.[50]

In 1935, in an attempt to counter the growing influence of the trade union confederation (the *CTCh*), the various entrepreneurial organizations amalgamated and created the *Confederación de la Producción y del Comercio*. Until the mid-1960s, however, their role and influence was extremely limited. Guillermo Campero has outlined the political weaknesses which led to their failure to project a coherent programme. First, the entrepreneurs, unlike the trade unions, did not have a formative socialization in common strategies of action. Consequently, many saw themselves as part of the established order rather than as agents of social change. Second, it was the political parties which had the 'real' project, so, unlike the trade unions, the entrepreneurial associations did not maintain day-to-day links with the parties of the right. Third, the heterogeneity of strictly economic interests was contrary to the formulation of a common project. And fourth, the ideological segmentation of those business leaders who did possess a more elaborated sociopolitical perspective.[51]

By the early 1970s, two tendencies had emerged in the entrepreneurial sector. The first, led by León Villarín and Domingo Durán, made up of small and medium-sized groups consisting of *transportistas* (transport workers), certain farmers in the south, professional guilds and small *comerciantes* (shopkeepers). They presented an anti-political vision and adopted a corporatist approach. Villarín proposed that the recently organized *Movimiento de Acción Gremial*, born out of the 1972 anti-government strike, should become an entrepreneurial political party to represent *'las expresiones de superación de una sociedad en la cual las superstructuras políticas, burocráticas y centralistas habían ahogado la expresión genuina de las fuerzas sociales'*.[52] This was a corporatist position in which the *gremios* appeared to be the representatives of a central figure of society: the working man, subject of the virtues of hard work and patriotism, opposed to the *político* and the 'theorizing parasite' who moved in a centralized and superstructural political sphere. In a post-Allende regime the *gremios* would have direct representation *vis-à-vis* the state without the need for mediators and with sole responsibility for the political economy.

There was also a more 'capitalist' sector within the entrepreneurs. It shared certain similarities with the previous group in that it also used the 'working man' symbol and adopted a partly corporatist stance. However, this sector shied away from the notion of a 'society of *gremios*' and the movementist logic of the corporatist *gremios*.

Instead, it placed considerable importance on the role of political parties and the armed forces, and supported the idea of a market economy and free enterprise. This diversity of orientation contributed to the weakness of a collective project. Yet these positions remained very general and only affected the leadership of the entrepreneurial movement. There was also little programmatic involvement outside the economic field. When an entrepreneurial sector tied to the *Sociedad de Fomento Fabríl* elaborated a declaration of principles for a military government, this was still prepared at the leadership and technical levels and had little to do with any collective fight involving all sectors of the entrepreneurs. Its objective seems to have been privately to propose lines of action to the armed forces. The document declared that the state, within a framework of a social market economy, should own the basic resources, control the financial system and the fundamental productive units, but that private and mixed enterprise should also occupy an important role.

The Chicago Boys had developed an important political relationship with the *gremialistas* but the principal objective of their ideological influence was the entrepreneurial world. Yet it is paradoxical that the main obstacle to their ambitions of increasing their political influence came precisely from this sector. Unlike the *gremialistas*, the entrepreneur was a pragmatic animal, suspicious of the ideas of the free market. The analysis of the relationship between the Chicago Boys and entrepreneurs leads to an examination of two important events: the 1967 Entrepreneurial Convention and the 1970 Alessandri presidential programme.

The Convention was a response to the growing unease felt by the entrepreneurial sector at the accelerating process of social change. It achieved sectoral unity in the name of defence of private property and anti-state intervention. The Chicago Boys participated in the presentation of a series of convention documents, but were unsuccessful in their attempts to take over the organization which was to head the entrepreneurial assault against the 1970 Allende presidential candidacy: Alessandri's presidential campaign team. The Convention succeeded in uniting the entrepreneur around the difficult issue of state economic involvement by delineating the differences between positive and negative intervention. But while this was a step towards a more general acceptance of liberal concepts and a more organic and expansive entrepreneurial movement, the conference did not go far enough to satisfy the principal Chicago economists proposal of opening up the Chilean economy. These elements led to a veto on the part of the entrepreneurs against the participation of the Chicago economists in the technical team responsible for the presidential programme. The economists had proposed their usual prescriptions which included the immediate elimination of all price controls and the introduction of market mechanisms for all productive sectors. The clash eventually led to a complete break with the entrepreneurs. The Chicago Boys thus realized that the neo-capitalist revolution would also have to be waged against the vast majority of businessmen. In this they were in agreement with some of the larger entrepreneurial conglomerates which were to become its main source of support.

The economic conglomerates. Chile's economic conglomerates (the so-called *grupos económicos*) played a critical role in helping to develop political and economic policy under the military regime. It was the fusion of the technocrats and the business sector which provided the right with a solid base in Pinochet's Chile.[53] The association of one of these groups to the Chicago-trained economists was decisive in the ascendancy of these economists.[54] From very early on in their evolutionary process, the Edwards group began to show an interest in their ideas. Carlos Urenda, a member of the group, claimed that the Chicago Boy economists *'garantizaban una orientación pro-libre empresa y nuestro deber era sostenerla'.*[55] The relationship between the Chicago Boys and the entrepreneurs grouped around Agustín Edwards was significant. It represented the most important source of support for these economists and their ideas, in both the period prior to the coup and that which followed. The entrepreneurial group headed by Edwards, Jorge Ross and Carlos Urenda showed a great interest, very early on, in the transforming experience implied in the University of Chicago's *Project Chile* and the development of a new generation of neo-liberal economists within the Catholic University. Since the return of the American professors to Chicago and the naming of Sergio de Castro as dean of economics, these entrepreneurs began to give their support to the principal activities of the economists. Unlike the vast majority of entrepreneurs, the Edwards group was highly ideological and politicized. They were ardent supporters of a neo-liberal economy and maintained, largely due to their principal orientation towards the non-productive financial sector and transnational companies, close links with influential social and political North American economic groups.

The first joint venture between these entrepreneurs and the Chicago Boys was the setting up of the CESEC in 1963. Arising out of an initiative of Edwards', the centre aimed to respond to 'the lack of right-wing economic thought'. They thus created an 'instrument to defend the principles of the free market and economic efficiency'. At first, the centre concentrated on analysing strictly economic matters, but with Frei's presidential victory and the disastrous position of the right after 1965, the need to generate a new ideology for the right became a priority. The centre thus became increasingly involved in political-economic analysis of the current economic situation, incorporating public opinion studies, polls and sociological studies in order to support the battle which the entrepreneurs were then waging against the government. These studies formed an important dimension of the Entrepreneurial Convention and in the 1970 Alessandri programme. Therefore, the CESEC served a political function and became the centre of undercover operations in the campaign against Allende. It also maintained the so called 'Campaign of Terror' through magazines such as the PEC and specially contracted journalists. After Allende's victory, the CESEC was disbanded and its archives destroyed, but it subsequently reappeared in 'subterranean form' and began to formulate an alternative economic programme in preparation for an eventual coup.[56]

The Edwards group helped the Chicago Boys in other ways. Its companies absorbed advisers, consultants and executives who had passed through the economics faculty at the Catholic University. The impact of these administrators on the companies was not merely reflected in the modernization of managerial practices, but also in a profound transformation in the logic which traditionally oriented the productive and banking sectors in Chile. Their monetarist leanings meant that they favoured the financial rather than productive aspects of these firms. Edwards also introduced the group to a series of foreign entrepreneurs who were organized in Chile via the Chilean branch of the US-based *Comité Interamericano del Comercio y la Producción* (CICYP). This organization disseminated Chicago Boy publications among national entrepreneurial groups which formed part of CICYP. In Chile, the CICYP was headed by Edwards group director Jorge Ross, and Edwards actively participated in the organization. Its main objective was to 'promote the principles of private enterprise and free initiative'. By the 1960s, CICYP members included the leaders of the most important Chilean companies, principally in mining and industry, but also in banking, oil, agriculture, commerce, construction and the media. Many were multinational corporations and Chilean monopolies such as the beer and tobacco companies. This entrepreneurial group sponsored the Chicago Boys by providing an extensive network which would enable them to become the 'organic intellectuals' in the creation of a capitalist refoundation of Chilean society.[57]

THE RIGHT-WING MEDIA: CONSERVATIVE AND LIBERAL SYNTHESIS

In the early 1970s, there was a process of political convergence between the Chicago Boys and the *gremialistas*, united in their fight against Allende. It was *gremialista* support for the concept of subsidiarity which brought them closer to the neo-liberal thesis of the Chicago School. In the face of democratic advance and the statist leanings of Allende's socialism, the *gremialistas'* emphasis on alternative organizations of civil society based on non-politicized intermediary organizations found an echo in the apoliticism and anti-statism of neo-liberalism and its strong critique of democratic constructivism. This convergence of neo-liberalism and corporatism became articulated in the 1960s in the work of Eyzaguirre, when he abandoned the corporatist elements of his earlier theories and adopted in its place the concept of the 'social market economy'.[58] He embraced the 'defence of the liberty of the individual' as his disciples began to accommodate themselves with liberalism, coinciding with the neo-liberal rejection of constructivism (state planning in the activities of civil society). This translated into a condemnation not only of communism and democratic socialism, but of regulated capitalism. Hayek believed that a planned society was impossible because there existed too many unknowns. One must remove the state's redistributive pretences, which otherwise would create an artificial social order dominating and suffocating the spontaneous order generated by individual action. This enabled the *gremialistas* to converge with neo-liberalism. Both endorsed the notion of a naturally spontaneous order, while Hayek readily recognized the concept of subsidiarity. This entailed the silencing of fundamental corporatist ideals such as the more detailed proposals of a corporatist regime, including a strong economic role for the state, the moral regime of the economy and social justice and its critique of liberalism. Yet their shared anti-constructivism arose from quite different origins. The social corporatists held communitarian ideals in which man was perceived as a social being. Neo-liberalism, in contrast, with individualist leanings, perceives man as an independent and free individual. The market, and neither the family or the intermediary organizations, being the social paradigm *par excellence*. Although Frei and Allende adopted a communitarian conception of society, they were viewed with horror by the *gremialista* intellectuals. The need to oppose the democratic constructivism of these governments explained why the *gremialistas* and the neo-liberals put their differences aside. By the late 1970s, these differences virtually disappeared.[59]

Another process inspired by these same rupturist intellectuals, and mirroring this nascent ideological synthesis between *gremialistas* and Chicago Boys, was the development of a series of new right-wing publications. In 1967, the Catholic University economists, aided by the economic groups, set up the *Página Económica* in *El Mercurio*, and in 1968, this same group began to edit the short-lived *Polémica Económico-social*. These publications espoused not only the usual recipe of economic neo-liberalism but also launched attacks on politics *per se* and, ironically, on the growing influence of university based *gremialismo*.[60] The *gremialistas* launched the magazine *Portada* in 1969, presenting not only an economic vision but a global position over Chilean society. Its vision was inspired by two figures, Jaime Eyzaguirre and Jorge Prat. In Eyzaguirre, the magazine valued a Catholic commitment and the concept of nationality as being determined by Hispanic values. From Jorge Prat, the magazine adopted a militant anti-communism, the idea of a strong, authoritarian, national unity presidency, and the concept of national decadence. By 1970, *Portada*'s break with the political project of the traditional right and a radical discursive transformation enabled a merging with *Polémica Económico-social*. This fusion of a conservative and anti-democratic political project with an economic schema influenced by neo-liberalism was a significant development. The explicit motive for the amalgamation was to achieve an objective common to both publications. Communicated in nationalist language, the effect was to establish the *bases de pensamiento para la unidad nacional*.

To understand this process of ideological fusion one must first examine the magazine's political diagnostic. In accordance with a right-wing fear of decadence, the revamped *Portada* put forward the thesis that Chile was enmeshed in global decadence owing to a corrupt party system and the subsequent increase in state intervention. This was a key point of contact with the neo-liberal economists who had themselves incorporated the nationalist-authoritarian project. The economists were also anti-statist and anti-political and both groups shared a fascination with the concept of subsidiarity. While it has corporatist origins, subsidiarity also has a neo-liberal basis: the notion of the minimal state and a free economy. However, there were also serious points of conflict between these two views. The magazine, therefore, opted for a compromise with an emphasis on the anti-political and corporatist option in the political and, simultaneously, complete support for neo-liberalism.[61]

In Chile, newspapers have always played an important formative role in political thought, and *El Mercurio*, owned by the Edwards group, played a vital role in the dissemination of neo-liberal and authoritarian ideals. It was the first newspaper to emphasize the need to organize a business administration school by letting it be known that, in 1955, Harvard University was involved in a process of setting up such institutions in Turkey and Italy. In 1956, on the arrival of the Chicago economists Rottenberg and Harberger, it published a long article by the latter, as well as the early works of those Chilean economists trained at Chicago. For Guillermo Sunkel, *El Mercurio* was the '*organo de referencia dominante*' of the political and economic elites which in the 1960s ceased to operate in the historic tradition of 'objective journalism' and began to act in the classic liberal sense, which sees the media as an instrument of political action. Even newspapers, it seems, were not immune to the political and ideological changes affecting a crisis-ridden right. *El Mercurio* began to reflect the new positions emerging from this sector in both style and content. In what amounted to a radical reinterpretation of the role of the newspaper until then, *El Mercurio* in a 1970 editorial, commemorating its seventieth anniversary declared that its output from now on had to be '*trasladados al público con urgente exactitud, manteniendo en medio del fragor de la tarea la serenidad para afirmar una directiva*'.[62] In effect, *El Mercurio*, employing Gramsci's hypothesis, had, by the end of the 1960s, adopted the role of an authoritarian and neo-liberal political party.[63] Throughout this period it attempted both to 'advertise' monetarist policies and call for the removal of the Allende government, echoing in both style and content the corporatist and nationalist demands of the *gremialistas* and the PN. After the coup, this role developed into one of 'educating' the dominant classes in the theories of the market in order to facilitate their implementation. With the demise of competitive party politics the newspaper was also to become a forum of representation for the political and economic elites and a tool by which to assess their demands.

The strategy of the right-wing media aimed to replace the democratic system. Unlike the traditional parties of the right, the political objective of these publications was to coordinate a 'new style' authoritarian strategy and to amass the new forces necessary for the revolution with the middle sectors and the armed forces as the vanguard. Hence prominence was given to nationalist ideology as well as to military personnel prepared to use violence to overthrow the Allende government. Within this context the *gremialista*–Chicago Boys alliance made perfect political sense. The economists needed an all-encompassing ideology with which to justify a rather uninspiring technical and economic revolution. The *gremialistas'* corporatist and florid ideology provided just the perfect combination of mysticism and authoritarianism for an economic plan which had no apparent moral attraction nor justification. The *gremialistas* lacked the economic sophistication with which to launch their specific revolution. Abandoning the 'impractical' elements inherent in economic corporatism in favour of neo-liberalism was a necessary compromise. By attaching themselves to the liberal technocrats, the *gremialistas* discerned a monumental opportunity to carry out the political and social elements of their ideology. This was clearly of great concern to Jaime Guzmán, who once remarked that he knew nothing of economics. In essence, the Chicago Boys craved an economic revolution and the *gremialistas* a political transformation of society. To achieve both would require a joint offensive on a society ill-equipped to accept the alienating nature of the changes to come.

3 The Right Unfettered

The final and definitive break with the democratic order took place on 11 September 1973, when the Chilean armed forces launched a military attack against the *Unidad Popular* government of President Salvador Allende. Although there was token resistance from left-wing forces and a minority of military personnel still loyal to the administration, victory for the coup plotters was quickly secured. 'The Battle of Chile', as the violent insurrection and the consequent resistance came to be known, had a major impact internationally. Not only was it ferocious, but it was also perceived to symbolize the essential conflict between left and right. In Chile, the coup marked a new epoch in the country's political evolution, the final rupture in a long democratic tradition.

THE RIGHT'S REACTION TO THE COUP

The armed forces emerged as the ideal inheritors for a right beset by crisis and thereby unable to assume political power directly. Not only did the military have a strong aversion to Marxism, compromise and political parties, it also lacked a global project, administrative know-how and had little experience of government. The right quickly became aware of the influence it might exercise over the military in addition to the new problems which such a relationship posed. To solve this predicament the *Partido Nacional* (PN) voluntarily dissolved itself three days after the military coup, and in so doing demonstrated its unwillingness to compete for power with the military. By the end of 1973, it ceased to exist as a structured entity. This was inevitable given that the new regime had simultaneously imposed a 'recess' of party and pressure group activity. It had not been clear whether the military would be prepared to accept pacts or explicit agreements in relation to its pursuit of power. By unilaterally disbanding, the PN pushed the armed forces into pursuing long-term aims. Consequently, the military rallied around the 'national interest' slogan with its concurrent pretence of neutrality and the 'common good'.[1] The leaders of the right were swift in making the necessary signals to prove their willingness to hand over sovereignty. Political action through parties was exchanged for negotiation and movements in order to attain positions of influence within the new state apparatus.

The first dilemma facing what was, in effect, a heterogeneous right-wing coalition arose from the question of the regime's future, or lack of it. Two main tendencies emerged within days of the coup: a *restauradora* position, supported by more moderate elements within the coalition, which favoured a return to the pre-1973 democratic system; and an authoritarian tendency which hoped to use the military to institute a radical change of Chile's political, economic, and social structures.[2] The conflict between these two tendencies ended in early October 1973, following the military government's decree proscribing all Marxist parties.[3] More significantly, the contents of the decree included references to the creation of a *nueva institu-cionalidad*.[4] This theme became the focus of official policy with Pinochet outlining in November 1973 three possible options *vis-à-vis* the future of the military regime: a short transition government, the establishment of a 'purifying' civilian–military administration or an 'absolute and permanent' military regime. He quickly rejected both the first and last option by asserting that '*jamas hemos pensado perpetuarnos en el poder y la primera alternativa se observa prematura'*, and as such the new civilian–military coalition would be '*profund-amente nacionalista, ajeno a lo que divide, como es el caso de los partidos políticos, porque existen ideales comunes que están por encima de lo meramente partidista'*.[5]

This marked the unequivocal defeat of the *restauradores*. Government documents and declarations now reflected the new 'foundational' nature of the regime.[6] As a result of this split within the initial *golpista* coalition, the military government lost the support of the more moderate elements within the right who had supported the coup as a lesser of two evils, including an important section of the traditional right. Its members now abandoned active political action and returned to various, mainly legal and entrepreneurial forms of private activity.

Why had the more extreme faction emerged victorious over the more moderate elements of the coalition? First, because of the ability of the *autoritarios* to adapt themselves to the military's limited polit-ical vision. This consisted of a desire to dismantle political parties and transfer total power to the armed forces, as well as a paranoid fear of anyone questioning this power or wishing to share in it. Second, the counter-revolutionary model was influenced by the manner in which the coup had taken place. The disproportionate level of violence carried out by the military against its enemies, the traumatic symbolism of the bombing of the *La Moneda* presidential palace, the death of President Salvador Allende and the intensity of the repression which followed could only be legitimized and justified if accompanied by radical social change. The authoritarian faction thus assigned 'meaning' to the tragedy.

With the defeat of the *restauradores*, the authoritarian tendency, incorporating *gremialistas*, Chicago Boys and nationalists, perceived the principal problem *vis-à-vis* the military to be one of persuading them to implement a programme of capitalist modernization. However, until April 1975, the option of a *dictadura duradera* did not imply a decision on the precise contents of the bourgeois counter-revolution. The authoritarian tendency had achieved a vague consensus in support of the regime with an ambiguous and eclectic programme of socio-economic changes.[7] The divergent internal elements shared only an unwillingness to return to the past. Such doctrinal rivalry was reflected in the composition and ideology of the regime between 1973 and 1975. According to Moulian and Torres, the dissolution of the right's political structures reflected a confidence in the military's ability to carry out specific change.[8] It also implied a change in the nature of 'doing politics', as well as reaffirming that, in certain circumstances, the political and economic elites did not need political parties or access to direct political power. They were less dependent than other social classes, possessing as they did a varied power network. Renouncing direct control of the state apparatus, therefore, did not deprive the authoritarian right of its influence over the decision-making process.

THREE DOCTRINES IN COMPETITION

Due to a lack of intellectual elaboration and the internal struggles within the regime, the initial period (1973–5) of the regime was characterized by a high degree of eclecticism and a lack of ideological elaboration. There was a struggle for hegemony between these now dominating and previously marginal ideologies, which were united only negatively around concepts of anti-statism, anti-communism and anti-liberal democracy. The policies and rhetoric of the regime throughout this period reflected this heterogeneous coalition. This was particularly evident in the government's most important policy document, the *Declaración de Principios del Gobierno de Chile*, released in March 1974, which set out the key tenets of the regime's ideology. The declaration also provided a valuable insight into the extent to which the various competing ideologies were able to impose themselves on the new ruling elite.

The nationalists did have limited influence in the *Declaración de Principios*, although purely at a rhetorical level. Concepts such as 'national unity' and the quest for an idyllic and heroic past, which were included in the document, were typically nationalist. The same could be said of the Spenglerian notion of decadence and the desire to resuscitate the image of Diego Portales.[9] Of more specific, although short-lived influence was the Doctrine of National Security (DNS), which, unlike the other ideological tendencies, was military in origin. It furnished the armed forces with the necessary political justification of their 'messianic' role. This was vital for a professional organization whose subordination to civilian rule had suppressed any independent political identity. The DNS perceived 'nation' and 'state' as living, interchangeable and supra-individual entities of which individuals are subordinate parts.[10] Its *raison d'être* was to establish and maintain what the doctrine termed the *Unidad Nacional*. This was understood not as the historic process of social consensus but as a national 'fact' or 'tradition', which if removed, could only be restored by the armed forces. This concept does not accept the existence of conflict, seen as contrary to the very essence of unity. Without what the doctrine refers to as 'national power', the nation would simply disintegrate. This power is recognized as the amalgamation of the resources possessed, developed and mobilized by a particular state to realize its 'national objectives'. For the doctrine, the fundamental definition for the Chilean state is the struggle against Marxism. This confrontation does not take the form of a conventional external war. It is a fight against subversion, against an enemy who has infiltrated every level of Chilean society. There can be no dialogue with this enemy, only elimination. The doctrine concludes that democracy has failed to accomplish this task; only the military, with its advanced organization and extensive resources, has the means to confront it. In this way, the DNS played a crucial role throughout this initial phase of consolidation.

Following the coup, *gremialismo* began to organize through linked yet autonomous groups. Many of its followers occupied various legislative and politically related government posts. Instrumental to this process was the *gremialista* sympathizer Miguel Kast. He was recalled from the United States to take up an influential posting with the national planning organization, ODEPLAN. From his position as a member of one of the country's most powerful state bodies, Kast gradually and consistently placed both *gremialistas* and Chicago Boys into key administrative posts.[11] The *gremialista* stranglehold was not limited to ODEPLAN, but stretched as far as the *Secretaría General de Gobierno* (led by the movement's guru, Jaime Guzmán), the *alcaldías* (the mayor's office), the *Secretaría General de la Juventud* and the *Secretaría General de la Mujer*.[12] By far the most influential civilian in ideological, judicial and political matters was the founder and leader of the *gremialista* movement, Jaime Guzmán.

Soon after the September coup, the *Junta* member General Gustavo Leigh, through his brother, asked Guzmán to help draft a new constitution. Guzmán not only agreed, but proposed to assist in strengthening civilian support for the regime, through the *secretarías*. Despite being acknowledged as the author of the *Declaración de Principios*, Guzmán himself claimed that '*para mi, lo estable es la docencia y la colaboración con el gobierno es algo transitorio y accidental*'.[13] A careful study of the *Declaración* disputes this and reveals how influential *gremialismo*, and Guzmán in particular, were in drafting the regime's most important document in these formative years. The whole Christian emphasis of the document, particularly the *integrismo católico*, and the concept of man as superior to society, as well as the importance attached to the 'common good', reflected unadulterated *gremialista* thought. Furthermore, the document included references to the *gremialista* concept of *poder social*, defined as '*la facultad de los cuerpos intermedios de la sociedad para desarollarse con legítima autonomía hacia la obtención de sus fines específicos*'.[14] Comprised of trade unions, *gremios* and family organizations, the *poder social* would protect the freedom of the citizen, thus safeguarding the autonomy of civil society. It was also intended to act as both an instrument of support for the state authorities and a link with the *poder político* through the intermediary organizations.[15] In this way, the government attempted to substitute the western liberal ideals of participation and representation with those of *gremialismo*.

The movement's political strategy suffered a serious blow after the military regime abandoned the corporatist notion of *poder social*. Those *gremios* which had successfully mobilized against the *Unidad Popular* government hoped to maintain their organizations, converting them into vehicles in support of the new regime.[16] However, having voiced concern over the regime's economic strategy, the *gremios* demanded direct participation in both economic and administrative planning. The military, unsurprisingly, were unwilling to entertain notions of power-sharing and, consequently, its support for the *poder social* quickly evaporated. In response, the *gremialista* movement began organizing and mobilizing the *secretarías*, perceived as politically less sensitive. Why did the military choose to adopt this archaic strain of thought? Clearly, the Catholic component within it conferred Christian legitimacy, an ethical basis capable of justifying the economic and social transformations imposed by force. Also, members of the movement were close to the increasingly influential Chicago Boys. Moreover, given its role as leaders of the anti-Allende protests, the *gremialistas*, more than any other ideology, had the kudos to keep together the disparate elements of the pro-regime civilian coalition.

During this first phase, the Chicago-trained economists played a relatively minor role in the government's economic programme. As with the *gremialistas*, they initially occupied lower-profile, yet potentially influential, administrative posts. With the help of Kast, Chicago Boys, such as Sergio de la Cuadra and Alvaro Bardón, established themselves in bodies such as ODEPLAN, and through the economy ministers, Raul Sáez and Jorge Cauas, many became increasingly influential in the civilian economic team of advisers.[17] It was a period of eclectic and pragmatic economic policies. A time for both rupture and continuity in economic affairs. While this initial phase had moved towards a *refundación*, there was still some concern as to the political effects of the measures adopted and a desire to maintain the political unity of the entrepreneurs. The economic programme adopted prior to the April 1975 economic 'shock' could be viewed as a rational response to the problems of hyperinflation, goods scarcity and balance of payments deficit, affecting the country in the post-coup period. Between 1973 and 1974, a rather traditional and conservative stabilization programme was put into operation by the non-Chicago economic team to overcome these problems. It included a reduction in public spending and in the budget deficit from 24 per cent of Gross National Product (GNP) in 1973 to 8 per cent in 1974 and a drop of more than 30 per cent in real wages and salaries.[18] Parallel to these austerity measures, all price controls were abolished, the currency was devalued, tariffs were reduced and the capital market was gradually liberalized. The stabilization programme failed. Production increased, but inflation reached 379 per cent in 1974 (a poor result despite a drop from 600 per cent in 1973). The fiscal deficit fell, but not as much as the government hoped or had expected. The current account deficit rose to over US$200 million in 1974, and unemployment increased dramatically. By the beginning of 1975, inflation reached the previous year's high levels, the balance of payments deficit was showing a tendency to rise and low copper prices on the international market threatened a serious crisis.

The internal debates over possible solutions caused a split in the regime's economic team. This was epitomized by the opposing positions of the economic ministers Raul Sáez and Jorge Cauas.[19] Sáez believed that in an underdeveloped country the state, in conjunction with the private sector, must still play a predominant role. Cauas, supported by the Chicago Boys, insisted on the need to reverse the state's tendency to monopolize the resource distribution process. Both options were placed before General Pinochet, and his decision, in April 1975, to opt for Cauas's monetarist *Programa de Recuperación Económica*, designed together with the Chicago Boys, marked the decisive victory over the *gradualistas* who had dominated the initial phase. To accomplish this they had needed to oust those obstructive technocrats, such as Sáez, in strategic positions. With Sáez removed from all positions of influence, the Chicago-trained technocrats had an open door through which to make their ascendancy as the hegemonic economic force within the regime.

The new economic plan consisted of nothing new; only larger doses of what had come before. Cuts of 15 per cent were made in a matter of months in public sector personnel, with the exception of the armed forces. As a result of these draconian measures, bank lending interest rates rose to an equivalent level of 178 per cent per year in the third quarter of 1975, GNP fell by 12.9 per cent, while industrial production dropped by 23.5 per cent. Unemployment reached 20 per cent and the current account deficit doubled, reaching record figures of US$491 million. Inflation fell, but was still unacceptably high at 343 per cent and real salaries and wages plunged to 60 per cent of 1973 levels. The economic strategy abandoned the state-protected industrial sector to the mercy of foreign competition and reoriented the government in style and substance, by removing economic decisions from any semblance of representative strategies. In essence, it postulated the separation of entrepreneurial interests from those of the nation.

How did a tendency so alien to Chilean political life achieve its objectives during this critical phase? How did the Chicago Boys realize a project which favoured a reduced number of entrepreneurs? And how did they succeed in imposing these ideas on the military and a bourgeoisie marginalized by the new economic strategy? The proximity of the main inspirators to power was instrumental in their successful implementation of the plan. The navy had been given exclusive economic responsibility and the ex-marine Roberto Kelly (Papa Kelly as he was known to the Chicago Boys), owing to his closeness both to the military and the economists, was given the task of finding able and sympathetic advisers. During the Allende government, he had built up an essential network through his attempts to devise an alternative economic strategy. Immediately following the coup his personal friend, the *junta* member, Admiral José Toribio Merino, appointed him director-general of ODEPLAN and instructed Kelly to bring him suitable names.[20] With the help of Kast, Kelly had, by April 1975, placed Chicago Boys and *gremialistas* in key government positions.

According to Arturo Fontaine Aldunate, the economists were favoured because they had been the most intransigent line in opposition to the *Unidad Popular*. They represented a resurrection of principles inherent to liberalism, a revival of the authoritarian principles of *portalianismo*.[21] Also important was their capacity to present the economic options as technical and scientific. This 'myth' was used to *sacralizar* words and deeds and to identify who had the right to discuss the political economy. To be accepted as a critic one had to possess the 'science', the *verdadera economía*. For Rolf Lüders, what influenced the regime was the idea that the plan implied a destruction of all forms of monopolies, not only at a commercial level but also involving labour. And this was a programme which appealed to the armed forces since it endowed them with more power than could be gained by alternative strategies.[22]

Chile's political economy had for some time been under the scrutiny of the International Monetary Fund (IMF) owing to the country's balance of payments deficit. The ideological similarities between the IMF executives and the Chicago Boys added to the influence of the latter, considerably increasing their status among those in the military responsible for economic management. The plan was presented as the only means by which to overcome effectively the problem of foreign dependency. The proposal of increasing the country's international economic prestige and expanding exports was highly appealing to the armed forces. The Chicago technocrats were the only nucleus of experts who knew what they wanted. They offered the government a coherent alternative, which also implied a complete break with the past and promised spectacular results. The model also had the backing of important sectors of society, such as the economic groups, who provided the plan with powerful allies eager to benefit from the untold financial gains it offered. The pre-shock period, consisting of moderate liberalism, was far too pragmatic to constitute an ideology capable of serving as a base for a 'great' economic and social revolution. Above all, however, Pinochet admired the simplicity of the proposed economic model, the determination and clarity of the Chicago Boys and the notion that it required the permanence of power.

Once the Chicago Boys had prevailed and the programme began to show signs of success, this initial group of technocrats became a political group providing a high degree of cohesion to the government's policies. Their objective was now to adopt the neo-liberal model as social theory, and to assimilate the *gremialistas*, thus injecting the required political expertise. These two movements were to become the economic, ideological and political pillars of the regime in the years to come.

THE CONSOLIDATION OF THE NEW RIGHT

The growing discontent which the economic shock caused led the military to call on the *gremialistas* to create a movement which would bring together supporters of the regime. Morale needed to be kept high in order to prevent the erosion of the heterogeneous and fragile government coalition. The importance of developing a morale-boosting, cadre-building movement was seized upon by Jaime Guzmán. To this end, he established the *Frente Juvenil de Unidad Nacional*. The *Frente* was set up in late 1976, as an authoritarian, organic and 'aristocratic' youth movement, and its organizational structure was essentially *gremialista*. Its basic unit was the *nucleo* or cell, based at the school, college, *población* or university. Each *nucleo* was officially autonomous but subordinate to a hierarchically superior *Consejo Nacional* which coordinated the cells and organized its activities. It consisted of 18 *consejeros* each representing the four sectors in which the organization was divided: *Juventud Secundaria, Juventud Universitaria, Juventud Comunal* and *Juventud Profesional*. Guzmán and Kast were among the more prominent *consejeros*.

The *Frente*, however, failed to develop into a mass movement not only because of Pinochet's lack of support but because the non-*gremialista* political right refused to participate in a movement designed primarily to take over the traditional role assigned to political parties.[23] The movement did, however, succeed in grooming and moulding young *gremialista* leaders from the *Frente* and the *secretarías* in readiness to occupy the many, and increasingly powerful, posts in the municipalities. The *gremialistas* built their power base within the realm of local government, through their stranglehold on the *alcaldías* and other public administration posts. This was a new generation, lacking the necessary pre-1973 political experience. They were young ideologues, socialized within the authoritarian regime, who represented, in essence, the right's new and dynamic political generation. As the municipalities were given ever-increasing responsibilities, the political power of these barely post-adolescent *gremialista* administrators became wide-ranging, covering areas such as health, education and welfare. Appointed by the president, they provided the regime with an invaluable source of ideological coherence and control.

Within the government hierarchy itself, the most politically indispensable figure was Sergio Fernández. While not an official member of the *gremialista* organization he was widely regarded as a devout sympathizer. As labour minister, he provided the movement with the means to fortify its position and increase its influence over many aspects of the government's key political and ideological decisions. In 1977, Fernández was appointed *Contralor*, with responsibility for organizing the *Consulta Nacional* (a plebiscite held in 1978 to seek support for the government's institutionalization strategy). In the following year, Fernández was promoted to the interior ministry. This marked the pinnacle of *gremialista* political influence, whose position was made all the more secure by the knowledge that they were the only feasible option for a military in desperate need of a legitimizing ideology.

What the *gremialistas* accomplished in the field of politics, the Chicago-trained economists achieved in the economic sphere. Despite the economically moderating role of the military prior to the so-called *siete modernizaciones* (a radical programme aimed at introducing the market into all aspects of the country's social relations network), the Chicago Boys dominated economic government policy.[24] Alvaro Bardón was appointed vice-president of the Central Bank in 1975 and economics minister the following year. Sergio de Castro became finance minister in 1976, while Sergio de la Cuadra was promoted to the presidency of the Central Bank. In December 1978, the orchestrators of the neo-liberal model were put in place, with José Piñera as labour minister and the orthodox monetarist, *gremialista* supporter, Sergio Fernández as interior minister. Together with de Castro, as inspirator of the government's economic policy, these three men embodied the Chicago Boys' invulnerability within the regime.

As an elitist movement, the Chicago Boys developed their *cadre* base at the economics faculty of the Catholic University. This was accomplished through the successful screening and control of both the economists and students involved within the faculty. Through the unreserved and systematic use of terror and intimidation, the state apparatus, with the tacit consent of the Chicago Boys, marginalized and barred from academia many of those who opposed the ideas and practical consequences of the economic model.[25] In the same way that the *gremialistas* increased their control of public and political life through the manipulation of the municipalities; so too did the monetarist technocrats guarantee future docile public administrators and economists for the regime through the control of the universities and their relevant faculties.

Critical to this process of domination had been the economic groups whose power and influence had increased dramatically throughout this period of regime consolidation. These were new groups which bore little relationship to those prior to 1973, groups, such as Cruzat-Larraín and Vial, whose roots and success lay not in the productive sector but rather in control of financial activity. In the past, it had been control of productive firms that had enabled the economic groups to expand into the financial sector. Now the reverse was the case; successful control of the financial sector permitted the acquisition of new firms for the groups. The operative concepts were now those of 'acquiring' and 'speculating' rather than those of 'creating' and 'producing', resulting in higher levels of centralization and control of firms belonging to a group. As the starting point was now financial rather than productive, a process of planning and control was developed with the sole aim of increasing a conglomerate's utilities. Decisions concerning their role and expansion plans were now increasingly taken at a level remote to the companies themselves, leaving very little power and room for manouevre in the hands of the executives. Two types quickly developed: managers who were responsible for the everyday running of the particular firm; and analysts whose role was to observe and assess the global implications of the national and international economy, planning the group's expansion strategy accordingly.[26] It was at this second level that the already close ties between the Chicago Boys and the economic groups intensified.

This intrinsic link has been denied by many supporters of the regime. They claimed that as a consequence of the 'neutral technician' characteristic of the economic team they could not have been under the influence of the groups.[27] Others refute such a link believing the argument to be alien to economic science and thus not worthy of analysis.[28] Despite these claims and assurances, the reality seems to have been very different. The Chicago Boys persistently supported the notion of a 'protected democracy' in which political parties had no role to play, while power and influence resided with the media, owned and controlled by the economic groups. The link was overwhelming. Through group-sponsored study departments, staffed by Chicago Boys, economic policy was geared to the benefit of the groups. In so doing, the state effectively renounced the right to economic control and management by transferring it instead to the private sector.

The economic shock of 1975 marked the final rupture with the political economy of the last four decades, and from then on the Chicago Boys tightened their grip on the Chilean economy, progressively evolving towards more extreme and globalizing forms of monetarist orthodoxy. Prior to 1975, the ideological concepts developed by the technocrats were unable to permeate into other areas, given that such concepts ran counter to the government's alleged support for the *poder social* and participatory labour relations. However, after 1975, the economic model, still in its fragile infancy, demanded even greater authoritarian and repressive measures to ensure its success. The relatively moderate policies of General Nicanor Diáz Estrada's labour ministry and General Gustavo Leigh's social programme thus came to an abrupt end. The 'pragmatism' of the first phase (1973–5) was therefore replaced by even tighter controls on trade unions. Labour policy came under the spectre of the DNS and the rigour of emergency norms were maintained despite *gremialista* rhetoric to the contrary. *Gremialismo* had fallen under the influence of national security. The central notion of worker–employer harmony was now modified to justify both the prohibition of strikes and of the 'depoliticized and autonomous intermediary organizations'. The *gremialistas* now conceded that until the government's objectives were realized the country would have to remain in a state of emergency.[29] The notion of 'common good' was redefined to include national security and economic development. Subsidiarity became dependent on the necessities of order. The individual, as an entity possessing natural rights, was thus substituted by a notion which saw no contradiction between the state and the person. Quite simply, the rights of the latter were to be subordinated to those of the former.[30]

THE INSTITUTIONALIZATION OF THE REGIME

There was a distinct militaristic view of politics and the state throughout this period at the expense of the *refundación* justification of the first phase. Pinochet's 1977 Chacarillas speech marked the end of this emergency mentality. On 10 July, Pinochet revealed what became known as the *Plan de Chacarillas*, an announcement of the government's political intention to institutionalize the regime and legalize its permanence in power. Pinochet asserted that the nation's *nueva democracia* would be authoritarian, protected, integrationist and technocratic. There were to be three institutionally normalizing phases: the first encompassing 'recuperation', in which '*el Poder Político ha debido ser integralmente asumido por las Fuerzas Armadas y de Orden, con colaboración de la civilidad*'; the second, a 'transitionary' phase in which '*habrá de pasar así de la colaboración a la participación*'; and finally, a 'consolidationary' stage would be implemented through which '*el poder será ejercido por la civilidad, reservándose constitucionalmente a las Fuerzas Armadas y de Orden el papel de contribuir a cautelar las bases esenciales de la institucionalidad y la seguridad nacional en sus amplias y decisivas proyecciones modernas*'.[31]

The erosion of the military's legitimacy, generated by the applied economic policies, the increasing conflict with the Catholic Church, the excesses of the security services and the country's international isolation, forced the regime to make political adjustments. The plan outlined on Mount Chacarillas was an attempt to resolve the political crisis and marked a victory for the *institucionalizadora/aperturista* tendency (also known as the *blandos*) made up of *gremialistas*. They feared a permanent militarization of a state in turmoil.[32] Guzmán supported this position by claiming that the armed forces, by definition, could not govern indefinitely without undermining their *raison d'être* while, in contrast, a gradual liberalization towards a solid and participatory political system could '*hacer aflorar antes la evidencia de las inevitables dificultades sociales, pero permite salvarlas gracias a la ventaja del que afronta oportunamente un riesgo calculado*'.[33]

This position was in sharp contrast with the views held by the nationalists (the *duros*). Since 1976, the hardline nationalist leader, Pablo Rodríguez, and his *anti-institucionalizadora* sympathizers, had been increasingly putting pressure on the government to advance immediately towards defining a new political model, based on the primacy of the armed forces. They blamed a 'socially unjust and politically disastrous' economy for the erosion of government prestige and believed that certain fundamental conditions had to be satisfied before any transition could be initiated. These included mass mobilization and fluid communication channels between government and intermediary bodies. Only then could organically organized legislative bodies be set up and a civic movement of the *fuerzas vivas de la nación* mobilized.

Unlike the *gremialistas* and nationalists, the Chicago Boys appeared calm in the face of growing dissatisfaction with the regime. Their only concern centred on the completion of the 'de-stating' process, regarded as a necessary prerequisite for political normalization. Adopting Hayek's interpretation of liberty, the technocrats insisted that without economic and social reforms any form of political freedom was meaningless. The Chicago Boys were also sceptical as to whether the proposed constitutional formulae would actually safeguard the stability of the system and eradicate the threat of a return to the past. From their viewpoint, a reordering of national, social and economic life was needed, but not through the *fetichismo legalista* of the *gremialistas*, for there was no *poder mágico* in a constitutional solution.[34]

Despite this, the economists, faced with imminent constitutional definition, centred their efforts on the discussions surrounding the basic tenets of the economic model which they wished to see consecrated in the future *ordenamiento jurídico*. They generally agreed on the basic principles for inclusion in a new constitution. Besides the right to private property, these included the notion of subsidiarity (constitutionally fixing a limit on public spending), *impersonalidad de las normas* (preventing the operation of 'non-neutral' measures) and the *tecnificación* of public decisions (juridically guaranteeing the use of 'experts' in all aspects of policy-making). A sudden increase in the number of vociferous Chicago Boy 'intellectuals' led to an abandonment of the previously restrictive and blinkered technocratic profile. The once silent economists became involved in the frequent discussions over the *nueva institucionalidad económica*.

The economic groups also participated in the ensuing debate through the press (especially in *El Mercurio*), largely owned by the groups themselves. They set up and funded magazines, such as the *Informe Económico* of the BHC group, and the more ideologically rigorous *Economía y Sociedad* (edited by José Piñera), to influence the government decision-making process. In 1979, the groups funded the neo-liberal *Centro de Estudios Públicos* (CEP) with a similar aim in mind. Staffed by the Chicago economists, as were the journals, it regularly organized international conferences and published an influential journal, *Estudios Públicos*.

Once it was clear that the institutionalization process would continue despite their protests, the nationalists also attempted to influence the course of events. The *La Tercera* newspaper was to the nationalists what *El Mercurio* was to the Chicago Boys. Through their regular columnists, Pablo Rodríguez, Gastón Acuña, Ricardo Claro and Alvaro Puga, the *duros* criticized the political economy and the institutional measures being debated. They dominated sections of the state television network, TVN, and the *Universidad de Chile*, where nationalists such as Pedro Felix de Aguirre, Jaime Pereira and Ambrosio Rodríguez used their positions of influence in an attempt to alter the course of the *apertura*. Pinochet's daughter, Lucía, created the *Corporación de Estudios Nacionales* (CEN) to oppose the constitutional formulae, political parties and liberal democracy as a whole. Despite a prominent founder, the organizing of seminars and the publishing of articles in various community newspapers, the CEN was of little influence. Unlike the CEP, which could be considered a genuine intellectual centre, the CEN was little more than a propaganda front for the nationalist elements within the regime. Even the marginalized traditional right began to organize. In 1978, Julio Subercaseaux, Víctor Santa Cruz and Héctor Correa, all former members of the now disbanded PN, founded the *Corporación de Estudios Contemporáneos* (CEC), which received considerable funding from those sections of the entrepreneurial groups disillusioned with the neo-liberal political economy.[35]

The *gremialistas*, as the vanguard of the institutionalization process, had the most to lose in this ideological conflict. Through their stranglehold on the influential *comisión constituyente*, established by the regime to plan for the country's future constitution, the *gremialistas* had seen significant parts of their political model adopted by the regime.[36] To consolidate this enviable position they saw fit to organize as extensively as the other competing right-wing tendencies. In 1979, the *gremialistas* founded the magazine *Realidad* under the direction of Ernesto Llanes, while Guzmán continued to represent the views of the movement through his columns in the quasi-*gremialista* weeklies, *Ercilla* and *Qué Pasa*. The movement also organized a cadre organization, *Nueva Democracia*, integrating professionals tied to the principles of *gremialismo*. While denying to be a political party, *Nueva Democracia*, certainly conducted itself as one. Indeed, it become the precursor to the *gremialista*/Chicago Boys *Unión Demócrata Independiente* (UDI), the country's third largest party.

For the first time since the coup, the right felt under pressure to organize, though in a very limited and exclusive way. It had always had an unofficial voice, in the *oficialista* press, in *El Mercurio, La Tercera, Qué Pasa* and *Ercilla*, to name but a few. Yet only after Chacarillas did it begin to develop an organized and officially recognizable identity. The level of right-wing competition which emerged after 1977 was an interesting and singular phenomenon, but should not be considered as surprising within this context. The Chilean right now had everything to play for, as the time for ideological definition was approaching.

After 1977, the economy began to show signs of success. The initial group of government technocrats became a political group capable of providing coherence and rationale to the administration's recent institutional plans. As noted in the previous chapter, this was accomplished through the full adoption of neo-liberalism as social theory and the full assimilation of the *gremialistas*.[37] The Chicago Boys' recently acquired 'global' ideology now extended its previously limited concerns, embracing the all-encompassing social theory of Hayek rather than the relatively narrow economism of Friedman. Their success in forging neo-liberalism as the dominant ideology lay in a recognition that the entrepreneurial groups were fascinated by the successful economic results and lacked the capacity to present alternative options. The business sector thus subordinated the problems of developmental strategy to the political guarantees granted to them by the government on issues of labour controls, law and order and respect for property.

Of more importance was the Chicago Boys' ability to 'neo-liberalize' the distinctly traditional *gremialista* movement. After Chacarillas and the increasing successes of the economic model, the *gremialistas* were forced to abandon the remaining vestiges of their corporatist habits and other central elements of their ideology. As these became increasingly incompatible with the growingly radical liberalism of the political economy, the *gremialistas* were unavoidably left without a coherent political vision with which to justify the *revolución capitalista* to which they now adhered. This doctrinal crisis goes far in explaining their reliance on the DNS in the ensuing post-shock period (1975–7). After 1977, neo-liberalism was able to fill the *gremialista* ideological void, providing a global vision of society which satisfied both the anti-interventionism and the depoliticizing elements of the initial *gremialista* project. There was now a reinterpretation of subsidiarity and the once sacrosanct intermediary bodies. These bodies were scornfully accused of monopolistic and oligarchic tendencies. It was the responsibility of individuals to defend freedom rather than the *gremio*, the neighbourhood group or the trade union. This spectacular *volte face* was justified by the assertion that these groups had, in the face of an omnipotent state, been necessary. As this type of state was no longer a reality, the *gremio* and trade union had become an irrelevant anachronism. While the general rhetoric articulated by the regime still breathed the air of traditional *gremialismo*, the actual substance did not.

Many commentators point to the inherent lack of a defined economic philosophy to explain this transformation.[38] Guzmán must have been aware of the unfeasibility of corporatism within a world order which abhorred both the state and any form of collective organization.[39] As a result, the *gremialistas* simply refrained from formulating any detailed economic programme. This function had been adequately performed by the government economists, fellow students at the Catholic University and comrades-in-arms. The *gremialistas* were more concerned with the realization of their politically authoritarian dream and the Chicago Boys were there to see it reach fruition. While the *gremialistas* were prepared to abandon the essence of their archaic philosophy to gain power, the neo-liberal economists needed certain aspects of *gremialista* ideology to justify their proposed project. They also needed members of the movement to implement the model. The neo-liberalized *gremialistas* seized this dual role, using their administrative skills and their traditional rhetoric to conceal the real nature and objectives of the counter-revolution.

Prior to Chacarillas, purely technical justifications had sufficed, but after 1977 the demands for political reform became forceful. An ideology was needed which could globalize the problems of both the political and the economic spheres of national life. This became the *raison d'être* of the neo-liberalized *gremialista* movement, which now espoused the mercantile individualism of Hayek and Friedman rather than the Catholic-inspired integrationist concepts of the *Estado Nuevo*. Superficially, *gremialismo* remained unchanged, in order to continue as a legitimizing force for the regime and its programme. In reality, however, a free market philosophy had taken grip, so much so that it soon became impossible to distinguish the *gremialista* from the pure neo-liberal.

General Pinochet's Chacarillas speech prevented the fragmentation of the civilian regime coalition and to some extent deflected the growing international pressure on Chile. Yet its lack of definition, in terms of timetable and future political model, exposed the plan as a strategy for delaying specific commitments on the transition process, an obvious device to side-step crisis by deflecting debate within the regime. But the crisis had been largely overcome by 1979, as the economy boomed and Chile became an increasingly popular member of the international finance community. This was reflected in a new feeling of *triunfalismo* on the part of the regime and its right-wing civilian coalition partners. Their economic confidence reached such high levels that their previous defensive position on political, social and labour issues was quickly forgotten. The military regime and its supporters, after six years of partial political and ideological confusion, now had the confidence to forge ahead with the long-awaited institutionalization process which would culminate in a *'verdadera revolución libertaria'* encompassing the entire social relations system.[40] However, satisfying this objective became a justification for prolonging the regime. Pinochet declared in 1979 that the country would have to delay the transition to allow the consolidation of the regime's political, social and economic transformations. This announcement marked the abandonment of the Chacarillas plan. Fulfilling the regime's development plans now superseded any future political itinerary.

4 The Right's Institutional and Political Legacy

By 1979, Chile's ruling classes had embraced the neo-liberalism espoused by both the Chicago Boys and the *gremialistas*. The free market concepts of Friedman and Hayek became hegemonic within a ruling elite which desperately needed to fill the ideological vacuum with which it had been plagued for so long. The Chilean right thus abandoned traditional political pragmatism and defensiveness, emphasizing instead 'ideological action' and 'revolutionary' alternatives for the country's structural problems. By 1979 it had the power, the political will and the confidence to surge forward, to expand and consolidate the achievements of the last six years.

THE SEVEN MODERNIZATIONS

With the appointment of the neo-liberal José Piñera as labour minister in 1978, the Chicago Boys expanded their already extensive influence in areas other than those directly linked to the economy.[1] With the so-called *siete modernizaciones*, encompassing labour, pensions, education, health, agriculture, justice and decentralization, the revolutionary dimensions of the neo-liberal project began to permeate all aspects of Chilean society.[2] The modernizations' objective was the infusion of market forces into the country's social relations network. This involved an extension of subsidiarity into non-economic spheres, underpinned by the official aim of ensuring efficiency and rationality in decision-making, expanding equality of opportunity and increasing the limits of individual freedom to cover all aspects of everyday life. The reforms involved the decentralization of public institutions in order to place greater responsibility in the hands of the private sector. According to its supporters, this would permit market decision-making to operate and thereby guarantee 'freedom of choice' in provision and access to basic social services. This was vindicated as necessary to free the individual from the 'monopolistic' *gremio* and trade union, to stimulate efficiency by submitting individuals' decisions to the logic of the market, and to transfer responsibility for social services from an inefficient state to a dynamic private sector.[3]

According to Pilar Vergara, the implicit aim of the modernizations was to create the material and cultural conditions on which the Hayekian-inspired *Nueva Sociedad* would rest; a society based on the Utopia of self-regulation.[4] The aim was to break up the previous value system, forcing it to readapt to the planned new order. The reforms thus served as a powerful re-socializing agent, displacing social demands and conflict from the state to the market. As a result of the deliberate atomization of social networks, individuals would now resolve their problems in isolation and within the market, rather than collectively through their social organizations. By seeking to fragment interest-group demands, the neo-liberal model sought to remove the *raison d'être* for organized collective action and consequently of politics itself. This was to be reinforced by the individualistic and competitive nature inherent in the concept of equality of opportunities, where reward was seen to be based on individual merit, thus substituting common interest with individualistic self-interest and competition.[5] Of all the modernizations, those relating to labour and pensions most reflected this thinking.

The Labour Plan

The *Plan Laboral* was an attempt to restructure civil society and its relationship with the state. Supporters of the scheme claimed it would conciliate trade union freedom with economic efficiency and social justice. They criticized the pre-1973 labour laws as infused with Marxist concepts of class struggle and monopolistic trade union superstructures, claiming they had 'led to politicized syndicalism and irresponsible collective conflict which punished both employer and economic development'.[6] The official aim of the labour reform envisaged a trade unionism based on depoliticized *gremios* in which worker freedom and collective action (albeit reinterpreted) would be guaranteed. 'Modern' strikes, which would minimize social cost and orient themselves towards purely wage demands, rewarding workers for high productivity levels, would replace old style, conflict-based, mass action. Thus a new era of responsible negotiation between employer and employee involving only those directly related to a dispute would follow, putting an end the 'damaging' involvement of the state.[7]

The new legislation proposed a legalization of trade unions by individual firm rather than by sector, under the principle of free affiliation. Only 10 per cent of company employees were needed to form a separate union which could then proceed to negotiate independently with the management.[8] Trade union federations or any association involving more than one union were prohibited from any form of collective bargaining, as were workers involved in services and the public sector. The right to strike was guaranteed but severely restricted, action being limited to a maximum time-period of 60 days after which an employee would be automatically dismissed. Companies were also given the right to employ scab labour the moment action began and lock out workers at any time. In essence, this was an attempt to create 'independent' unions, each bargaining separately and competitively, taking part in collective action in a decentralized manner which would pose no threat to the rationality and stability of the economic model. In a classic case of divide-and-rule the reform's planners, in a single swoop, introduced free markets, a decentralized structure and political demobilization into labour relations.[9]

The Pension Plan

The rationale behind the *Plan de Pensiones* was based on a partly correct critique of the traditional pension schemes as inefficient and regressive. This often led to workers' contributions being used by the state to target and benefit specific interest groups. The Frei administration (1964–70) attempted unsuccessfully to reform the system, but the pension scheme seemed to be the eternal 'sleeping giant' no one wished to wake. The government proposed to replace the 'pay-as-you-earn' system with individual savings plans (AFPs). Workers were to continue contributing but to private companies rather than public institutions. They were free to select a company of their choice which would invest their contributions in the capital markets. Consequently, the rate of return obtained by an individual depended directly on successful investment in highly profitable companies. Once affiliated to these profit-making financial institutions, the worker's 'fate' became closely intertwined with that of the enterprises in which their funds were invested.

According to Alejandro Foxley, another practical consequence of the scheme was that by relocating social security funds from the public to the private sector the command over a huge volume of long-term investment resources was thus transferred. The economic groups acquired control of 75 per cent of these resources. This was the result of workers choosing to invest in the larger groups, perceiving them to be less of a financial risk, inadvertently strengthening the most powerful conglomerates. Workers thus became the unsuspecting agents reinforcing the pattern of asset concentration that characterized the economic model.[10]

The new scheme was remarkable in that it implied the fundamental change of a system which had been culturally and economically ingrained for a majority of Chileans, accustomed to a relatively well-developed welfare state. The new plan, however, explicitly excluded the growing number of workers not privy to stable employment. It simply attempted to build a system in which employees and the success of both the economic model and the groups were intrinsically linked. To take any form of collective action was to threaten the stability and success of the economy so posing a serious threat to the future of workers' pensions.

The Social Sector Modernizations

These followed similar principles of transferring resources from central government to the private sector, by developing a private market for education and health from which individuals would buy the best services available in a competitive environment. The education system was privatized as far as possible, decentralized and responsibility transferred to the *gremialista*-dominated *alcaldías*. The universities lost their long-cherished autonomy and became subjected to the principles of the free market. Complete lack of government quality control seriously damaged both the reputation and the quality of the Chilean higher education system. Within the health system, *libre elección* and the *rol subsidiario del estado* became the key phrases, and the role of the state was reduced. The private sector was given the task of providing health care through the use of insurance schemes, while the already impoverished *Servicio Nacional de Salud* was abolished and replaced by 27 regional bodies each managed by presidentially appointed administrators. Through these reforms, the neo-liberals attempted to reduce the political nature of Chile's educational, social and welfare institutions, subjecting them to the market, with the explicit intention of atomizing both state power and civil society.

While the *gremialista* notion of communitarianism had inspired the regime's rhetoric during its first years, by the end of the 1970s, the Hayek-inspired Chicago Boys and their loyal political allies, the neo-liberalized *gremialistas,* had become the dominant force within the military regime. They succeeded in extending their theories of the market into every aspect of Chilean life. Their vision of society, expressed through the seven modernizations, became all-encompassing and was seen as infallible by a majority of both the political and economic right. All that was now required were the political and legal assurances which would ensure the permanence of the neo-liberal model. The 1980 constitution was to serve this function.

THE 1980 CONSTITUTION

With the ratification of the constitutional project in a plebiscite in 1980, the Chicago Boys and *gremialistas* reached the pinnacle of their success. They had consolidated their positions of influence to such a degree that the eventual constitution reflected their attempts to raise to a constitutional level the basic principles of the all-encompassing neo-liberal model, as well as the mechanisms to enforce it. They were successful in consecrating a political, social and economic model organized according to the laws of the market. As the regime and its civilian supporters did not question the hegemony of the economic model (so pervasive were the Chicago technocrats), the internal debates which culminated in the constitutional proposal taken to plebiscite centred on other issues marginal to the economic system. These concentrated on the questions of transition timetable, the role of the president, the validity of universal suffrage, the forms of representation and the role of both the armed forces and political parties.

The Right and the Constitutional Debate

Although the *gremialistas* favoured a relatively lengthy transition process, in order to give the modernization reforms time to consolidate, support was given to a specific and defined time limit. This was seen as essential to prevent the loss of regime stability in the face of growing internal and external pressure, especially over human rights. On whether there would merely be a reform of the 1925 constitution, accompanied by a short transition, or a new complete and definitive one, the *gremialistas*, like the government, opted for the latter.[11] Guzmán believed that the flexibility of a new constitution would allow the military government to maintain its power intact and complete its mission, while simultaneously deflecting potential criticism by more clearly defining the transition. He also claimed that it would commit the government to gradual but effective re-democratization by removing the political risks of regime instability and loss of credibility.[12]

While no longer advocating corporatist forms of representation, the *gremialistas* continued to distrust the concept of universal suffrage. It was perceived as a mechanism which established artificial levels of equality. Men were, after all, essentially unequal, thus any process which sought to alter this was flawed and dangerous. It was also prone to 'mass distortions', since individuals change and emotions are elevated during elections when the electorate were liable to make irrational decisions. The system was also unable accurately to reflect or measure the 'intensity' of voters' opinions, through the simplification of positions which are in reality highly complex. Universal suffrage was also accused of causing a permanent struggle at the mass level, candidates having periodically to submit themselves to the verdict of the people, thereby forcing rash and demagogic promises to be made. Above all, the *gremialistas* believed that this liberal electoral process would lead to the infiltration of Marxist ideas with demagogy serving as an instrument for so called 'totalitarian' ideologies, taking over the popular will through global myths.[13]

While universal suffrage and the notion of liberal democracy itself were viewed as essentially flawed, the *gremialistas* were forced to accept them as options of *mal menor*.[14] Hence, they proposed a *democracia protegida* to prevent the rise of totalitarianism, statism, terrorism and demagogy. Universal suffrage would become the predominant, but not the exclusive, method of generating political authority, used only in electing the president, the Chamber of Deputies and two-thirds of the Senate. Universal suffrage would also have to recognize and respect the essential values of *chilenidad* – the dignity of man, the family as the basic nucleus of society, social integration in opposition to the class struggle, the state as objective and impersonal and the autonomy of intermediary groups.[15] Individuals or ideologies in contradiction with such values faced political exclusion.

The *gremialistas* also wished to create an institutional framework for the 'responsible and constructive exercising of universal suffrage' to avoid the rise of demagogic practices. They called for a strong presidential system, since legislatures were seen as doctrinaire and inefficient and therefore counter to what the *gremialistas* believed to be the increasing 'technification' of government. They wished to establish designated institutional bodies which would safeguard the contents of a future constitution against the possible demagogic and populist tendencies of elected government. The military would play a crucial role acting as guardians of the *institucionalidad* with majority representation in the proposed quangos as well as extra powers placing it in an autonomous position *vis-à-vis* a future elected government.

While sharing much of the *gremialistas'* economic thinking, the traditional right approached the question of regime stability and efficiency from a totally different perspective. They emphasized political rather than coercive legal norms, relying more on the integrity of the party political system and universal suffrage as a system capable of guaranteeing individual and collective rights. Democratic stability could only be maintained through the free exercise of liberal democratic rights, although the old right was clearly divided on the issue of whether to exclude Marxist parties and ideologies. They favoured a shorter transition phase and an *Estatuto Constitucional Provisorio* rather than a new 'revolutionary' constitution.

The nationalists participated in the debate from the same position as always, categorically rejecting any constitutional process, and viewing concessions towards a democratic system as signalling a return to the pre-1973 political model. More preferable was an organic democracy through the institutionalization of the military's political power. Organic channels of representation would substitute political parties, while universal suffrage would be replaced by organic suffrage and indirect presidential elections. While tacitly supporting the neo-liberal modernizations, the nationalists refused to adapt to new circumstances. Unlike the *gremialistas*, and to a lesser extent the traditional right, they were unwilling to succumb to the Chicago Boys' ideological pull. The principles of the movement remained intact, thus frustrating attempts to influence the regime and consequently leading to political marginalization.

Because of the model's unchallenged status, the Chicago Boys were relatively indifferent to the problems surrounding the structuring of the state's political organs. As technocrats they were willing to leave the legalistic intricacies of formulating a constitution to those more capable of doing so. As long as sufficient time was provided to consolidate the modernizations and the mechanisms created to secure the model's permanence, the Chicago Boys were content to allow the *gremialistas* a free hand in formulating Chile's future constitutional framework. The technocrats were well aware that while including traditionalist concepts such as the family, the nation and the common good, the *gremialistas* would, nevertheless, protect the neo-liberal model within a new constitution.

The Constitutional Process

The lengthy constitutional process officially began in the immediate post-coup period with the creation of the *Comisión Constituyente*, chaired by Enrique Ortúzar. Despite initial appearances, it was a *gremialista*-controlled institution, in quality if not in quantity. Early members included the Christian Democrats Enrique Evans and Alejandro Silva Bascuñan, Jorge Ovalle from *Democracia Radical*, and the ex-parliamentarians from the now disbanded *Partido Nacional (*PN), Sergio Díez and Gustavo Lorca. By 1977, both Evans and Silva Bascuñan had resigned, while Ovalle had been removed under the direct orders of Pinochet.[16] The regime's attempt to introduce a certain level of political diversity within the *Comisión* was merely a smoke-screen to hide the real power-base within it: Jaime Guzmán. He provided the intellect, the political will, the ideas and, most importantly, the personal and ideological link between the General and Ortúzar's commission. While asserting absolute autonomy and independence, the *Comisión Constituyente* was nothing more than a government tool, enhancing a level of respectability and legality. In November 1977, the commission was handed a presidential document outlining Pinochet's constitutional requirements. Unbeknown to them, Guzmán had been instrumental in its formulation, illustrating the extent of *gremialista* influence in the regime. When in October 1978 the Ortúzar Commission presented its *anteproyecto,* the degree of government interference had been so great that unofficially the document became known as the *Proyecto Pinochet.*[17]

As expected, and in accordance with *gremialista* thinking, the *Comisión* proposed a strong presidential system and an eight-year term of office. The president, the deputies and two-thirds of the Senate would be elected via universal suffrage, the remaining third being designated by various government authorities. The armed forces were to be given a central role as the protectors of the institutional system. They would constitute a majority in the new and all-pervasive super-quango, the *Consejo de Seguridad Nacional* (COSENA), and be given the power to make it autonomous from government control. Marxist parties would be constitutionally prevented from organizing under threat of draconian punitive measures and individuals accused of holding such views could risk losing all political rights. In accordance with the Chicago Boys, the proposed project guaranteed the neo-liberal economic model by removing the Central Bank from state control and by including measures which would constitutionally prevent the state from expanding or acting contrary to the principle of subsidiarity.[18] In an attempt to appear both legalistic and pluralistic, the regime submitted this *gremialista*-inspired document to the scrutiny of the *Consejo de Estado*, widely believed to have represented the views of the traditional right. Chaired by the former President of the Republic, Jorge Alessandri, its role consisted of modifying the Ortúzar proposal with the explicit aim of submitting a final draft which would then be adopted or rejected through a plebiscite.

While maintaining the essential political and economic dimensions of the *anteproyecto*, changes were undertaken which reflected the relatively moderate sentiments of the *Consejo*. Weary of a system that concentrated too much power in the hands of the president, the *Consejo* reduced the term of office to six years and proposed giving more responsibility to a future Congress. Curtailing certain aspects of the military's proposed independence and strength also became an objective for Alessandri and his team. The armed forces' chiefs lost both their security of tenure and their in-built majority in the COSENA. Alessandri also reduced the quorum necessary to reform the constitution and limited, albeit slightly, some of the enormous power given to the Central Bank by Ortúzar and his commission. By far the most significant contribution made by the *Consejo* concerned the establishing of a transition mechanism, an area ignored by the *Comisión Constituyente*. The *Consejo* proposed that prior to the actual transition process, a designated Congress should be established, consisting of 120 deputies and 40 senators, which would assume increasing political responsibility as the transition progressed. This transition, beginning in March 1981, would last five years after which full democratic elections would be held. Although the *Consejo del Estado* was set up with Pinochet's support, it seemed unlikely that the proposals would be accepted. With the advice of Guzmán, and Chicago Boys such as Baraona, de Castro, Piñera and Kast, Pinochet made 175 unilateral changes to Alessandri's proposal, strengthening both the power of the armed forces and the president and disregarding the proposed transition timetable.

The Campaign for the Constitutional Plebiscite

Having delayed the institutional process for more than seven years, Pinochet gave the opposition less than four weeks to comment and debate the proposed scheme. On 10 August 1980, he announced his intention to submit the revised constitutional plan for approval by plebiscite. This sudden decision caught the opposition unaware with Pinochet clearly using the element of surprise to his advantage. Throughout most of the period prior to the vote the opposition remained divided over what tactics to employ, whether to abstain and condemn the whole process as fraudulent, or to campaign for a NO vote. Despite its final decision to actively oppose the YES vote, the opposition faced a number of obstacles resulting in a vote which was not only far from fair, but was also condemned by most international observers. Apart from the relatively brief electioneering period, which limited the effectiveness of any opposition, political space in which to work was severely curtailed. Challenging public debate did not take place and the political parties remained actively proscribed and repressed. The campaign was marked by intimidation and pressure. Moreover, the lack of an electoral register did not facilitate the process, since it made it impossible to check the validity of both voters and votes.[19]

On the eve of the vote, Pinochet made a final appeal to the electorate, announcing a package of economic measures, including a series of tax cuts, in a blatant attempt to win over wavering voters.[20] The vote took place on 11 September 1980 and not surprisingly the constitution was approved by 4.2 million to 1.9 million votes, with one million abstentions being counted as YES votes.[21] Thus, the government obtained 67 per cent of the vote to the opposition's 30 per cent.[22] While it seems highly unlikely that the regime could have garnered such a high level of support if the plebiscite had been free of fraud, it does seem credible that it could have obtained a plurality of the votes. Both fear and substantial support for the Pinochet administration could have harvested such a success, but Pinochet was taking no risks.

The Constitution

Despite Pinochet's dramatic intervention, the constitution marked the culmination of neo-liberal supremacy within the regime, as expressed by the Chicago Boys and *gremialistas*. It established an eight-year transition period, in which Pinochet would continue as president, after which a single-candidate plebiscite would be held, presumably with the general himself. This would give Pinochet the opportunity to remain in power until 1997.[23] The permanent elements of the constitution would only come into effect after the proposed single-candidate plebiscite in 1989. Until then, in a clear abandonment of his Chacarillas commitment, the military would continue as the sole expression of political power, as stipulated in Article 24 of the constitution. This satisfied the Chicago Boys' and *gremialista* demands for ample time to fulfil the needs of the model without the 'inconvenience' of democratic interference.

The most controversial section of the new constitution was Article 8, which defined the political system as a *democracia protegida*. This banned any person or group which contradicted the essential values of the 'Chilean spirit' from engaging in political activity, but was primarily a mechanism to exclude Marxists from the political system. Those convicted of such an offence would lose most of their civil and political rights. An individual would no longer be allowed to hold public office, be appointed as a university rector or lecturer or be allowed to teach. They would also lose the right to work in the media and hold any position in labour, student or business organizations. This would apply for 10 years, or 20 in the case of 're-offenders'.[24]

The constitution, reflecting *gremialista* ideas, did not adopt full universal suffrage. It limited its use to the election of the president, the deputies and two-thirds of senators. The remaining one-third would be nominated by the commanders-in-chief of the armed forces, the president and the Supreme Court.[25] The constitution made no provision for direct local and regional elections, opting instead to create presidential appointees at the regional, provincial and neigh-bourhood levels.

The concentration of political power is an underlying feature of the 1980 constitution. In placing very little power in the hands of the legislature, the regime chose to concentrate this faculty in the hands of the president. In western liberal democracies, in theory at least, the executive proposes and the legislature legislates. In the Chilean constitution both these faculties were given over to the president and his ministers. Also, by extending his term of office to eight years, what was created was more akin to a medieval monarch than a modern democratic president.[26] The president was to become the 'principal functionary' of a heavily entrenched neo-liberal system, removing the source of power from elected representatives and placing it instead in the hands of unelected and unaccountable military-dominated bodies. The COSENA was one such body, consisting of the president of the Republic, the presidents of the Senate and the Supreme Court, each of the four commanders-in-chief of the armed forces and the director-general of the police.[27] It had veto power over issues of national security, meaning that it could comment on any constitutional issue and interpret what constituted national security. It was the supreme source of power, with every constitutional body, including the president and Congress, subject to its authority. Another such institution was the *Tribunal Constitucional* which incorporated lawyers appointed by the president, the Supreme Court, the COSENA and the Senate. As with the members of the COSENA, these lawyers enjoyed security of tenure and were responsible for upholding the constitution. They had the power to declare any law unconstitutional, and prohibit any organization, movement or political party which contravened Article 8. It also had the authority to decide in which cases individuals had acted in a spirit deemed to be in contradiction with the article. Not even the president was exempt, although in his case Senate approval was necessary before he could be removed from office.[28] Economic management was removed from government control through the creation of an autonomous Central Bank with responsibility for monetary policy. The constitution also restricted the state's ability to expand by including the notions of *no discriminación* and subsidiarity.

These were constitutional mechanisms designed to weaken elected administrations, to block government attempts at reform and prevent any substantial changes being made to the neo-liberal socio-economic order. By concentrating power both in the executive and in unrepresentative, quasi-military bodies, the constitution attempted to remove all but the most general of issues from democratic scrutiny and control.[29] The constitution thus conformed to neo-liberal aspirations, as expressed by the government economists and the *gremialistas*, desiring an individualistic vision of society enmeshed in law. Yet it left many issues undefined. No mention was made of political party organization or a possible electoral system. Article 24 and the constitution's notable omissions marked a further and powerful form of control which were to impact upon the country over the next eight years.

Both the modernizations and the constitution thus presented a critical vision of Chile's history, of statism, politicization and party division which, according to its supporters, had condemned the nation to chaos and stagnation. Central to this was the state's role in destroying the creativity of individuals, of paving the way for the rise of demagogy and protecting inefficiency. Political freedom was only possible with economic freedom which had in the constitution been defined around the concepts of property and the free market. The latter was perceived as the cornerstone of the new political system. Its objective centred on the atomization of the state's decision-making process and its conversion into a sum of individuals which would make collective action unnecessary and irrelevant. A reduced state was likened to a stronger state, not only because it would now become bureaucratically manageable but because it would prevent the proliferation of political actors under pressure to influence decisions which were irrelevant to them. The Utopia inherent in this neo-liberal project was one in which organized collective action, politics and societal change became irrelevant. As the market alone could not guarantee this, authoritarian and military power together with exclusion mechanisms were essential to ensure the permanent and all pervasive nature of the model.

Before it became safe to hand over power to civilian authority, the neo-liberals had insisted on two preconditions: the real transformation of society in accordance with the principles of mercantile competition, demand atomization and state reduction; and the creation of a new leading political class which would be socialized by the system and willing to continue the work of the Chicago Boy and *gremialista* old guard.[30] After the consolidation of these preconditions, the Chilean new right had created a constitution-in-waiting which would, if successful, make structural change very difficult to implement. They had in effect created a near perfect system, one that could not be changed with ease (the constitution made it virtually impossible to obtain the necessary quorum to modify it) and which conformed precisely with the wishes of its creators.

5 The Re-emergence of Party Politics

The political context changed dramatically for the right after 1983. Economic recession, government intransigence, the development of an effective opposition and the growth of social mobilization led to a crisis in the Pinochet regime. Until then, however, political and economic conditions for the government had been favourable. Following the initial economic stabilization and restructuring policies applied until 1978, the Chicago model had sought to perfect an approach which would automatically adjust the economy to domestic and international business cycles. Foreign capital poured into the country, assisted by the liquidity of an international financial system overflowing with petrodollars, and feeding an economic boom.[1] Easy credit allowed entrepreneurs to borrow large sums of money at low interest rates to facilitate programmes of expansion and diversification. It also enabled exporters to neutralize the effects of an increasingly overvalued peso.[2] The middle sectors could not resist the opportunity to borrow cheap dollars and thereby consume imported goods and services, previously the reserve of the upper classes.

Politically, the model helped to subdue those social groups excluded from the policy process. The positive effects of capital inflows were more visible than the negative consequences. The prevailing affluence among the upper and middle classes, and among some sectors of the working class, muted most of the discontent that existed. By 1980, many economic indicators had turned favourable, while official discourse successfully concealed some of the less favourable indicators, including falling levels of domestic savings, deteriorating balance of trade figures, an overvalued peso and an ever-increasing gap between rich and poor. Admirers of the model were thus increasingly confident that the socio-economic transformations had been a success. The military regime and its civilian clique of supporters felt satisfied with the political climate as they did in their economic achievements. The opposition was intrinsically divided and therefore unable to mobilize; the left was still reeling at the split of the *Partido Socialista de Chile* in 1979; the Christian Democrats had entered into an internal process of reorganization and a significant democratic right had as yet not emerged to challenge the hegemony of its authoritarian counterpart. The ratification by plebiscite of the 1980 constitution, however fraudulent it might have been, helped to institutionalize the regime, not only domestically, but with the international community as a whole, especially following the electoral successes of Thatcher and Reagan. Indeed, both the United Kingdom and the United States ended the boycott of exports to Chile, including the sale of arms, and where in 1980 only eight countries had supported Chile in United Nations' human rights votes, in 1981, there were over 20, including the United States for the first time.

THE ECONOMIC CRISIS, 1981–3

By opening the domestic economy so extensively, the Chicago Boys also left it vulnerable to the negative effects of extreme fluctuations in the world economy. The boom hit a crisis when confidence collapsed in 1982. Reagan announced his intention to stem the rise of US inflation, and oil prices stabilized. The resulting squeeze on money supplies meant that outstanding debts could not be serviced. Local currencies throughout Latin America were radically devalued, making dollar debt more expensive and interest rates higher. Businesses found themselves unable to pay their considerable debts. In Chile, the first cracks appeared as one of the country's largest firms declared bankruptcy.[3] Interest rates began to rise dramatically, and smaller firms not tied to the large economic conglomerates began to collapse.[4] Foreign banks refused to lend additional money to Chilean financial institutions. By the end of 1982, international reserves had fallen by almost US$1.5 billion and the balance of payments deficit rose to US$1.1 billion.

Despite mounting pressure from the entrepreneurial groups, the Chicago Boys refused to act, maintaining an unswerving commitment to economic adjustment. Government intervention would have been seen as an admission that the economic model had failed. Chilean policy-makers also believed that the world recession would be mild and short-lived and that international liquidity would soon be restored. By 1982, it became evident, however, that previous economic conditions would not be revived. The Chicago Boys-led economic team therefore announced the unthinkable in June: the devaluation of the peso. The political consequences were catastrophic, the regime having repeatedly insisted that devaluation was not an option. The neo-liberal system was severely shaken and the government's credibility lay in tatters. The devaluation represented a retreat from the radical neo-liberal model. Yet the regime refused to initiate reflationary measures to ease the pressure from usurious domestic interest rates. Pinochet backed the Chicago Boys in their resolve to apply automatic adjustment. By 1983, business failures and unemployment reached unprecedented levels. The government was finally forced into an official acknowledgement of the economic crisis in January 1983, when it ordered the intervention of five banks, the liquidation of three others, and the direct supervision of two more. Paradoxically, the state assumed control of over 80 per cent of the once private financial system and gained indirect control of firms which were deeply indebted to it.

The failure of the neo-liberal model to resolve the problems of growth, investment, employment and an increasingly unjust distribution of national income had been obscured until 1981 by apparent success according to certain indicators publicized by the government, and above all, by an international economic situation that allowed an excessive flow of foreign capital into Chile. This capital was dedicated to financial speculation and consumption based on growing indebtedness. The collapse of this financial system, combined with the dogmatism and incompetence of the economic team, laid bare the profound weaknesses hidden beneath the triumphant official discourse. What had been called the 'Chilean miracle' finally showed its true colours: increasing economic concentration in the hands of a few groups engaged in irresponsible plundering and speculative manipulation, one of the highest external debts in the world, the destruction of national means of production, acute economic stagnation, 30 per cent unemployment and the lack of an economic project with solid investment bases for the future.[5]

THE POLITICAL CONSEQUENCES OF THE ECONOMIC CRISIS

The Chicago Boys had committed two fundamental errors: they failed to recognize the severity of the economic crisis, destroying many of the arguments which underpinned their theories; and they failed to insist on a shorter transition period than the one finally adopted by the regime. To have promised a speedy return to democratic norms would have deflected some of the economic criticism being levelled against the government and its civilian economic team. These two mistakes led to the marginalization of these economists from the government. The economic disaster caused the discrediting of neo-liberalism as the regime's legitimating ideology by nullifying its revolutionary pretensions. This in turn led to a weakening in the support for the government nucleus on the part of the political and economic elites: the middle and upper sectors, as well as the entrepreneurs. However, at no time did they question the fundamental aspects of the system. They did not renounce their economic liberalism, nor did they abandon their adherence to the authoritarian and conservative political project, the so-called protected democracy, consecrated in the 1980 constitution.

However, the 'rescue' mission which the regime had assumed began to be questioned by the very forces which until then had comprised its base of support. For this elite, the mission of the military government was no longer to *refundir* Chilean society, but to conduct a transition process towards an efficient and stable democratic order. The idea of a revolution destined to create a new order which would supersede the formalism of traditional democracy was replaced by appeals to the mechanisms of formal democracy as a principle of legitimization and foundation of social and political stability.[6] The economic crisis revitalized the debate about the economic model, but now the voices of groups close to the centre of power were augmented for the first time by diverse business associations and organized interest groups. A majority of the sectors in the dominant coalition lost faith in the model's capacity to succeed. Doubt led to growing isolation of the technocratic team, weakened the team's capacity to govern and caused its progressive disintegration. This 'entrepreneurial revolt', headed by the most affected small and medium-sized entrepreneurs, marked the end of unquestioning acquiescence on the part of the regime's most loyal supporters.[7] Spurred by the alarming political consequences of Chile's seemingly bottomless economic crisis, the entrepreneurial organizations sought to organize in opposition to the model. By mid-1983, under the aegis of the *Confederación de la producción y del comercio* the entrepreneurs called on the government to introduce reflationary policies to reactivate the economy.

The first signs of mass popular discontent appeared in May 1983 with a series of huge protests which lasted until November 1984. These *protestas* were to change the face of Chilean politics. In May 1983, the copper workers' union changed its first call for a general strike to one for a national day of protest. Support for the action was expressed by Chileans staying home from school, partially disrupting daily activities, briefly demonstrating in central Santiago, honking car horns, banging pots and turning off lights at a prearranged hour. The massive success of the first day of protest surprised both the government and the opposition and inspired the latter to repeat this form of social mobilization. These protests united the middle and popular sectors on the same side of a political confrontation for the first time in several decades. A cooperation which was later eroded by government efforts to co-opt some business associations economically in order to dissuade them from participating in the protests. Cooperation was also mitigated by middle-class fears of the radical forms of mobilization manifested by youth groups in the *poblaciones*, the marginal urban townships. As a consequence, subsequent mobilizations became concentrated among more militant groups of youth, students and the urban poor.[8] The middle classes were also badly affected by the crisis, with debts multiplied and the disappearance of bank deposits and savings. This trend alienated these middle-class sectors from the military regime. The isolation of the government produced a genuine opening in which organized sectors could publicize their discontent without risking a massacre.

THE RIGHT'S RESPONSE

The interior minister, Sergio Fernández, proposed a programme of political liberalization to diffuse any problems which might arise out of the country's present economic difficulties. Pinochet rejected these proposals, which included the immediate legalization of political parties, and Fernández resigned as a consequence. This reopened the bitter disputes between the various sectors which made up the right-wing coalition. Criticism against Pinochet's position was led by the *Nueva Democracia* group which represented the *gremialista* sector and which had close associations with Fernández. During February 1983, rumours spread that the nationalist sector would enter the government. This implied that the regime was ready to adopt a politically hardline stance and that the neo-liberal economic model would be drastically altered. This came to nothing, however, after Pinochet named an interior minister who represented a continuist position rather than a nationalist one. Yet soon after, Pinochet made a speech that was highly critical of the liberal democratic model and called on his associates to create a civilian–military movement in support of the regime. The task was delegated to Federico Willoughby, a prominent nationalist leader. Pinochet's strategy of playing off the so-called *blandos*, supporters of immediate political liberalization, against the nationalist *duros*, meant the regime lacked any kind of coherence during this period.

The government made no political response to the crisis until August 1983 when it named the moderate nationalist leader, Sergio Onofre Jarpa, as the new interior minister. Jarpa's plan consisted of opening up a dialogue with the democratic opposition and of replacing the neo-liberal economic team with a more pragmatic and flexible group. His aim was to decompress political tensions rather than carry out more wholesale liberalization, something which the *Nueva Democracia* group was demanding as the only solution to growing mass discontent. Jarpa also hoped to break up the opposition coalition by marginalizing the left from the more right-wing opposition sectors willing to talk to the regime. In essence, to split the moderate opposition coalition *Alianza Democrática* (AD) from the more hardline *Moviemiento Democrático Popular* (MDP).[9] For Pinochet, Jarpa's decompression strategy implied a mechanism to buy time until 1989, when the government could apply the permanent elements of the constitution, thus ensuring the continuity of the regime; in essence, to neutralize the mobilizing capacity of the opposition. AD's participation in Jarpa's dialogue led to serious tensions in the opposition camp and to a change in the nature of the protests. These now concentrated in the more popular areas of Santiago, became more confrontational and attracted fewer and fewer participants. The Christian Democrats and the middle classes even began to perceive these protests as part of the communist conspiracy.[10]

Jarpa's strategy failed. In 1980, the opposition might have been willing to accept a Brazilian-style negotiated and gradual transition. However, by 1983 the country was in the midst of an economic crisis and the opposition at the height of its mobilization programme. This was bound to create difficulties in the government–opposition dialogue. Throughout the negotiations, the regime refused to propose concrete solutions to the institutional crisis, reinforcing the view that the government was buying time in order to deactivate the opposition's mobilizing capacity, but the opposition was simply too confident to compromise. Moreover, owing to the fragmentation of the right, Jarpa was unable to unite the pro-government civilian coalition in support of his plan. His strategy was further undermined by a hardline group (consisting mainly of nationalists) whose influence on Pinochet had greatly increased since the collapse of the Chicago Boys' hegemony. These sectors opposed any strategy which would imply a softening in the government's approach to the democratic transition process. The failure of Jarpa's dialogue was largely due to the government's attempt to promote only a limited liberalization programme at a time of crisis, when opposition expectations were high. Even the more moderate sectors who were prepared to talk adopted a maximalist position. Unable to find the moderate voice he had sought, Jarpa resigned. The collapse of the talks accelerated the creation of political parties, especially within the right.

THE RE-EMERGENCE OF THE POLITICAL RIGHT

Jarpa's plan had one significant effect: the *de facto* creation of a series of political parties which were still illegal but now tolerated.[11] The economic crisis, the *protestas* and the government's response had shown that an accommodation with opponents of the regime was not a viable option. The right finally became aware of an unavoidable truth: that the system could not be fine-tuned. With the failure of Jarpa's decompression strategy, the right opted for the only alternative available: to face the fact that it would have to adapt and mobilize if it was to ensure the survival of the regime's principal political and economic accomplishments. In the face of this growing opposition and mobilization, supporters of the regime attempted to form a united right-wing movement. However, fragmentation, which had usually been a feature of the left, plagued this nascent process, and seemed to be defined in terms of how far to associate with the military regime and the figure of Pinochet himself. It also faced a dilemma in its ideological opposition to political parties *per se*. How could the right organize itself around a party system if it opposed such movements? There were also clear ideological and tactical differences. Under these uncertain circumstances, its fragmentation seemed inevitable. By 1987, three main tendencies had emerged.

The Neo-Liberal Right

The neo-liberal right became the strongest of these tendencies and, within this sector, the *gremialista*-based *Unión Demócrata Independiente* (UDI) emerged as the most influential right-wing movement during the latter stages of the military regime. Other parties established during this period included the *Movimiento de Unidad Nacional* (MUN), the precursor to *Renovación Nacional*

(RN), today Chile's largest right-wing party, and a neo-liberal faction of the *Partido Nacional* (PN), Chile's most important conservative movement prior to the 1973 military coup.

Unión Demócrata Independiente (UDI)

UDI was set up in August 1983 by *gremialistas* from the *Nueva Democracia* movement, as well as Chicago Boys and other representatives of the bureaucratic technocracy of the military regime. Its creation was a logical conclusion to the ongoing fusion between the principal right-wing ideological currents during the military government. The nationalist leader Federico Willoughby was particularly scathing in his attack: '*Yo llamo agencia de empleos al gremialismo y empresa de demoliciones a los Chicago Boys, estos dos grupos se han juntado para tener un organismo de nombre de señora y matrimoniarse con cualquiera de los partidos tradicionales.*'[12] With Jaime Guzmán as its unquestionable leader, the party proposed to bring together supporters of the 'principles of a free society' (defined as one in which the markets and the intermediary organizations shoulder the main tenets of the decision-making process), followers of the 1980 constitution and those who believed in a gradual transition towards a 'full' democratic system. The short-term objective consisted of defending the model in the face of the pragmatic economic line now being adopted by the government. From the outset, it sought to adopt a hardline political position and throughout this period its rallying cry was a call for the proscription of the radical left-wing coalition, the MDP. Although politically and socially conservative, the party was economically very liberal. UDI was classified as an urban right, economically modern but at the same time paternalistic and authoritarian, representing those most loyal to the military regime's economic and political model. Despite its claims to be an independent movement, UDI was, and still is, the party most closely associated with the military, representing an attempt by Guzmán and his followers to secure the prolongation of the regime's 'achievements' in a post-military Chile.

Movimiento de Unión Nacional (MUN)

It was clear that Jarpa would need a vehicle to support his political decompression project. MUN was therefore set up in 1983 as a force in favour of the *apertura*. It proposed a joint effort to adopt 'a path of understanding and dialogue', to be achieved via a process of political liberalization and by correcting the errors of an inflexible and insensitive political economy. Andrés Allamand, a young charismatic politician, former leader of the secondary student opposition to Allende's Popular Front government and a former PN activist, became the MUN's provisional secretary-general in October. His leadership reflected the nature of its constituency: unlike UDI, most of its members had not been active participants in the military regime and were on the whole former PN congressmen weary of reviving the historic party of the pre-1973 traditional right.

The MUN constituted a support apparatus for Jarpa's 'liberalization from above' strategy. Pinochet believed it would form the basis for a mass-based movement in support of his government and his eventual presidential candidacy in the proposed plebiscite. However, once Jarpa's strategy faltered, the movement adopted an increasingly independent line from both Jarpa and the government. It sought the centre ground and became the only significant right-wing movement to contemplate a future without Pinochet. It even criticized the 1980 constitution because of its lack of coherence *vis-à-vis* the permanent and transitory articles. However, Allamand was aware that adopting a position too close to the opposition could prove counterproductive and thus damage the movement's prospects for bringing together more hardline right-wing elements. The collapse of the Jarpa Plan (which failed to provide any government concessions, constitutional modifications nor acceptance of any moderate demands) placed the MUN in a very difficult position: to side with the opposition or reinsert itself into the government's civilian coalition. Although seeking to distance itself from the military regime, the MUN was still a right-wing movement whose members had supported the 1973 coup and the military government. Siding with the opposition would have inevitably alienated most of its popular support. It felt it had no option but to remain essentially a pro-regime political movement, although unlike UDI, a critical one.

Partido Nacional (PN)

The reorganization of the PN represented a rebellion by certain sectors of the traditional pre-1973 right, especially those who before 1965 had belonged to the *Partido Liberal*, which had then opposed Jarpa's conservative leadership of the PN and now wished to become a semi-opposition, and supporters of a shorter transition period. The process of rekindling the PN was a long and arduous one, owing to the protracted negotiations with the MUN. The party was divided at the most fundamental level: its former members could not even agree whether to revive the historic party or set up a new organization. A mediating commission, set up in December 1983, sought to bring together these opposing tendencies, proposing a virtual *de facto* amalgamation with the MUN, because of the latter's close ties with the government and its clear differentiation from the opposition. This position was rejected by many in the PN who hoped to bring the party closer to the democratic opposition. The PN thus suffered a double tension: offers and pressures to participate in the unity of the right and rapprochement with the opposition and in particular the Christian Democrats.

The Nationalist Right

The nationalist sector, including organizations such as the *Movimiento de Acción Nacional* (MAN), *Avanzada Nacional* (AN) and the *Frente Nacional de Trabajo* (FNT), was characterized by a high degree of loyalty to the regime, but was unable greatly to influence the government. It nevertheless gave its unconditional support to Pinochet and represented the most reactionary and intransigent tendency on the right.

Movimiento de Acción Nacional (MAN)
The MAN was set up in 1987 by associates of the nationalist think tank, the *Corporación de Estudios Nacionales* (CEN). Despite its rhetoric to the contrary, it adopted a revisionist ideological position by claiming that nationalism was embedded in representative formulas and the separation of powers. Although it differed from other ideologies in rejecting the monopolistic role of parties in the political arena, the MAN nevertheless abandoned the nationalist concept of organic democracy and removed any concepts which could be interpreted as fascist. This relatively pragmatic approach was a recognition of nationalism's weak position within the political arena. It attempted to foster links with other right-wing groups and supported the notion of a broad alliance. Yet its differences with the neo-liberals were too fundamental and the party dissolved itself after only a year of existence.

Avanzada Nacional (AN)
AN emerged from the confused political arena of 1983. It consisted of nationalist sectors and adopted a position of unconditional support for the military government and the 1980 constitution. But what

differentiated it from the MAN? While the MAN represented orthodox nationalism in its corporatism, at least on paper, AN promulgated the notion of 'military revolution'. Its rhetoric was military and it fostered the cult of the armed forces. AN was characterized by its attempts to mobilize the *pinochetista* base of support and organized rallies in which the dictator was present. It became in essence Pinochet's party.

Frente Nacional de Trabajo (FNT)

The FNT was set up in 1985 by Jarpa after his resignation as interior minister, principally as a vehicle for his political ambitions. It sought to bring together anti-communists and other right-wing elements who did not share the free market orientation of the Chicago Boys. If UDI represented the internationalization of the right, the FNT was an attempt to reintroduce the notion of a nationalist right.[13] Jarpa's principal support base for his 'popular national movement' came from sectors such as the lorry drivers, the corporatist *gremio* leader Domingo Durán, agricultural entrepreneurs and, most importantly, from the military itself.[14]

The Democratic Right

The democratic right represented those in favour of reasserting the strategies and ideology of the historic right and were the right-wing sector most critical of the regime. In respect to its political strategy, a central preoccupation centred on forging an alliance with the Christian Democrats. This was a position loyal to the spirit of the pre-1973 traditional right which prior to 1964 had an 'understanding' with the centre party. However, it enjoyed only limited success in bringing together the right's historic social bases, traumatized by the experiences of the *Unidad Popular* and weary of fraternizing with the Christian Democrats. Although it failed to institutionalize itself, individual representatives of the democratic right, including more moderate elements within the PN, joined with the opposition in its campaign against the regime.

RENOVACIÓN NACIONAL: THE UNIFICATION OF THE RIGHT

The nature and outcome of the political confrontation which developed in the post-1983 period threw into question not only the continuation of Pinochet's leadership, but also the fundamental aspects of the societal model and the political regime (which had shaped the ideology and historical project of the officialist right). Three fundamentals were therefore at play: the ultra-capitalist socio-economic model, the authoritarian political regime and the *pinochetista* leadership. The right was tensioned between the *pinochetista* strategy of linking the three above projects and the opposition's desire to destroy all three. This limited the right's capacity for political flexibility. Despite agreement around fundamental aspects of the dominant political and economic model, the right was not a unified sector, being essentially divided around one fundamental question: the possibility or impossibility of preserving the model and the regime with a leadership different from that of Pinochet.

However, the approaching plebiscite put into sharp focus the need to set aside any differences in defence of the fundamental aspects of the regime. To this end, MUN made a public statement in favour of unification at the start of 1987. It called on the PN, FNT and UDI to create a single party, *Renovación Nacional* (RN), whose consensus would be based on certain principles and a common vision of the transition process. It strove to adopt a common front on issues such as support for representative democracy, the breakup of centralizing state power, the concept of a social market economy, a rejection of totalitarianism and support for the 1973 military coup. Consensus on the transition would centre on reaffirming the legitimacy of the 1980 constitution and the military's return to barracks by 1989. AN was excluded because of its opposition to the liberal democratic system, as were the democratic right-wing parties because of their support for the opposition. For to have opened up the new movement further would have led to unreconcilable fragmentation. Andrés Allamand sought to avoid possible power struggles by proposing that each party sacrifice its leadership in favour of unity. However, the allocation of posts and leadership 'quotas' by sector became an issue of internal debate within each party.[15]

Allamand's strategy was threefold. First, to persuade the military that an alternative candidate to Pinochet was needed for the plebiscite. The new movement would have to convince the regime that its achievements could continue without him. Second, to separate the radical left-wing MDP from the opposition. RN would thus seek to create a *realidad bipolar* with the opposition: the moderate left on the one hand and RN on the other. Third, to ensure that RN, rather than the Christian Democrats, negotiated with the regime on the issue of an alternative candidate. The PN rejected the invitation, opposing the exclusion of the democratic right and objecting to the presence of the FNT and UDI, perceived by the PN as anti-democratic. The PN thus allied itself with the democratic right sector linked to the opposition AD.

The resignation of Ricardo Rivadeneira as the consensus president of RN in December 1987 marked the starting point of the internal crisis which led to the breakup of the organization in April 1988. The differences between the disparate integrants of RN became apparent during the power struggle which ensued to replace Rivadeneira. His resignation was implicitly linked to the high degree of internal tension caused by disagreements over the plebiscite conjuncture. Rivadeneira represented the moderate wing of the party and was critical of the military regime. The sector represented by UDI sought to pressurize RN into quickly declaring its support for the YES and for Pinochet as the single candidate (which would have entailed the General remaining in office for a further eight years).[16] Two tendencies thus developed. First, a sector comprised of former MUN activists which perceived RN as an independent party *vis-à-vis* the government. It wanted RN to adopt a highly critical stance towards it and promote concern for human rights abuses. Although this group sought to defend the government's socio-economic model, it criticized its political manifestations and favoured speeding up the democratization process. Second, a group centred on UDI and other conservative elements. This sector constantly put pressure on the new party to move closer to Pinochet. It saw RN as a basis of civil support for the military regime and as the inheritor of its achievements.

Strategic Differences

The MUN sector was the first to call for open presidential elections as an alternative strategy to the plebiscite. This became a consensual position within the MUN: in July 1987, the party's political commission approved a proposal from Jarpa to support the notion of open elections.[17] Although it publicly supported the plebiscite formula, UDI privately favoured competitive elections. Jaime Guzmán himself stated that 'if Pinochet wants to be re-elected, he would be better advised to choose a system of open and competitive elections ... and not a plebiscite'.[18] However, once the pro-*gremialista* Sergio Fernández was reinstated as interior minister (with the aim of coordinating Pinochet's candidacy for the plebiscite) and made clear the government's intention of proceeding with the plebiscite, the political parameters turned upside down. UDI hardened its position and once again declared its support for the plebiscite mechanism. However, this did not lead to further conflicts within RN. Once it became clear that the plebiscite would proceed, despite opposition from certain sectors of the right, discussions on possible electoral mechanisms ceased. Debate now centred on the issue of the single candidate. The Allamand-led sector consistently favoured any candidate other than Pinochet. The Guzmán sector, on the other hand, gave its unconditional support to the General's candidacy. Rivadeneira's resignation was announced at this precise point. Which sector won control of the party now became critical.

RN's political commission elected Jarpa as provisional president prior to the internal elections to be held in March 1988. Although publicly Jarpa's election was portrayed as a consensus decision, his nomination had been bitterly opposed by UDI. Despite obvious differences between Jarpa and the MUN, the latter had given its backing for several reasons. First, both Allamand and Jarpa shared the same pre-1973 political tradition in the PN. There was a common ideological bond which explained in part their desire to unite in opposition to the *gremialistas*. Second, by uniting they could secure a bloc within the party capable of counteracting UDI's influence in the forthcoming internal elections. Third, Jarpa seemed to be the only candidate capable of defeating any potential UDI candidate.

The principal unifying element within RN was its desire to continue the regime's socio-economic reforms. There was general agreement over the main pillars of the neo-capitalist revolution.[19] This goes some way to explaining the fusion of various tendencies within a single political party. The conflict within RN, however, centred on how best to ensure the continuation of this project. While UDI adopted a strategy of intrinsically linking Pinochet's leadership with the consolidation of the model, the Allamand sector attempted to depersonalize the model. Once the possibility of competitive elections had been extinguished, MUN opted to favour a plebiscite with a consensus candidate in order to avoid the confrontation which a Pinochet candidacy would have entailed. MUN realized from very early on that the right might lose if Pinochet were chosen as the candidate. UDI, in contrast, partly blinded by ideological zeal, adopted the view that only a Pinochet candidacy could emerge victorious. There also existed differences over other fundamental issues such as constitutional reform, primarily over Article 8. UDI had a natural tendency to reject any kind of modification to a constitution it had inspired virtually single-handed. The sector led by Allamand favoured repeal of the draconian measures included in the article. However, the moderate sector in RN was outvoted by Jarpa and Guzmán, both being virulent anti-communists.

In January 1988, RN's political commission voted in favour of officially accepting the plebiscite as a mechanism for presidential succession. It also agreed to support any candidate chosen by the commanders-in-chief of the armed forces. The document asserting RN's position stated that the party had full confidence that the armed forces *'ejercerán plenamente las altas responsabilidades y atribuciones que la constitución política les entrega...y que actuarán con acierto y amplitud de criterio, buscando asegurar la estabilidad institucional y concitar el respaldo mayoritorio de la ciudadanía'*.[20] Rather than quashing differences, this ambiguous declaration caused further controversy. The various sectors within the party differed on the document's interpretation. Allamand, for example, stressed the conditional nature of the support (that it required the backing of a majority of Chileans thus implying that Pinochet would not be a viable option) and that RN had not expressed support for any particular candidate. UDI, on the other hand, stressed that this was a declaration in support of the YES option and that the party had full confidence in the choice of the commanders-in-chiefs of the armed forces. It seemed clear, therefore, that the declaration was a consensus document cobbled together by the party's various tendencies, thus accounting for the implicit ambiguity.

RN Internal Elections: Breakup of the Party

Internal elections to choose the party leadership were due to be held in March 1988. This period represents the most divisive and acrimonious in the party's history, since the outcome was crucial to its future direction. A choice had to be made between two competing strategies and internal groups: the *Alianza*, made up of the MUN and the FNT, whose objective was to re-elect Jarpa as president; and a group centred on UDI, known as the *Verdadera Renovación*, which sought to organize pro-UDI electoral lists throughout the country; the explicit aim being to elect Guzmán as president and promote Pinochet's candidacy. The differences were simply conjunctural: unconditional support for the constitution versus support for it but recognition that it needed to be reformed; closer ties to the regime

versus an emphasis on the independence of the party; and unconditional support for Pinochet's candidature versus the possibility of an
alternative candidate.

Verdadera Renovación favoured the complete replacement of the
party hierarchy, preferably with its own, mostly young UDI candidates, reflecting the party's generational makeup. The MUN and
FNT wished to include experienced as well as young members. They
therefore sought integrated electoral lists. Although leaders from
both factions stressed that the party was seeking to find unitary lists
in all districts and regions, in the majority of the metropolitan region
and in the most important provinces, including Valparaíso, Arica,
Antofagasta and Arauco, two competing lists emerged. Those
presenting unitary lists did so mainly because in those areas no faction
was powerful enough to present its own separate list. The campaign
was fiercest in Santiago, where there were six unitary lists compared
to 14 competitive ones. The regions presented 27 unitary lists and
only nine competitive ones.

Mutual accusations and recriminations soon emerged. *Alianza*
leaders denounced the intervention of public functionaries and
municipal employees in the internal electoral process, one MUN
leader even stating that the sector knew 'that activists from the *poblaciones* have offered preferential treatment in the allocation of
housing subsidies and work in the PEM and POJH (government work
programmes) in return for support for their lists'.[21] This accusation is
not far-fetched given UDI's powerful presence in the *poblaciones*.
After years of promoting its activities through the *alcaldías*, UDI had
built up a significant constituency of support within these working-
class areas. *Alianza*, therefore, claimed that party members receiving
the PEM and POJH had been pressured into voting for the UDI lists.
The military government was also concerned at the possibility of
those most hostile to the regime winning the RN elections, since a
UDI victory would ensure RN's unconditional support for a Pinochet
candidacy.[22] The situation deteriorated on 7 March, when during a
meeting of RN's political commission, Guzmán convened a press
conference and called for the resignation of the party directorate,
including that of its president, Sergio Onofre Jarpa. Guzmán
denounced *Alianza* electoral 'irregularities' and stated that to avoid
the postponement of the electoral process, which would detract the
party from its fundamental task (to ensure a YES victory), it was
essential for the party to appoint a leadership which could provide
guarantees to all the sectors in the group. Guzmán proposed that the

leaders of each of the sectors find a truly consensus president and general-secretary. In practice, this would mean an agreement between Allamand and Guzmán. Positions hardened as a result and mutual recriminations increased. As one *Alianza* supporter claimed:

> Guzmán thought he would have an easy victory, but he never imagined that our list had the organizational capacity and underestimated Jarpa's capacity to set up unitary lists. He therefore sought to pressure us by threatening to break up the party and by using the municipal apparatus to pressurize the activists, above all in the working-class areas. On seeing that even by doing this he could not win and by realizing the political error of involving Pinochet in the campaign, he realized the huge costs of losing the election and so came out with the call for the directorate's resignation, without having consulted anyone, and decided to make his statement public.[23]

Alianza adopted a 'legalistic' position *vis-à-vis* the crisis, claiming it was not political but the result of grave acts of indiscipline on the part of Guzmán. Allamand's and Jarpa's attempt to brush off the crisis as a simple disciplinary problem points to two fundamental issues. First, Guzmán's aim was to prevent Jarpa from challenging Pinochet as a possible presidential candidate. It was thus crucial for *Alianza* to maintain the conflict within the political commission, where the sector had a majority and where Jarpa's legitimacy would not be questioned. Second, a moderate faction within *Alianza* (led by Allamand) believed it was essential to marginalize UDI, enabling MUN to structure the party with greater independence *vis-à-vis* the government. This would pave the way for the participation of more moderate elements within the right. Despite the UDI boycott, the MUN-dominated leadership held a series of elections between March and April in those areas of the country where the Allamand tendency could ensure victory. The electoral process was not free of anomalies and tensions. There were daily confrontations between opposing supporters, including the storming of RN's Santiago headquarters by UDI activists, where violent clashes ensued between the two groups.

UDI's position in relation to the crisis consisted of marginalizing itself from the party's institutions, namely the political commission and supreme tribunal. UDI recognized it would be unable to influence events from the party's internal organs, where MUN was in a majority. They therefore sought to delegitimize Jarpa and take control of the party, believing that pressure could best be exerted by paralysing the party rather than working through its legal and proper channels. Guzmán thus believed he could force *Alianza* into reaching a compromise: essentially, equal representation within the party. By creating a climate of ungovernability (through the boycott of the elections and the party structure) Jarpa and his supporters would be forced to back down and reach some kind of agreement with UDI outside the usual party organisms. Guzmán argued that the crisis was political and not discipline-based, as claimed by *Alianza*, representing a confrontation between two incompatible groups with different ways of doing politics. *Alianza*, however, succeeded in keeping the conflict within the party structure and refused to converse outside RN's official organs. At a meeting of the RN's supreme tribunal, Guzmán was accused of infringing the party's declaration of principles, as well as transgressing the norms of the party constitution and the law of political parties. Reconciliation was futile and Guzmán was expelled taking the majority of UDI members with him and reestablishing the *gremialista* party as a separate entity. Not only was the unity of the right thrown into question, but so too was Pinochet's candidacy. The now independent UDI began to work on unconditionally supporting Pinochet as candidate, while a slimmed down RN proposed to support any candidate nominated by the commanders-in-chief of the armed forces.

Allamand's principal objective during this period had consisted of constituting RN as a political force which 'acknowledged the proximity of the end of the military government and [was now] prepared to represent the centre-right in the budding democracy. The task was to recover and to renew a proper political identity'.[24] Thus by the time of the 1988 plebiscite, the right had divided into those who wished to continue with the essentials of the political and socio-economic model of the last 15 years and those who saw the emergence of a democratic regime as inevitable and so wished to occupy the traditional space of the political right. Of the two conservative parties which dominate post-Pinochet Chile, RN represents the former while UDI the latter. Their strategy for the 1988 plebiscite bore this out.

THE 1988 PLEBISCITE

Following very questionable referendums in 1978 and 1980, the Pinochet regime organized in 1988 what was considered to be a technically fair plebiscite, in accordance with the transitory elements of the 1980 constitution. It required that the commanders-in-chiefs of the armed forces and the director-general of the police unanimously select a successor to Pinochet as president for an eight-year term beginning on 11 March 1989. Before taking office, however, the nominee had to be ratified in a popular, yes-or-no plebiscite to take place in October 1988. If the candidate was rejected, parliamentary and presidential elections would be called and the country would subsequently progress towards a system of 'protected democracy'. If, on the other hand, the government candidate was successful, he would remain as president until 1997. No opposition candidate was to be allowed to stand, and Pinochet consequently declared his intention to be the sole contender on 25 April 1988. However, the *Junta* had given him the green light some months back, despite opposition from some members, most notably General Fernando Matthei, commander-in-chief of the air force.

With the exception of a few of the smaller democratic right parties the totality of the right opted for the YES in the plebiscite. However, this concealed wide differences within the pro-regime civilian coalition. While UDI was unconditional in its support for Pinochet, RN had preferred an alternative candidate. In fact, many on the right, both independent and otherwise, would have favoured a civilian candidate, younger and less confrontational than Pinochet. More prudent political analysts, as many were on the civilian right, had hoped for a more moderate centre-right alliance in order to ensure an orderly and peaceful transition, thus alienating the radical left. However, the right once again opted for the historic tendency of *mal menor*, of choosing the lesser of two evils. These differences frustrated the possibility of forming a right-wing coalition in support of the YES. It is possible that the subsequent lack of coherence seriously damaged what was already a very weak government campaign.

Once the split in RN had taken place, discussions within the right centred on the plebiscite campaign. The *gremialista* sympathizing interior minister, Sergio Fernández, stated that the campaign should be organized by those groups directly dependent on the government. This position angered RN for two reasons. First, because the party was highly critical of the intervention of public functionaries. UDI had deployed this tactic in the internal RN elections and Allamand recognized the same was likely to happen again. He was also highly critical of the politicization of the armed forces. Second, Allamand believed the campaign should be carried out by the political parties, which he believed would be more efficient. Parties could rely on a more solid social base of support and had better representation than the military and government officials. It was clear that if the parties were given the lead, RN would benefit most, since it had substantial support and a relatively well-organized structure. However, with Fernández as official campaign organizer, it was UDI which would have the greater influence. Despite agreeing to create a united campaign, RN's participation was at best lukewarm. It concurred with neither the style, tone nor content of the YES campaign and consequently offered only cautious support.

Relations between RN and the regime did not change much during this period. While the party did reiterate its support for the government and the YES campaign, it did not make any declarations in relation to the imminent Pinochet candidacy apart from expressing support for the independent decision of the armed forces. Jarpa even stated that if Pinochet were chosen, it would be better for him to stand as a civilian rather than as an officer. RN's main concern was to convince the public that a YES triumph would entail a real change. It did so through a declaration which called on the armed forces to withdraw from politics and the running of the state, and in which it stressed its support for human rights and respect for freedom of expression. It also called for the modernization process to be consolidated within a civilian and democratic government; support for the economic system, although changes must be made to it and support for constitutional reform.[25] The success of Allamand's critical stance was reflected in the moderate positions adopted by the party.[26] UDI also began to develop its own policies, unlike RN, joining the officialist campaign from the outset and with great enthusiasm. It never criticized the intervention of public functionaries in the campaign and upheld the government's right to use public officials.

During the plebiscite campaign both RN and UDI rejected the traditional schema of left, right and centre. They affirmed that there were two divisions: those who supported a free society and those who defended a 'socialist, centralized and statist' one. In the plebiscite, therefore, not only would the continuation of Pinochet be at stake, but so too would the confrontation between two opposing societal projects. The democratic opposition's slogan of 'dictatorship or democracy' was thus challenged by the right's slogan of 'free society or communist chaos' and the confrontational nature of the plebiscite thus became a confrontation between two systems. RN's criticism of the opposition (grouped around the *Concertación*, a broad-based coalition of moderate left, centre and democratic right-wing parties) focused on two claims. First, that the *Partido Comunista de Chile*

(PCCh) was hegemonic within the opposition coalition, and that the *Partido Demócrata Cristiano* (PDC) had lost the leadership of the *Concertación*. The aim of such a strategy was clear: to discredit the opposition parties. Second, that the opposition had failed to define its position in relation to the plebiscite and the 1980 constitution, allowing RN to claim that the *Concertación* was hypocritical in seeking constitutional guarantees to ensure a just and valid plebiscite while refusing to recognize the legitimacy of the constitution.

Present in both parties, but more defined in UDI, was the right's support for the socio-economic achievements of the military regime. For RN, praise for the government in this respect was balanced by an admission that mistakes had been made on this front and by criticism of the human rights situation. On the other hand, both parties compared the regime's achievements with the chaotic situation before 1973. Achievements which could not be held together by themselves were sustained through references to the threat of a return to the past. Especially with the *gremialistas*, the discourse in support of the regime's work was infused with sordid and dark references to an evil past that would re-emerge if the NO vote won. RN employed less of this doomsday rhetoric, but UDI's declarations, rather than RN's, were subsequently used in the officialist campaign. This is where the main difference between the two parties lay. Within RN there was a desire to realize a campaign with a high political content, that by voting YES it was possible to have a transition from an authoritarian government to a fully democratic one. There was also recognition that the government's and Pinochet's image had to change, and as such, campaign publicity should stress the real changes that a YES victory would imply. Yet RN's attempts to alter the tone of the campaign failed and the *gremialista* point of view prevailed. Impact was the name of the game, and all kinds of tactics were used, however unprincipled. As such, the main themes used in the officialist campaign, the so-called 'Campaign of Terror', included the threat of a return to a chaotic and disastrous past; excessive ridiculing of the opposition parties; identifying them with Marxism and international communism and the dangerous consequences of a NO victory. There was never any self-reflection or self-criticism. Although Pinochet imposed himself as the regime's single candidate and expected to win, a brilliant opposition campaign together with a lacklustre performance from government supporters led to the General's defeat by 55 per cent to 44 per cent in the 5 October plebiscite.

POST-PLEBISCITE REDEFINITIONS WITHIN THE RIGHT

The failure of the YES did not imply a political problem for UDI, blaming as it did, the weaknesses of the YES campaign primarily on the regions.[27] The party claimed that if their campaign in the capital (extensive house-to-house canvassing, for example) had been carried out in the whole country, the YES would have won. UDI also blamed the economic crisis, product of the international recession, for the adverse results, expressing surprise at the fact that the socio-economic success of the government had not translated into electoral gains. Its analysis was superficial, lacking any recognition of the failure of its own political strategy, instead blaming the electorate.

RN attempted to make a more detailed analysis of the failure by concentrating on the weaknesses of the military government's and, therefore, of UDI's political strategy. It blamed the plebiscite mechanism for the defeat, since it permitted the opposition to unite and free itself from the need to elaborate a government programme. RN also blamed socio-economic mistakes made by the regime. However, most of the blame was placed on public functionaries and individuals tied to the state apparatus who carried out a flawed electoral campaign and who on occasions published false opinion poll data (to give the impression that Pinochet was doing very well in the period prior to the plebiscite) with the aim of hegemonizing their position in the process, even conning Pinochet himself.[28] This resulted in the deterioration of the relationship between RN and UDI.[29] It improved only when RN's demand for Interior Minister Férnandez's resignation, as the orchestrator of the officialist campaign, was accepted. UDI's attempt to turn failure into triumph was thus frustrated.

RN and UDI did not significantly modify their political discourse after the defeat. With differing intensity, both parties continued to voice support for Pinochet and his socio-economic policies. Their attitude *vis-à-vis* the democratic opposition did not change either, apart from both parties' desire to negotiate with it. The right recognized the relative weakening of its position after the plebiscite. It became infused with, especially in the case of UDI, a previously unheard of sense of realism which forced it to contemplate defeat in the forthcoming presidential and congressional elections. Reaching an accommodation with the opposition, in the form of constitutional reform, now became a priority, even for UDI. In essence, electoral failure had forced the right to compromise. With Fernández's resignation, Carlos Cáceres, a relatively independent right-wing political heavyweight, took charge of the interior ministry with the aim of steering the regime towards the 1989 general election. Cáceres's objectives were threefold. First, to continue with the process of economic modernization and ensure, as far as possible, its continuation. Second, to negotiate with the opposition on the question of constitutional reform. The opposition parties' position in this respect had strengthened following the plebiscite and its demands for substantial reform of the constitution now had more weight. And third, to ensure a smooth electoral process in which the right's prospects could be maximized.

The military, however, refused to negotiate directly with the opposition, instead relying on Cáceres and General Jorge Ballerino to act as mediators. Pinochet's distrust of politicians remained as fervent as ever and entering into talks with them remained anathema to him. Although the notion of constitutional reform did not generate resistance from the armed forces, a process of persuasion did take place, largely carried out by Cáceres. UDI, while supporting the need for reform, proposed only limited changes, while RN and the opposition sought to dismantle some of its more important elements. However, RN was successful in marginalizing UDI from the negotiations, which involved the opposition and RN itself. According to Cáceres, 'UDI was more or less marginalized from the debate. It was principally RN, the *Concertación* and the government. Jaime Guzmán, the individual most linked with the whole institutional issue, did not feel comfortable with the notion of reforming the constitution.'[30] By opting to take the lead in the constitutional reform negotiations, RN sought to act as the bridge between the government and the opposition, thus securing for itself a reputation as a responsible and democratic interlocutor for the right, firmly placed in the centre of Chilean politics. The party also took much of the credit for the successful negotiations, which included a change in the congressional quorums necessary for approving legislation and, more importantly, the repeal of the draconian Article 8.

Perhaps one of the most important consequences of the plebiscite for the right was the manner in which it revealed the respective strengths of its constituent parties. RN's relative triumph in being proved correct about the plebiscite mechanism and the subsequent electoral strategy, together with its positive behaviour in the immediate aftermath of the plebiscite, consolidated its leadership position within the conglomerate of pro-regime organizations.[31] Yet RN opted for a strategy of *camino propio* whose long-term objective consisted of turning RN into the most important party of the right, as an alternative in its own right, and thus marginalizing UDI from the political arena. Strengthening its independence from the government was another of the essential points of the *camino propio* strategy. In this, it realized the importance of differentiating itself not only from the regime, but from those parties associated with it. Both its moderate policies and attempt to move to the centre (becoming a mediator between the government and the then opposition) were elements designed to move towards those positions. To continue with this policy, RN realized it would have to work with the following electoral premises: first, it would have to present its own candidate in the next presidential elections or at the very least support someone with a proven record of independence from the regime. Second, the failure of the plebiscite left RN in a strong position in relation to the other YES parties. If it wished to consolidate itself in the long term as the principal party of the right, any alliance must have RN as the hegemonic force within it. It must take charge in the design of the government programme, electoral campaign strategy and have priority in the choosing of deputy and senatorial candidates. Third, RN must continue to present a moderate face if it was to succeed in being perceived as a centre-right party.[32]

UDI's position, on the other hand, was considerably weakened by the plebiscite debacle. The strategy had been UDI's and it had failed. From that moment it attempted to revitalize the alliance which was structured around the YES. Yet UDI was aware that the collapse of the alliance fundamentally responded to RN's distancing itself from it. Having lost the plebiscite, however, it was keenly aware that its relatively weak position would not enable it to challenge the opposition in the December 1989 presidential and congressional elections. Yet the deteriorating relationship with RN made an alliance extremely difficult. Pinochet's defeat though had, in theory at least, removed the most important obstacle in the right's attempt to unite around a single banner. The democratic opposition *Concertación* coalition had been very successful and the main tenets of it were likely to remain for the forthcoming elections. Whatever their differences, the right would have to do the same if it were to have any chance of presenting a credible challenge. On the eve of democracy, the right had moved away from the figure of Pinochet, albeit in differing degrees, and even UDI now realized that Pinochet was more of a hindrance than a help. It was now forced to contemplate a future without him. With elections only one year away, the dilemma which the right now faced centred on whether it was to become a presidential force or a congressional one and what the future held for a potentially minority movement within an overwhelmingly presidential political system. UDI and RN, the principal inheritors of the pre-1973 political right, would now be forced to decide whether the future of the movement lay together or apart. However, an apparently irreconcilable tension came into operation which even to this day affects the right's evolutionary process: RN and UDI, since their tumultuous beginning, have been unable to reconcile their differences yet must face the truth that they can neither work together nor survive apart. The development of the right in post-military Chile has been defined by this conundrum.

Part II
The Right in Democracy

6 New Identities and Faces

The right lost its democratic credentials in 1972 after it began to advocate insurrection. However, the 1981–3 economic crisis undermined its confidence in authoritarianism as the optimum model for guaranteeing the political and economic privileges promised by the military after the 1973 coup. Moreover, the general political climate, both domestically and internationally, was now more congenial to democracy. The great ideological battlelines which had been drawn in the early 1970s were now a thing of the past. The right no longer perceived that there existed a violent threat to the capitalist model of transformation. Universal acceptance of neo-liberalism only helped to reinforce the self-confidence of the political and economic elites. By the mid-1980s, the international community, most notably the United States, had substantially altered its foreign policy towards the region. Whereas Latin American authoritarian governments were at least tolerated in the 1970s, because they represented a first line of defence against the perceived threat from communism, foreign policy now began to stress the importance of democracy. Most favoured dictators, in Central America, Argentina, Paraguay and elsewhere in the region, were abandoned and democratic opposition movements were courted by the international community. The Chilean right, more than any other movement representing the economic and political elites in Latin America, now realized the time was ripe for a change if its privileged position was not to be irrecoverably undermined. Therefore, the reconstituted right, or more specifically the *blando* tendency, began to call for an orderly return to democracy. It also redefined the meaning of the term; while in the pre-1973 period, democracy stressed the notion of broadened participation and a more just system of economic redistribution, in the mid-1980s it began to emphasize the notion of rebuilding competitive democratic institutions.

One central question which must be asked but which may yet remain unanswered, is whether the new right's 'new found' support for democracy is procedural, that is, accepted on the basis of a utilitarian calculation, or substantive, that is, valued in itself.[1] For some on the right it was both, for others it was not. Although the present analysis attempts to go some way in answering this question, through an analysis of the party right, we can safely argue that it has now accepted the democratic framework. The acid test, however, will be to see how far it has moved towards substantive support for democracy. We must remember that we are referring to a movement with at least three major sets of collective actors and ideological systems, essentially conservative, liberal and authoritarian. These are clearly distinctions which are not easy to make, especially in the Chilean context. As we have seen in previous chapters, there is an uneasy coexistence of symbolic elements belonging to these ideological traditions in the same political discourse. The practical implications of this mix are important, in that the role a right-wing party is likely to play in democracy will differ according to whether or not it conveys the predominance of liberal, conservative or authoritarian elements. As these labels are far from static we must examine the configuration of right-wing coalitions and ideas before being able to assess the role that a right-wing party can play in the democratic process. This is important because of the paradoxical weakness of right-wing parties: weak in terms of party structure but strong at the level of civil society. A key element in explaining Latin American instability (although this has been less marked in Chile) has been this imbalance. Examining the structure and relative strengths of the right-wing parties will enable us to assess how this disequilibrium has been corrected.[2] We must therefore be wary of over-emphasizing the role of ideology to define such parties, particularly when acknowledging that the two principal representatives of the Chilean right, *Renovación Nacional* (RN) and *Unión Demócrata Independiente* (UDI), are ideologically similar. While ideology is important, we need a more enduring basis of comparison.

Right-wing parties need to build a large electoral coalition to succeed electorally, especially given Chile's binominal electoral system, which promotes the creation of large electoral blocs. During the military regime, the right was more of a pressure group than a political party. Therefore, a significant transformation would require not only the capturing and identification of a larger electoral base, but also the corresponding adaptation of the organizational structure of the old party apparatus in order to be able successfully to compete in the electoral process. Under this scenario, 'old guard' party leaders are likely to be displaced by a new cohort of politicians. We are therefore faced with the prospect of analysing new identities and faces on the right. Most analyses assume that the question is to explain how specific right-wing groups, which rejected democracy in the 1970s and early 1980s, reversed themselves. But there has not only been a change of strategy but a change in the self-identity of the right. There have been new recruits, and groups associated with the traditional right have taken on new roles and stances. We are therefore essentially looking at new forms of organization as legislatures, parties and elections regain major importance. These are all issues which must be examined to enable us adequately to assess the role of the right in the new democratic order.

RENOVACIÓN NACIONAL

One of the most dynamic transformations in the Chilean political class was the emergence of a new wave of 'renovated' centre-right politicians. This generation, composed of young professionals with little or no formal political experience, strongly identified with the economic (although not the political) legacy of the regime, and were eager to incorporate the right into the nascent democratic political framework. This group of individuals sought to revitalize the right through the continued defence of a social market economy, a progressive distancing from the military government, and a firm commitment to a democratic political system.[3] The renovation of the right was most closely associated with the rise of a new class of young politicians in RN who introduced a modern perspective and approach to the country's process of redemocratization. Under the leadership of Andrés Allamand, the party's president from 1990 until 1997, this tendency within RN, known as the *Patrulla Juvenil*, sought to put the right back on the democratic political map.[4] Recognizing that the right faced an historic opportunity to 'renovate' its message and role in the transition to democracy, this younger generation became the impetus behind such a project. Unlike the more traditional *caudillos* of the right, who saw politics as a 'hobby' for the pursuit of personal interests, the modern generation brought a certain professionalization to political life. Its professional training and exposure to the mechanized age equipped it with a rational and efficient approach to politics.[5] Moreover, there were certain former PN *grandées*, the so-called *transatlánticos*, who also adhered to Allamand's political project, among them Francisco Bulnes, Juan Luis Ossa and Pedro Ibáñez. Although they did not belong to the younger generation associated with the *Patrulla Juvenil*, they were politically moderate, economically liberal, and opposed Jarpa's authoritarian style. Many of them were wealthy entrepreneurs who provided financial backing for the modernizing wing of the party.

The *Patrulla Juveníl* faced, and still faces, strong opposition from more hardline and politically traditional sectors of the party, principally the group originally centred around Sergio Onofre Jarpa, who acrimoniously resigned from RN in July 1997 following a decade of political antagonism with younger members of the party. The historical makeup of RN meant that such an ideological and strategic duality was inevitable. From the onset, RN brought together a seemingly unholy alliance of right-wing modernizers, such as Allamand, and moderate nationalists and conservatives, many of them former PN stalwarts.[6] The cultural, generational, ideological and political differences between these two competing sectors is indeed stark. Jarpa and Allamand's stylistic differences embody the difficulties which surround the two sectors' marriage of convenience. Jarpa is a politician representative of the old school, a hermetic personality more often than not referred to as *Don Sergio*. Allamand, known as *Mr Apertura,* is referred to informally as *Andrés*. Jarpa is a predictable politician, whose adversaries, especially those within the government, know how he works. Allamand, on the other hand, is unpredictable, known to be a politician of surprises. Jarpa adheres to oral rather than written culture and prefers to be guided by instinct rather than by well-devised political projects. Allamand is a politician of the technological age who downloads his speeches onto computers and likes the party to produce countless documents and projects for public consumption. Jarpa's greater commitment to the military regime allows him to withstand the right's self-criticism on issues such as human rights. He is a conservative and a nationalist. Allamand, on the other hand, is liberal and progressive. Jarpa is a centralizer, who attempts to impose with his 'aristocratic' presence and refuses to surround himself with teams of advisers, while Allamand is a team player. Jarpa is a virulent anti-communist and will not meet with the left, while Allamand has friends across the political spectrum. Jarpa has lukewarm relations with the media; he will give on-the-record interviews, but is unlikely to provide his personal view on a given issue. Allamand has strong ties with the media and will provide off-the-record information.[7]

These personal differences have been played out in the wider context of RN politics and embody the differences between these two competing sectors. At a basic level, this was a struggle for the leadership of the party, a battle over how RN should function as a movement. A struggle between old style personalist *caudillo* politics and the new world of 'organizational structures', mobile phones and fax machines. This was also a generational battle between the modernizing young guard and the anti-left old guard. There is also a correlation between those who in some way participated in the *ancien régime*, such as Jarpa (interior minister during the military government), and the young cadres who did not. The latter believed themselves to be more independent *vis-à-vis* the military and acted accordingly. This invariably led to bitter disputes between both wings of the party, especially over such sensitive issues as the role of the armed forces in the new constitutional order and the vexed question of human rights violations.[8]

These disputes came to a head in the events leading up to the party's Third General Council in Valparaíso in August 1990, when both Allamand and Jarpa sought to win control of RN. Allamand's first challenge to Jarpa's presidency took place on 9 April during a meeting of the party's political commission.[9] At this meeting, the *Patrulla Juvenil* wing presented a motion which maintained that, in the face of sustained growth (the party became the country's second largest following the December 1989 general election), it was now necessary to modernize the party by establishing a clear political programme and a reform of the party's structures. It also called for candidates to the party presidency to declare themselves before the meeting of the party's supreme decision-making body, the general council. Francisco Bulnes, an ally of the modernizing sector of the party, explained that this procedure was critical given that '*no lo puede hacer una directiva improvisada que se maneja muy bien en el área chica, pero que llegue siempre tarde a los grandes temas*'.[10] This position ran counter to the personalist approach adopted by the RN president. Jarpa opposed an election mechanism which demanded that candidates present themselves in advance of the general council. Despite opposition from pro-Jarpa members of the political commission, such as Miguel Otero and Angel Fantuzzi, the motion was passed by 13 votes to two. The traditionalists, however, refused to claim defeat, and as one Jarpa supporter declared, it was still possible that '*el estilo de viejo cuño que ha imperado en RN retome su gran sitial y que Jarpa resulte finalmente aclamado, sin candidatura previa, como presidente de su partido*'.[11] The traditional wing of the party thus had a clear distaste for modern politics, especially the concept of internal elections; leaders should be chosen by consent rather than through the ballot box. The modernizers, on the other hand, felt this was the only strategy which could oust Jarpa and replace him with Allamand. The RN president could only be removed using modern methods of political brinkmanship, the traditional right's historic weakness. However, fearing a competing electoral list at the general council meeting, the right's generalized fear of internal competition prevailed and Jarpa finally decided not to stand for re-election; thus a unitary list was presented to the council.

Although Allamand became president, the party directorate was engineered in such a way as to represent both wings of the party: Félix Viveros became the party's secretary-general. As a former leader of the PN's *Juventud Nacional*, Viveros, together with Allamand, was one of the founders of the *Movimiento de Unión Nacional* (MUN). He had been responsible for Jarpa's senatorial campaign and was loyal to both men. The five vice-presidents consisted of Enrique Larra, a pro-Jarpa politician; Alberto Espina a pro-Allamand party activist; Carlos Reymond, who was not linked to either side; Gonzalo Eguiguren, the most fervent Jarpa sympathizer who also cultivated a good relationship with Allamand; and Miguel Otero, a virulent opponent of Allamand's. He had flirted with the possibility, as many others had, of presenting an alternative list once Jarpa had decided to stand down from the presidency. The pro-Jarpa lobby had insisted on his participation in the new directorate as a precondition for supporting Allamand. Moreover, Senator Sebastián Piñera, a moderate right-winger who had voted NO in the 1988 plebiscite, much to the consternation of the right, was excluded from the leadership as a further precondition for the support of the traditionalists.[12] The unitary list, with Allamand as president, was 'elected' at the party's general council on 5 August. Elections for the political commission were, however, competitive and all sections of the party were represented. Allamand supporters won six seats, as well as having the support of two parliamentary representatives on the commission. Jarpa obtained the support of four members, as well as that of three parliamentarians, while seven members of the new political commission did not express their loyalty to either side.[13]

Allamand's victory was all the more impressive given that the modernizing tendency represented a minority in the party. However, three factors ensured that the modernizing wing would prevail. First, the right's traditional unifying instincts. Not supporting the number two in the organization, Allamand, when the number one had opted to retire from the leadership, was viewed as a recipe for internal conflict. Second, the right's historic pragmatism forced many to accept that only an Allamand-style party could be successful in attracting voters in sufficient numbers. Third, financial considerations prevailed. The conservatives were well aware that RN was financially insolvent. The party thus needed the considerable resources that the *transatlánticos*, as well as wealthy modernizers such as Sebastián Piñera, could provide.[14] The election of Allamand as president marked the most important turning point for the party and its modernizing wing. It represented the first sign that a new breed of politician, a new generation, was about to take over the party right. The change in leadership also posed new challenges for RN's competitor, UDI. Allamand at the time was 35 years old and thus represented a threat to UDI's claim of being the party of the 'young generation'. Moreover, UDI faced a party which sought to elaborate a modern ideological project in a direct challenge to UDI's own brand of ideological 'political modernity', although of a more conservative type.

On winning the presidency, Allamand's priorities and challenges were clearly marked out. First, to establish his personal leadership and confront the *jarpistas* and those RN deputies with strong regionalistic instincts, resentful of the party's centralizing bias. He also needed to harmonize the 'feudal gentlemen' of the right, the inorganic pressures of the entrepreneurial sector and navigate between the conservatives and liberals of the party. Second, he had to re-establish the ideological pillars of the right, given that the centre-left government had adopted the social market economy, rallying cry of the Chilean right. Third, Allamand faced the challenge of resolving the party's organizational and financial problems. Fourth, he sought to move RN towards the centre, with the aim of winning over traditional Christian Democrat supporters. His strategy involved distancing the party from the figure of Pinochet without alienating the right's *pinochetista* supporters. Fifth, there was a need for him to establish good relations with the entrepreneurs, a crucial element in the party's financial and political drive. Without their support the party may well have languished at the expense of the more 'entrepreneur-friendly' UDI.

UNIÓN DEMÓCRATA INDEPENDIENTE

UDI's evolution as a party was markedly different from that of RN. As such, its organizational structure and the make-up of its leadership is very distinct. While RN is characterized by its attempts to transform itself into a modern, liberal, western-style right-wing party, UDI has pursued a very peculiar political path. Although it is politically and socially very conservative, its economic ideology represents the most extreme form of neo-liberalism. This reflects the party's historical trajectory incorporating both the *gremialistas*, responsible for the military regime's social and political ideology, and the neo-liberal economists who were largely responsible for economic policy during the Pinochet administration. This ideological fusion has generated what we could describe as technological conservatism, a phenomenon which has very few parallels outside the Chilean experience.[15]

Several features have characterized UDI and its leadership since its inception in 1983. These, rather than ideology itself, have differentiated the party from other right-wing competitors. First, the party leadership is drawn almost exclusively from former student activists from the Catholic University.[16] The domination of student activists in UDI is highlighted by the composition of the party's parliamentarians. While only five out of 46 RN congressmen during the Aylwin administration (1990–4) were student leaders at university, 12 of the 16 UDI parliamentarians had participated in university politics. Moreover, most were law students who studied under the aegis of the movement's founder and indisputable leader Jaime Guzmán.[17] The fact that the future economic policy-makers of the military regime (the Chicago Boys) were economics graduates from the same university helped facilitate the eventual ideological fusion between these two seemingly incompatible political groups.

Second, the party is generational in composition. UDI's hardcore party activists are almost exclusively in the 35–50 years age bracket. This corresponds to Guzmán's tutelage of the Catholic University's law faculty during the military regime. Before Guzmán's assassination in 1991, it was difficult to find UDI members of his generation or older, since no one was able to overshadow Guzmán or dispute his pre-eminence.[18]

Third, most of the leadership gained valuable political experience in the municipalities or other government departments during the military regime. These institutions represented the principal '*escuela política para la derecha. Allí formaron a varias generaciones de dirigentes y no es casual la gran cantidad de diputados, y hasta senadores, cuyo origen de acción política fue en el municipio*'.[19] As a consequence of the military government's neo-liberal doctrine of breaking up the 'centralizing state' and its paranoid insistence that it apply the Doctrine of National Security to its control of local authorities, policy-makers concentrated on establishing control in the *comunas* before attacking the state as a whole. Prior to the 1992 municipal elections, 84 mayors were UDI members, all of whom controlled very large budgets. Most of these are now prominent UDI leaders and parliamentarians. This intrinsic relationship between UDI and the previous regime has played an important part in the party's continued adherence to the military government in general, and to Pinochet in particular. Unlike in RN, there is no breast-beating nor any internal debate around the issue of loyalty to the military administration. The political socialization of UDI had been nurtured by the military regime from 'the cradle to the grave'.

Fourth, Catholicism has played a fundamental part in UDI's development. Although RN has a strong Christian component, many of its members are not practising Catholics. Religious differences between the two parties are similar to those which divided the traditional right into conservatives and liberals. However, UDI's Catholicism is integrationist rather than confessional as was the case with the pre-coup *Partido Conservador* (PC). Moreover, unlike the former PC, before the creation of the *Partido Demócrata Cristiano* (PDC), UDI does not have the backing of the Chilean Catholic Church. Its implicit responsibility in human rights abuses during the military government would make it virtually impossible for the Catholic Church officially to sanction the party. However, UDI has close links to the conservative Catholic *Opus Dei* movement, founded in Spain in 1928 by the Spanish Bishop José María Escrivá de Balaguer. There are around 2,000 *Opus Dei* members in Chile, as well as 15,000 sympathizers and approximately 20 bishops. Two of UDI's most prominent leaders, the former president Jovino Novoa and the mayor of Las Condes Joaquín Lavín, are members of the organization. Other UDI sympathizers are also closely associated with *Opus Dei*, such as Bishop José Miguel Ibáñez Langlois, editor of *El Mercurio's Cronica Literaria* (known by the pseudonym Ignacio Valente) and Lucía Santa Cruz, a journalist with *El Mercurio* and a researcher in the UDI-linked *Instituto Libertad y Desarrollo*.[20]

Fifth, UDI has been marked by its extreme homogeneity reflecting in part its evolutionary process as a movement and party. The fact that virtually the totality of its leadership emanates from a very tightly knit sector grouped around the 'mystical' leadership of Jaime Guzmán has infused UDI with a high level of party discipline which is difficult to find outside Leninist structured left-wing parties. This homogeneity, and the party unity which this implies, is still a powerful force, despite Guzmán's death. There is still an uncanny similarity between all party leaders and parliamentarians. Their ability to espouse the party line virtually word for word is such that it is difficult to remember which UDI personality is actually speaking. Their political, ideological and cultural sameness makes it very difficult for any party activist to force their individuality into the open; they are indistinguishable from each other, simply cogs in the party wheel.[21] Although Guzmán's death opened certain subtle fissures, he had ensured that his legacy would continue. Admiration for Guzmán has been such that his influence still holds strong. He had moulded certain individuals as his successors and these have enjoyed the same level of loyalty.

Although no discernible tendencies are visible, certain differences or nuances can be gauged. These have been relatively minor and are insignificant when compared to the disagreements affecting RN, but they are nevertheless a source of potential future conflict. One such division centres on the party's religious emphasis. This is primarily because UDI comprises both the Catholic *gremialistas* and, to a lesser extent, former members of the military government's economic technocracy who tend to be secular. The latter have nevertheless maintained a lower profile. Although they have coexisted relatively peacefully, internal problems do sometimes arise, although these very rarely make it into the public domain. Julio Dittborn, a prominent UDI leader and deputy, is representative of a sector which does not conform to UDI's traditional cultural makeup, as do others who joined the party after the death of Guzmán, such as the former right-wing presidential candidate Hernán Büchi. Both men are openly agnostic and culturally liberal. Dittborn, especially, has often been at odds with the party hierarchy over issues such as divorce (he is separated from his wife, as is Büchi). This dichotomy between traditionalism and cultural liberalism is likely to accentuate as the party widens its appeal and welcomes a more disparate membership. UDI is a party whose strength lies predominantly in the large urban centres, most notably in Santiago and to a lesser extent in Concepción. A tension has, therefore, developed between the central party and parliamentarians and activists representing constituencies outside the capital. Provincial congressmen have protested against what they perceive as the party's centralizing tendencies.[22] Former UDI Senator Eugenio Cantuarias, who represented the eighth region until losing his seat in the December 1997 elections, had been the most confrontational voice in opposition to the party's lack of commitment to the regions. In 1991, he resigned from the party's directorate in protest. This friction must, however, be placed in context. The problem of regional participation is one which affects all parties. Chile is a very large country where travel is often difficult and inconvenient. It is also a very centralizing country where most political activity, as in other countries, is directed from the capital, which includes around one-third of the total population.

Chile's nascent right-wing political leadership has, therefore, to confront a new political reality. Moreover, it faces this challenge from a position of relative weakness, especially when contrasted with the considerable power it wielded during the military regime. It must adapt not only to a new, potentially volatile electorate, but to new institutions and processes, inherent in any democratic system. Regardless of Pinochet's attempts to destroy Chile's dominant party system, the role of political parties is as strong and vibrant as ever. The right, despite the hostility of a large part of it to this form of political representation, may need to insert itself into this competitive arena if it is to survive and develop as a viable electoral alternative.

7 Party Organization, Finance and Support

The history of right-wing parties is one of attempting to reconcile the often conflicting imperatives of maintaining internal cohesion while pursuing external growth. A right-wing party's evolution is tied to the way in which its leadership mediates these tensions in search of an electoral majority. To understand a party's strategy, ideology and electoral effectiveness we must examine not only its social base, but its internal institutions, and how these have adapted to the new political reality. The right's traditional success in defending its established interests has meant that it has not needed to develop complex party structures, traditionally relying on the state as the supreme 'organizer' of its political domination. However, this is no longer the case. Such an approach is all but impossible in an age of mass politics. Once the structural diversification of the economy has been produced, the political and economic elites need an improved and more sophisticated political machine capable of winning elections to ensure the compatibility of their diverse interests.[1] The process of disintegration brought about by the neo-liberal revolution led to the fragmentation of the class structure, the rupture of traditional patterns of social integration and the rise of new and distinct class groupings. The right may not succeed electorally unless it successfully captures these new constituencies. The nature of its political organization is likely to determine how successful it is in winning over these groups.

In sharp contrast to parties on the centre and left of the political spectrum, those on the right have traditionally been structurally weak. The Christian Democrat, Socialist and Communist Parties have always been organized along long-established and well-defined lines, maintaining close links with rank-and-file supporters whose views are more often than not represented accurately and forcefully. Political leaders outside the party structure are virtually non-existent, and when these have emerged they have rarely exercised more power than elected party representatives. Power in centre and left-wing parties is therefore formalized. Groups outside the formal structures, who wield any kind of influence, have never taken ultimate decisions nor blocked the decision-making capacity of the party leadership. However, within the right, the number of individuals or

small groups who wield sufficient power to influence political deci-
sion-taking and are capable of undermining the autonomy of right-
wing parties, are numerous. Parties on the right, therefore, are more
often than not mere instruments for organizing the electorate with
the sole aim of facilitating the agenda of democratically illegitimate
individuals and groups. This has inevitably weakened the party right
in Chile by promoting the emergence of a political class which is
docile and manipulable to external pressure, particularly that of the
various entrepreneurial sectors and representatives of the large
economic conglomerates.

The right's attempt to strengthen its political structures has been
weakened further by its personalism and lack of political culture. The
view that party membership results in a loss of independence *vis-à-vis*
political decision-making is still prevalent. Being an independent is
still seen as a morally superior position compared to party activity.
Party activism, however, is an associational formula, which organizes
its members and gives them rights and imposes certain obligations.
Political efficiency relies on the direct influence exercised through
specialized organizations of participation. Moreover, this lack of a
political culture has promoted division within the right and worked
against attempts to unify it. It has been unable to accept that diversity
is an essential factor in any political movement. The maturity of a
political party can be gauged in terms of how well it can limit these
differences and prevent them from escalating into damaging and
public internecine struggles which can tear the heart out of a movement.[2] These issues have become central to the right's attempts to
formalize its organizational and decision-making structures and thus
break free from centuries of party inefficiency and weakness. This
process has by no means been a uniform one and the mantle of political modernization has not been taken up with equal enthusiasm by all
within the right. In this, *Renovación Nacional* (RN) and *Unión
Demócrata Independiente* (UDI) have differed substantially.

FORMAL PARTY ORGANIZATION

The military government had been criticized for not including legislation covering the political parties in the 1980 constitution. This was
not surprising given the regime's scant regard for institutionalized
forms of politics. When it did legislate, however, it introduced
measures which imposed strict restrictions, controls and exclusions.

This made it very difficult for parties to register as legal entities as very large numbers of signatures were required. The 1987 *Ley Orgánica Constitucional de Partidos Políticos* also sought to regulate the internal structure of every party. Moreover, the law introduced a system of internal elections which in theory were intended to democratize the party system. This has meant that the nature of a political party has become very difficult to gauge from a simple analysis of its internal organization. An overview of this 'uniform' structure would nevertheless be useful in that it will enable us to assess better how each party has used this 'imposed' structure to make the most of its strengths and best reflect its cultural and historical characteristics. Although both UDI and RN share a common formal structure, they are in reality very different parties organizationally. The internal structure of Chile's right-wing parties are essentially divided into three main areas: territorial, functional and operational. However, RN and UDI have developed these areas to a differing degree, reflecting their particular strengths and weaknesses as well as their political and organizational priorities.

Territorial Organization

The fundamental organizational structure of UDI and RN reflects the administrative division of the country into communes, districts and regions. The commune is the *célula básica* of the party's internal organization and provides the vital link between rank-and-file party members and the national leadership. The district organization, in contrast, is designed to promote the party's strategy and ideology according to decisions made by the national central directorate, carry out training programmes designed by the party's technical teams and assess the needs of the commune as well as the district. The duties of the regional organization include supervising the activities of the district party, electing councillors to the general council, the principal decision-making organ, and assessing the activities of their particular senators.

The national organization is, nevertheless, the most important in terms of decision-making powers and visibility. Its principal body is the general council which meets at least once a year, incorporating all senators and deputies as well as national councillors elected by the regional councils. The central directorate, the political commission, the supreme tribunal and the national leaders of the functional organizations can attend but have no voting rights. The general council has responsibility for policy-making, choosing the candidates for congressional elections and for electing the central directorate, the political commission and the supreme tribunal. It approves or rejects the annual budget and has responsibility for ratifying party rules already approved by the political commission or the central directorate. The political commission incorporates the central directorate, the last five party presidents, three senators and five deputies elected by the parliamentarians themselves, the presidents of the regional councils and 15 non-parliamentary members chosen by the general council. Other former presidents of the party, the president of the supreme tribunal, the national presidents of the functional organizations and the remaining parliamentarians have non-voting rights. The role of the political commission includes exercising day-to-day party policy and has responsibility for implementing those sanctions against party members decreed by the supreme tribunal. The central directorate incorporates the national leadership of the party and includes the president, four vice-presidents of equal standing, a general-secretary and a general treasurer. Its functions include proposing policy to the general council and assuming ultimate responsibility for party policy as well as representing the party in a public capacity. It also proposes changes to the party's rules and statutes, administers the party's finances and has the power to reorganize the internal organization with the exception of the general council, supreme tribunal and political commission. The parties also have an internal disciplinary structure made up of five-member regional tribunals chosen by the regional councils and a seven-member supreme tribunal elected by the general council. The tribunals have responsibility for interpreting the party's rules and statutes, overseeing the internal elections process and internal discipline. They have the power to sanction any member by either suspending them from the party, sanctioning them orally or in writing, or expelling offenders. The supreme tribunal also acts as an appeals court for decisions made by the regional tribunals.[3]

Functional Organization

The parties are also organized along interest lines covering specific areas such as the workplace, universities and neighbourhoods. These bodies are intended to ensure party representation and activism on a 'daily basis'. Functional areas include the trade associations, the trade unions, youth, the townships, social action, professional and the universities.[4] These bodies exist to help socialize potential members who would otherwise not become involved in the party in terms of its territorial organization, which often requires a greater degree of activism. Moreover, there is a long tradition in Chile of political parties infiltrating workplace and cultural, as well as sporting, organizations. Each party's particular strength in any given functional area reflects the nature of that party and the sectors it wishes to attract.

Operational Organization

Both RN and UDI have developed, to a greater or lesser extent, an operational organization with responsibility for providing professional and technical support to the party's internal administration and organization. The efficiency and effectiveness of a given party will depend greatly on its operational organization. These bodies consist mainly of professionals, technicians and administrators who are answerable to the central directorate. Their work involves coordinating, administering and planning the party's work, managing the membership and the organization both in terms of its territorial and functional roles, internal communications, the press and public relations, political marketing, and providing technical support to the leadership and parliamentarians.

THE REAL ORGANIZATION

Although this is a general sketch of RN and UDI's organization it fails to provide an accurate picture of the parties' strengths and weaknesses. Although both adhere in principle to the Law of Political Parties there is much scope for them to concentrate on areas in which they are most effective. Although both have territorial and functional organizations their relative effectiveness varies greatly. Assessing the formal structure of both parties does little more than provide a context from which to examine each party's 'real' organizational framework, transcending formal structure.

Renovación Nacional

The party's main focus has centred on the idea of strengthening the role of political parties. Under Allamand's leadership, RN attempted both to place the party system back in the central arena and to re-evaluate the right's hostility to Chile's dominant political system. Consequently, Allamand sought to renovate the structure of the party. In this vein, one of RN's main priority since its inception in 1987 has been organizational in nature and has centred on developing an institutionalized, mass-based, modern and efficient West European/US style right-wing party. As a result, it has built an elaborate and extensive professional organizational, communicational and technical structure unmatched by any other Chilean political party whether on the right or left (with the possible exception of the Christian Democrats). The party has also introduced modern technology and marketing techniques.

At an early stage, modernizers in RN realized that the party's weakness was organizational. To some extent this was inevitable given that the party was still an incipient organization. Strategists highlighted a series of shortcomings including the existence of an infrastructure which was incapable of meeting the challenges of the political situation at the time, insufficient financial resources, lack of rank-and-file participation in the internal activities of the party, an inability to channel the support of prospective sympathizers and a hierarchical and exclusive decision-making process.[5] In order to maximize the potential of the rapid influx of members which RN experienced in its early years, the party developed an organizational plan with a series of fundamental objectives. These included the creation of an organic, institutionalized and modern internal structure with the necessary human, physical and financial resources to achieve the party's political objectives; the setting up of channels to facilitate the process towards internal party democracy and the decentralization of the party's activities; methods to increase the organic participation of the rank-and-file in the resolutive and deliberative functions of the party, and create a permanent body of technical teams to provide administrative and political support. In order to achieve these objectives, the party developed a support organization around two key areas: political support, and training and research.

Political Support

Back-up support for the party in terms of its political activities is divided into several areas. First, a territorial coordination unit is responsible for strengthening the party's territorial organization and acts as a bridge between the regions and districts. Moreover, regional and district units have been set up to provide administrative support to their respective areas of influence. Second, a functional organizations coordination unit with responsibility for strengthening the party in this area, and where RN is still relatively weak. In its quest to develop an efficient party machine, RN has to a large extent ignored developing what could be described as the more corporatist elements of party organization: those covering social sector activism. To this end, RN set up a series of functional departments covering the universities, the professional and technical sectors, the *gremial-syndical* movement, the entrepreneurial and commercial world, 'social action' (with responsibility for organizing the party's activities in the *poblaciones*), neighbourhood organizations and cultural activities. Third, a technical coordination unit which aims to bring together specialized teams of party workers. This field has been highly developed and represents RN's strongest organizational advantage. The unit consists of several departments, including an electoral department whose functions include the elaboration of electoral strategies, opinion poll work and electoral data analysis; a marketing department whose tasks include structuring an external support team made up of private companies and professional specialists, to analyse and evaluate the party's position in the general political context, the maximization of RN's corporate image, the evaluation of strategies used by other political parties and the design of a publicity strategy; a membership department to maintain and update membership records; a communications department to perfect channels of communication between the central directorate, the political commission, the parliamentarians, the communal, district and regional directorates and the party's *Instituto Libertad*, as well as responsibility for publishing the weekly *Informe Político y de Prensa*, the party's principal internal publication, which represents the basis for the work of the communal, district and regional directorates, and the *Informes de la Acción Parlamentaria,* which provide support to the party's parliamentarians;[6] and a press and public relations department whose principal function is to publish the party's most important publication, *Renovación*, in existence since the party's inception.[7] *Renovación*'s role has been to disseminate party doctrine and other specialized political information to a wider audience. As such, it is less concerned with the minutiae of party activity than with espousing RN's general ideological trends. The press and public relations department also publishes a daily press bulletin containing a resumé of activities and declarations. It is also responsible for developing the public relations functions of the party, paying particular attention to RN's television profile.

Training and Research

The party has worked diligently to develop the intellectual support and technical backup necessary to ensure that a variety of complex issues are well coordinated and presented. The technical team has been subdivided into 22 thematic areas covering a wide range of issues such as foreign policy, human rights and justice, regionalization, agriculture and telecommunications. Each thematic commission is made up of parliamentarians with particular congressional responsibility for a given area, party members or sympathizers and members of the political commission. The area coordinators have responsibility for defining party policy in relation to their particular area and for responding quickly to government policy initiatives. The *Instituto Libertad* is RN's principal research body, which while enjoying independent status, is intrinsically linked to the party, particularly through its modernizing wing. Its role is to support RN's legislative work, political research and leadership training. The institute consists of several departments, including legislative support, a training department with responsibility for the 'national programme of leadership training' for party activists, and a 'school for leaders' which trains party candidates. The institute also organizes seminars, lunch meetings with university students and provides audio-visual material for party supporters. It is responsible for several publications including a weekly bulletin analysing government legislation, current political issues and a resumé of the activities organized by the institute, specialized political and legislative studies and bulletins analysing press reports.

Despite continuing organizational shortcomings which are inevitable in a still relatively young party, RN has developed a complex, and relatively efficient, bureaucracy which has attempted to ape the large right-wing parties of the industrialized world. Its technical and intellectual backup is probably one of the most developed in Chile, bar the Christian Democrats. Moreover, the *Instituto Libertad* is recognized as one of the most effective party-linked academic institutions in the country. However, RN suffers from a series of organizational weaknesses commonly associated with mass-based and media-oriented political parties. It has failed to build and promote an organic relationship with its membership. The party's principal mechanism for the dissemination of ideas is via the media and its formal rank-and-file organizations remain underdeveloped. Irrespective of the fact that RN is an amalgam of disparate political tendencies, the party has failed to create a truly loyal mass of supporters. Although it maintains a constant high media profile, which is effective in terms of delivering the necessary votes at election time, an inability to moti- vate a committed and loyal following has resulted in supporters tending to drift from party to party at various points. Moreover, the party is still lacking in terms of internal democracy. Although the Law on Political Parties stipulates that internal elections be held for all party posts, competition at the national level is almost non-existent. Competitive lists for the election of the political commission are common, but the right's historic fear of dissent has resulted in unitary lists for the national directorate in every election since the party's inception. This list is chosen by the political commission and rubber- stamped by the general council, marking a substantial difference from other Chilean political parties such as the Christian Democrats and the Socialists where competition for the top posts, including party president, is often fierce and public. And although in the past this often led to internecine warfare and splits, internal party competition today has often been constructive and beneficial for the parties involved. The right's lack of a party political culture has meant that it is yet to learn these lessons. Rather than act as a safety valve for internal dissent, leadership elections in RN simply stifle debate which could thus be channelled and controlled effectively, forcing it to spill over at times, which the party leadership may find difficult to control. This is compounded by the right's personalism and individualism which has only acted to exacerbate internal tensions. The right, and especially RN, often acts like a spoilt child and has yet to learn the rules of the party political game.

Unión Demócrata Independiente

UDI remains a hierarchical, non-democratic, elite-based, cadre orga- nization. Often described as a Leninist-structured party, UDI has systematically failed to develop the national and regional organiza- tional structure necessary for a modern western-style political party.[8] UDI persistently criticizes RN for being a party of 'public opinion' defining conduct and principles via the media, while recognizing itself to be an organically organized, *Falangist*-style movement attempting to 'cut across society' and represent all social sectors.[9] Therefore, the party aspires to represent society 'vertically' rather than 'horizon- tally': to represent the views of the whole of society rather than promote the aspirations of one particular class or determined economic interests. Consequently, UDI claims to be a popular party, seeking to displace the left as the traditional standard-bearer of the urban working class.[10] In its bid to represent interests rather than individual voters, UDI has tended to be organically stronger in terms of functional rather than territorial organization. Where it is strong in the territorial is at the more local rather than national level, reflecting the vanguardist nature of the party. As Pablo Longueira, a party deputy, remarked:

> Until now, we have focused our strategy on rank-and-file commit-tees, the nuclei base. Initially, our organizational evolution was focused on the universities, in order to obtain a critical mass, an intellectual elite with political ideas, the majority of whom were in the previous government, in the *alcaldías*, in the ministries and, in parallel, we had a strong emphasis on recruiting youth leaders. From 1983, when UDI was first set up as a party, we decided to maintain that structure but to widen it to include the *poblaciones*. After the 1989 elections we have tried to structure the party along national lines. RN is a party which is tied to a particular class and therefore exists everywhere. There are representatives of the traditional right throughout Chile who become active during election periods. However, RN is not a party which works systematically throughout the year. To achieve this, we have organized a network of rank-and-file nuclei whose task is to act as social leaders who ensure that our membership remains intact. Our organization is not conducive to growth. We therefore have to go out and find these social leaders because behind everyone of these is a larger electorate.[11]

The party continues to suffer from serious organizational weaknesses. Unlike RN, UDI is yet to become a national party with representation in most communes and regions of the country. It is still principally an urban party, most active in those areas where, through the *alcaldías*, it built up a network of supporters. However, because this support exists mainly in those areas with the largest population concentra-tions, its relative strength has been greatly exaggerated. UDI still lacks what can be regarded as a modern party machine, still operating from the cramped Suecia Avenue headquarters in Santiago which it has occupied since it split from RN in the late 1980s. Because of the building's association with Jaime Guzmán, it seems unlikely that the party will move to premises better suited to the needs of the organi-zation. It is this amateurish approach to party politics which marks UDI out from other parties. Very little research seems to be carried out, although several research institutes are associated with UDI, such as the *Instituto Libertad y Desarrollo* and the *Fundación Jaime Guzmán*. Nevertheless, attempts to establish a purely party political research institute similar to RN's *Instituto Libertad* have failed owing to a lack of interest from UDI-sympathizing intellectuals. Minutes at meetings are apparently not taken, and those which are, are not maintained. The party has no archives in which study documents and other material could be kept.

This maverick approach, which contrasts with RN's professionalism, highlights a further defining characteristic: UDI's 'mysticism'. The party's 'amateurish' organization masks its 'opaqueness', a desire not to 'reveal' too much. Activities, disagreements and strategic plans all take place behind closed doors. Meetings are attended by a core leadership group, reflecting the party's hierarchical structure and the formalization of party activity is anathema to UDI. Organizing along similar lines to RN runs counter to the party's historical and cultural legacy. With Guzmán as supreme leader for so many years was there ever a need to create a complex and modern party machine? Guzmán took care of everything: strategy, ideology, tactics and membership. However, this may no longer be sufficient in an age of media-based mass politics. The party's spectacular growth in membership following Guzmán's death raised questions about the party's organizational strategy. What may have been successful for a small, elite-based party may no longer be sufficient for an organization seeking further to expand its membership.[12]

UDI has been most successful at the local level, in the so-called *núcleos de base*, and in organizing outside the strict confines of direct party political activism, for example in the neighbourhood organizations and the mothers' centres. Most of this activity has been concentrated in the urban working-class areas and the *poblaciones*, centres traditionally associated with the left, and particularly the Communists. The most important department in terms of the party's 'popular' work is the *Departamento de Organizaciones Sociales de Base*. It has direct responsibility for the creation of *cuerpos directivos* to represent neighbours via the *Directivas de Juntas de Vecinos*. The party has sought to create as many neighbourhood groups as possible. In many instances, UDI has set up rival organizations to compete with those *Juntas* which it has been unable to infiltrate successfully. The party has also stressed the role of mothers' centres, whose function is to establish support schemes and training in issues such as welfare. Youth clubs and sporting centres are also targeted. Moreover, UDI has a well-established rank-and-file leadership training programme in the *poblaciones*. The five-person communal directorates consist of activists trained by this programme, who are subsequently responsible for training other potential local leaders.

This *blitzkrieg* on working-class local organizations is intended to deliver *una llegada rápida a las personas* and the party admits that this approach has been cloned from both the Christian Democrats and the Communists, UDI's main electoral competitors in the *poblaciones*. UDI, a hierarchical party with strong central control and internal unity based on the authority of its leaders, has sought to develop popular roots that are different from those associated with a mass-based party, in the classic sense of Duverger. In western-style mass parties there is a 'feedback' between the leadership and the mass, a system of *retroalimentación*. However, UDI has attempted to 'ferment' its ideology on the mass, to sow its seeds. As such, the party has a longer-term perspective than other political parties. Like the Communists, UDI is seeking to convert prospective sympathizers rather than engage in a game of interaction between the leadership and the mass, in which there is only partial commitment to the party. UDI is, therefore, seeking *un lazo de compromiso más fuerte* exactly because it wishes to convert these individuals; to become members of UDI's ideology and to articulate it within a very coherent organization.[13] One commentator has summarized UDI's paternalistic and 'left-wing' approach to popular activity and how it has sought to capture the hearts and minds of the urban working class:

The party promises nothing, it only offers what it has: principles, hard work and courage. In its communal branches UDI organizes home craft classes. The students provide the materials and the effort, and the party provides the rest, which is considerable given that it brings in a social worker once a week, and the famous *técnicos de los martes* to Conchalí [a working-class suburb in Santiago]. Here, communal leaders share cakes and biscuits with [José] Piñera, [Hernán] Büchi y [Julio] Dittborn. Tea time is about comradeship and not politics, since the township leaders want this to be a party of friends. Despite the fact that 50 per cent of the activists do not understand the vanguardist nature of the free market, the politics classes are only for those who are interested or those who are climbing up the structures which UDI has created knowingly exploiting the legacy of the military municipalities. It is not surprising, therefore that UDI's base is very similar to that of the PC [Communist Party]: fat ladies from the countryside, who see men as useless home decorations. Because of their rigorous work, UDI is often referred to as communists of the right, and in religious terms, evangelical. The truth is that 90 per cent of its activists are Catholic, with many of them of the *Opus Dei* variety.[14]

THE SOURCES OF PARTY FINANCES

The issue of party finances in Chile is shrouded in mystery. Although annual accounts are published they fail to reflect accurately the financial state of the parties.[15] The fiasco surrounding the 1989 presidential election, when the entrepreneurial sector threatened to withdraw financial support from RN if it insisted on presenting Sergio Onofre Jarpa as the right's presidential candidate, is simply a reflection of the sensitive nature of this issue in RN and UDI.[16] Both parties claim to be the poorer relative of the other and are constantly complaining about lack of resources. One UDI leader claimed that he would 'gladly swap our finances for those of RN ... We are in fact quite poor. Apart from our administrative staff, none of us receives a penny for our party work.'[17] Similarly, an RN sympathizer admitted that he had the 'impression that UDI has had more [financial] support'.[18] Although it is difficult to assess which party is wealthier, the consensus seems to favour UDI, since the fact that RN has consistently supported the state financing of parties, while UDI has repeatedly opposed it, may reflect the latter's confidence in obtaining sufficient finance from alternative sources.

What is clear is that the most important source of financial support for both parties emanates from the entrepreneurial sector (especially at election time), although UDI has consistently denied such an assertion. UDI's relations with the entrepreneurial sector and the large economic conglomerates is very close owing to three principal factors. First, the relationship between RN and the business world has always been lukewarm at best. This stems from RN's lack of support for the entrepreneurial-backed 1989 Büchi presidential campaign, as well as the party's support for the government-sponsored labour and tax reforms in the early 1990s, which sought to redress the balance in labour/employer relations and in the tax system. RN's economic ambivalence contrasts with UDI's hardline support for neo-liberalism. Second, many UDI sympathizers were responsible for the privatization of state companies during the military government. These individuals stayed on as executives and thus have access to considerable resources which they make available to the party. Those associated with UDI include the privatized energy firms Endesa, Enersis and Chilectra. Third, the highly intellectualized nature of UDI's economic ideology has attracted several of the entrepreneurs tied to the large economic conglomerates. These entrepreneurs are the same group (although not the same individuals) who took the Chicago Boys under their wing during the early years of the Pinochet regime.[19] Those associated with UDI include those economic groups linked to Eleodoro Matte, Roberto de Andraca, Juan Hurtado and Hernán Boher.

A further source of financing, although still in its infancy, are the party internationals. The 1991 visit of Jose María Aznar, the leader of the then opposition Spanish right-wing *Partido Popular*, highlighted the political and financial difficulties which the Chilean right faces in obtaining international support, owing to its links with the military regime. This has led to international isolation. Aznar chose only to meet with the Christian Democrats rather than the right. He even refused to meet RN leaders although he did visit the party's headquarters. However, the right's lack of ties with the international community stems not only from its associations with the military. The Chilean right lacks international connections; there is no party continuity and its organizations remain weak. Moreover, it has historically adopted a strong sense of nationalism which has not been conducive to developing international contacts. RN and UDI are aware of the problems caused by their military links and recognize the difficulties faced by both parties in their attempts to integrate into the international political community. While Aznar repudiates the Francoist past of his party, the Chilean right has refused to do the same with Pinochet. However, the new generation of right-wing leaders is taking seriously the issue of integration with the international community. This is important given the large amounts of money received by the Socialists and the Christian Democrats via their respective research centres, especially from Germany, Spain, Italy, Holland and Belgium.[20] The Konrad Adenauer Foundation, linked to the German Christian Democrats, provides considerable sums to research centres tied to their Chilean counterparts, while the Friedrich Ebert Foundation, linked to the German Social Democrats, helps fund the Socialists.

Allamand's initiative to insert his party into the international political community did net results. RN has opened up contacts with the US Republican Party and to a lesser extent with the British

Conservative Party. In Western Europe, it has consolidated contacts only with the Hanns Seidel Foundation, linked to the Bavarian Social Christians, which provides funds for the party's *Instituto Libertad*. Moreover, the party (together with UDI) has become a member of the Union of Latin American Parties (UPLA), founded in 1992, and which groups together 19 regional centre-right parties and organizations with parliamentary representation. Following nearly a decade of negotiations, RN has also recently been allowed to join the Pacific Democratic Union, a regional grouping associated to the International Democratic Union (IDU), which represents 74 Christian Democrat, conservative and centre-right parties around the world. The Chilean right's association with the military regime had been the principal cause of this long delay. However, UDI is unlikely to be accepted as a member for some time to come, given its close links with Pinochet.

As in the United States, a considerable amount of funding is provided by individual party members themselves. Wealthy party leaders, such as RN's Sebastian Piñera and former UDI member José Piñera (Sebastian's brother), often fund their own campaigns, provide assistance to other party candidates and contribute financially to the everyday running of their parties. Funds are also raised by selling political analytical and informative services. This source of income is more prevalent within RN, through its research institute. Both parties still lack a systematic mechanism for obtaining financial support, UDI more so than RN, although this can be explained by the informal links between the former and the entrepreneurial world, which makes the setting up of a formal fund-raising structure unnecessary. UDI's cultural makeup would make such an organization anathema. More can be obtained by a 'nod and a wink' and personal appeals for funds than by institutionalizing fund-raising. However, RN has attempted to set up such a machinery, as it cannot to the same extent rely on the goodwill of the business community.

TRADITIONAL SUPPORTERS AND NEW RECRUITS

The electoral right must be studied in the context of the interaction between the new right-wing political leadership and its various social constituencies. It must show how these actors grapple with the new logic of coalition-building. We must, however, desist from defining these parties simply as institutions which derive support from the political and economic elites. Poly-classist coalitions are important for the right. For the left, given the electoral weight of its principal source of support, class appeals represent the shortest route to achieve electoral success. In the right, however, only a fraction of a mass right-wing party's electoral support will come from the upper classes. It builds majorities by slicing up the social spectrum and its appeals must transcend class differences. The right represents an institutionalized form of collective action through which alliances are forged between the dominant classes and other social strata. To facilitate an examination of this poly-classist coalition, Edward Gibson has devised the concept of core and non-core constituencies, which provides a useful framework for an examination of right-wing coalition-building, to emphasize how a party relates to a specific class while simultaneously affirming its multi-class nature.[21] The core constituency represents the sector which is most important in shaping a party's political agenda, in the provision of financial and ideological support, and in shaping its identity. However, support from a party's core constituency is not sufficient to guarantee electoral success. It must forge alliances with other social sectors. However, a party's fate will also be dictated by its ability to mobilize outside the core constituency (the non-core). We must, therefore, assess how mass support is generated and how this impacts on the evolution of the party.

The social sectors which both UDI and RN aspire to attract is intrinsically linked to their vision of what their respective parties represent. Although, as right-wing parties, their natural and principal representative base (core constituency) originates in those sectors most privileged economically, socially and politically, both have sought to widen their political appeal and seek to attract those social sectors not traditionally thought of as natural and unquestioningly loyal right-wing voters. It is within this competitive arena (rather than in the area of ideology) that the right's differences have become most evident. This quest to widen their base of support has had wide-ranging repercussions in terms of party organization and parliamentary and electoral strategy, since both parties reflect the groups they wish to attract.

The Middle-Class versus Working-Class Vote

RN has focused its attention on capturing the middle-class vote, most notably small and medium-sized entrepreneurs, employees, teachers

and the self-employed, by far the most numerous and politically important sector in Chile.[22] On the other hand, UDI has pitched its ideological message and organized its party machinery and strategy around an
attempt to capture the urban working-class vote, particularly that of
the urban townships (*poblaciones*). As one UDI deputy remarked:

> As a mass electorate our message is basically directed at the
> popular sectors. Within that sector I would signal out those men
> and women who respond to certain values, such as work, family and
> the nation, which are very close to the hearts of the popular sectors
> and which have never before had a chance to express themselves
> politically. This is because the parties which respond politically to
> those values have never had a popular strategy.[23]

Although still outnumbered in the *poblaciones* by the left and the
Christian Democrats, UDI has had spectacular successes in organizing within these working-class areas, principally because of its
municipal activities during the military government and because of its
particular fiery brand of populist politics.

Democrat versus *Pinochetista*

Andrés Allamand attempted to shift the party towards the political
centre as he acknowledged the need to compete for the same votes as
the Christian Democrats. Allamand argued that the party would
never be in a position to win an electoral majority unless it was able
to capture that centre ground, especially given that repeated polls
indicated that most voters defined themselves as such.[24] RN sees no
option but to enter the competition to win over this mass of potentially floating voters. The party's organization and structure, as well as
its policies and strategy have reflected this electoral reality. UDI, on
the other hand, attracts a more hardline voter, principally those with
the most unquestioning loyalty to the legacy of General Pinochet (not
an insignificant minority). As such, the *duro* base of the right is not
marked by a vision of the future but by past cleavages. In this respect,
the right-wing commentator Arturo Fontaine highlighted that:

> the right-wing voter goes down the list of candidates to see who to
> vote for. They see who was involved in the military regime. This is
> the key division. It is more than a decision based on the future,
> because the current government has presented an economic project
> very similar to that of the right.[25]

Traditional versus Technocrat

RN's electoral base comes principally from those identified with the pre-1973 traditional, economically conservative party right, thus attempting to reactivate the supporters of the former Liberal, Conservative and National Parties. Many RN leaders are former activists of Chile's historic right-wing parties. Meanwhile, UDI remains essentially an anti-party movement, which stresses the *gremial* rather than the political. It has thus sought to attract those sectors with little or no background in party political activity. These include an elite group of young, previously apolitical professionals, technicians and students who are attracted to UDI's technocratic style, infused with reactionary religious dogma and uncompromising neo-liberalism. The party is thus aiming to create a 'political vanguard' to act as leaders for the mass of the popular rank-and-file.

However, several potential problems exist in terms of which sectors each party is attempting to attract. First, because of the right's weak party culture, its support is more dependent on individual candidates than on party loyalty. Moreover, both RN and UDI are relatively new parties. Unlike the Christian Democrats and the Socialists, both were formed in the Pinochet era. This lack of party loyalty explains how in some parts of the country, RN quadrupled UDI in its share of the vote and that the latter surpassed RN in others. This does not occur with parties which have consolidated their relative positions. Second, the central figure for the right continues to be Pinochet. The structure of the right's representation, and possibly of its electorate, is more *pinochetista* than the modern and politically liberal leaders of RN, and even in some cases of UDI. What will happen to the right once the figure of Pinochet begins to fade? What will then differentiate the two sectors? If the present government is successful in formulating a security and public order policy and is economically and administratively efficient, what is to stop this electorate migrating to other parties? Moreover, RN is treading a very fine line in its quest to attract the centre. Will this not alienate its traditional supporters? This explains much of the party's vacillation in terms of whether to present a moderate or a hardline face. For example, many RN leaders will in private, and even sometimes in public, express their support for a divorce law. However, after criticism from the Catholic Church, RN promised the Pope that it would not endorse such a measure. While the party is aware that it will need to capture the centre vote, it must do so without alienating its core group of supporters. UDI's strategy within the right means that it can rely on the permanent support of those social groups responsible for the military's economic modernization programme, who are more sceptical of the virtues of democracy. Third, the right obtains only around one-fifth of the middle-class vote and one-tenth of the working-class vote, while it attracts over half the upper-class vote, by far the least numerous sector of Chilean society. This distribution makes it highly unlikely that the right can obtain a parliamentary majority if political and economic circumstances remain as they are. Moreover, among the working class, the right obtains most votes from the least educated sectors which are the most vulnerable to political change and the most sensitive to changes in government public spending priorities. If some have so easily shifted their loyalties from the left to the right, what is to stop them reverting to type in the future?

8 The Right in Action

The preceding examination of the social base and internal institutions of *Renovación Nacional* (RN) and *Unión Demócrata Independiente* (UDI) facilitates a deeper understanding of the policy orientations, strategies and tactics of both parties: in essence, how the former shape the latter. Moreover, an examination of both parties' policy agenda and how this is expressed politically can reveal the degree to which they have been successful in inserting themselves into Chile's nascent democratic framework. For over 17 years, the right's actions were determined by their relatively direct access to power within an authoritarian framework. Today's challenge is to find a mechanism for participation as an opposition force within a democratic framework. The rules of the contemporary political game are radically different from those of the military regime and as such the new right is, relatively speaking, a new contender.

PARTY POLICY

RN and UDI are similar parties in terms of economic and social policy. To varying degrees, both combine conservative social thinking with liberal free market economics. In this sense, their ideology is consistent with that of many right-wing parties, both in the developing and the industrialized world. In the Chilean case, the critical area of investigation must concentrate on the parties' political policy agenda. This is for two reasons. First, it represents the competitive arena in which the greatest differences lie, not only between RN and UDI, but also in relation to the wider mainstream national political context. Irrespective of certain nuances, there exists today a general consensus among left and right on the concept of a social market economy. Where differences between left and right are most stark is in the area of social and political policy. This is most evident in terms of attitudes to moral issues, such as divorce, birth control and sexuality. However, this is not an area of fundamental differentiation within the right itself, which tends to espouse traditional moral values, at least in public, despite the private misgivings of many within the modernizing wing of RN and certain socially liberal members of UDI, although these represent a small minority. The clear point of departure for RN and UDI, in terms of policy, lies in the political, where we find many discernible differences and where the greatest sources of conflict between the two originate.

Second, an examination of both parties' political differences provides us with the most useful basis for analysing their relative commitment to democracy. Support for the free market and conservative ethical values do not in themselves preclude support for democracy. However, their attitudes to the polity enable us adequately to assess to what degree RN and UDI feel an inherent bond with a western-style liberal democratic system. Since the initiation of the transition process, political debate in Chile, at least at the elite level, has focused on three principal and defining areas, and these lie at the heart of the country's political agenda: civil–military relations, violation of human rights and constitutional reform. Indeed, it is the effective resolution of each of these three issues which will ultimately mark the real success of the democratic transition and consolidation process.

The Role of the Armed Forces

The 1980 constitution set up a 'protected democracy' under the tutelage of the armed forces.[1] As such, considerable political power lies in the hands of the military, whose high degree of autonomy would be deemed unacceptable in any western liberal democracy. The commanders-in-chief have tenure during their term of office and responsibility for nominating those military officers chosen for promotion or retirement, although the president selects the final choice from a short list drawn up by the armed forces. They are also voting members of the all-powerful *Consejo Nacional de Seguridad* (COSENA) and each branch names one of the nine designated senators.[2] The *raison d'être* behind this position lies in what Oscar Godoy has called the *constitucionalización del cuarto poder*: the Latin American military has throughout its history intervened in times of crisis and continues to hold an 'underground position of intervention'. It is therefore preferable, according to this argument, to insert the armed forces into a country's institutional order, providing it with an established space in the state apparatus.[3] The exact nature and role of the armed forces within this institutional order has been a constant source of tension between RN and UDI. Both parties profess admiration and respect for the military and recognize the 'invaluable' role it has played in transforming Chile's political, economic and social system. Nevertheless, such respect masks a number of fundamental differences in their approach to the armed forces and civil–military relations.

It is not surprising that UDI's stance is uncompromising and unambiguous. The party does not disguise the fact that it wishes to be a civilian alternative to the military regime, that is, to represent the civilian inheritors of the Pinochet legacy. In its declaration of principles UDI states that the armed forces are a symbol of the country's unity and guarantors of the institutional order and, as such, offers it its *'inconmovible lealtad'* and asserts *'la necesidad indispensable de incorporar eficazmente su aporte activo a la seguridad y desarrollo del país'*.[4] UDI's links with the military are not only theoretical. The activities of the party, as well as members of its predecessor movement during the Pinochet regime, the *gremialistas*, has been extensively documented in an earlier chapter. These intrinsic links have remained in place, despite the demise of the military government. UDI not only maintains contacts with former personalities and ministers of the authoritarian government, many of whom are UDI members or sympathizers, but, especially through Guzmán, continued to liaise, albeit unofficially, with the military. One glaring example of this relationship lay in the *Comité Asesor de la Comandancia en Jefe*, set up by the military prior to the handover of power to the civilian authorities. Headed by General Jorge Ballerino, this committee attempted to reproduce the structure of the civilian administration in military form; in essence, to create a 'shadow cabinet' which analysed the government's strategy and thus guide the right's political behaviour. Carlos Cáceres became the civilian spokesperson and Rolf Lüders the principal adviser to the committee, which also had close links with UDI and Hernán Büchi's *Instituto Libertad y Desarrollo*. According to one RN insider, the committee was created as a result of *'la desconfianza que tienen los militares comprometidos con el régimen anterior en los partidos que representan actualmente la derecha'*.[5]

UDI's intrinsic relationship with the military is demonstrated symbolically every year on the 11 September, the anniversary of the coup, with party activists organizing visits to army units and its leaders paying public homage to the former *junta* members, while the party hierarchy attends the various celebrations organized by the military high command. Crowds of UDI supporters, bussed in from the *poblaciones*, gather outside Pinochet's home to proclaim their loyalty. The wealthy, predominantly youthful, sympathizers organize motorized cavalcades in the streets of uptown Santiago. This annual 'civic–military operation' regroups the *fuerzas leales* dispersed by the electoral defeats of 1988 and 1989. The aim of this *cabal* is to bring together Pinochet, his civilian supporters and those military officers which comprise the general's praetorian guard. The military component revolves around Pinochet under the guise of the annual September 'Army Month', while the civilian component is orchestrated by UDI (in its capacity as the *derecha cuartelera*). This relationship between UDI and the military is fundamental in nature. As one right-wing academic summarized Pinochet's relationship with the party:

> They get together privately with Pinochet and they do not talk about the weather. It is common sense that there is a very strong relationship. It is also evident through the degree of passion which many UDI leaders express when having to defend or talk about Pinochet and the *ancien régime*. This emotional streak indicates a strong level of affiliation which does not only function at the rational level but also at the emotional and sentimental level. This is nurtured via the physical relationship with the leader.[6]

The unambiguous link with the military helps to reinforce UDI's anti-party posture, one of its defining characteristics. After all, political parties within a democratic framework should not act as the civilian representatives of the armed forces. This lack of political independence has hindered UDI in terms of developing a modern and efficient party structure: it has meant UDI acting as spokesperson and unquestioning defender of the military. Hence, the party's dogmatic reluctance to consider the possibility of negotiating reform of even the most uncontroversial and undemocratic elements of the constitution's military articles and the organic law of the armed forces.

In an attempt to attract the centre ground without alienating its core constituency, RN's approach has been more measured and conciliatory, and the party has striven to adopt an equidistant position from both the left and UDI. Consequently, RN has criticized both positions in asserting the existence of those who *'aspiran a utilizar a los institutos armados como instrumento para obtener logros políticos que en la competencia democrática difícilmente alcanzarán* [and those] *que quieren que los uniformados desempeñen un papel preeminente y permanente en la vida política, lo cual contrariaría una de nuestras mejores tradiciones cívicas y vulneraría principios esenciales del régimen democrático'*.[7] Indeed, its position on the 11 September commemorations has been unambiguous, thus marking a fundamental break with the party's past as a vehicle for rallying the civilian supporters of the military regime. RN has neither organized nor participated in any official act of support for the previous regime, an important turning point in its attempts to attract the centre ground.[8] As Arturo Longton declared, when commenting on the party's non-participation in the rallies outside Pinochet's residence, such celebrations *'corresponde a otro partido'*.

In contrast, RN's position towards reforming the military elements of the constitution and the organic law of the armed forces has been riddled by ambiguity. This reflects fundamental internal divisions between RN modernizers and traditionalists, often publicly expressed. The traditionalists, party hardliners whose power base lies in the Senate, have repeatedly rejected reform. The modernizers, who dominate the Chamber of Deputies and the party leadership, have increasingly softened their stance in this area. Although in the past the latter publicly supported the status quo, in private it expressed a willingness to contemplate backing certain reforms, but only when the political climate became more conducive. Today, however, the modernizers' support for weakening the power of the military is both vociferous and public. And while such a position is undoubtedly essential to RN's attempts to become a modern centre-right party, it remains impossible to reconcile with the views of the still large and influential sector of traditionalists. UDI, in contrast, faces no such dilemma. It will continue to resist attempts to modify what is, after all, its political legacy without fear of losing its core support or causing a split within the party.

The Violation of Human Rights

The 1978 amnesty law passed by the armed forces granted an amnesty to all military personnel who committed acts of violence between 1973 and 1978, the period in which most human rights abuses had taken place.[9] The amnesty law was intended to 'pardon' crimes which the military defined as *excesos*. According to the authorities, such violations were the result of armed resistance by members of the Allende government. In combating 'subversion', the security forces found it necessary to adopt special measures because *'haber pretendido librar este combatante con los métodos propios de un período normal, hubiese significado sucumbir ante la subversión'*.[10] Since left-wing subversion had the characteristics of a foreign-backed civil war, the violation of human rights was justifiable. By 1978, the military government claimed to have secured 'social peace'. Moreover, the process of institutionalizing the regime, which culminated in the approval by plebiscite of the 1980 constitution, no longer justified such excesses. Furthermore, Article 8 of the constitution, which has now been repealed, sought to deny political as well as civil rights to those individuals and groups which according to the military government supported 'totalitarian' ideologies and which attested against *la chilenidad*, effectively banning left-wing parties and movements from operating legally.

In an attempt to redress the balance in favour of the victims of these violations, the government of President Patricio Aylwin (1990–4) set up the Truth and Reconciliation Commission (also known as the Rettig Commission), which sought to investigate all human rights abuses resulting in death between 11 September 1973 and 11 March 1990, the date when the military transferred power to the civilian authorities. The Rettig Commission investigated the events surrounding the execution of around 2,000 people and the disappearance of a further 700 between 1973 and 1978. It also sought to examine the death of around 500 opponents of the regime and 40–50 killings of officials and supporters of the military government after 1978.

How to resolve effectively the human rights' issue became one of the most politically sensitive and emotionally charged debates in Chile at the time of the democratic transition. Seeking redress had potentially serious implications for civil–military relations. However, human rights is no longer a priority issue for public opinion. There is general apathy among those not directly affected by past violations, even among politicians on the left. In a poll commissioned by the *Centro de Estudios Públicos* (CEP) in March 1989, 28 per cent of respondents cited human rights as an issue which the government should prioritize. By September 1994, this figure had dropped to just over 7 per cent.[11] Although the military and the right have called for an Argentine-style *Ley de Punto Final*, significant differences exist between RN and UDI on their perception of the human rights issue.

UDI has adopted a particularly hardline and uncompromising stance towards the issue of human rights violations. This stems not only from its unquestioning support for the military regime but also its highly particular interpretation of human rights. In the party's declaration of principles it states that '*el ser humano tiene una dignidad espiritual de la cual emanan derechos inherentes a su naturaleza que son anteriores y superiores al Estado'*.[12] Yet it also recognizes that certain personal rights can be restricted by the political authorities during what it calls *régimenes de excepción* when '*la soberanía, la juridicidad y la paz interior*' are threatened. These restrictions can be implemented '*en el grado y por el lapso requeridos para conjurar el peligro y restablecer la normalidad amenazada o quebrantada*'.[13] UDI has justified the violation of human rights in *gremialista* terminology by stating that '*todos los derechos humanos reconocen límites, exigidos por el bien común*'.[14] The party upholds the notion that there exists a hierarchy of rights. It is therefore justifiable to violate certain 'lesser' rights in the defence of other more important rights. Human rights are also seen as universal, that is to say, they are not associated with a particular political system. This emanates from UDI's procedural support for democracy, which is not valued in itself but perceived as the best available system for achieving certain goals, such as economic development and personal security. Therefore, by separating human rights from democracy, UDI has claimed that an authoritarian system is not necessarily incompatible with human rights. Moreover, it states, other regime types may better defend and promote these rights. UDI has highlighted two types of *anormalidad*: those that do not imply a system breakdown and those that do. The former can be dealt with adequately using existing constitutional states of exceptions. The latter, however, requires restricting fundamental political rights. The party believes the pre-1973 period represented a situation which required special measures to be adopted, in which the partial restricting of human rights proved insufficient to prevent the violation (in the form of demagoguery and statism) of more important rights. Under this 'thesis of inevitability', UDI supported the 1978 amnesty law.

UDI has consistently reiterated that it supported the investigation of abuses committed after 1978, both by individual military personnel as well as by the radical left. However, it has stated that officers bear individual responsibility and that the armed forces should not be admonished as an institution. Nevertheless, UDI has been consistently lukewarm in supporting the investigation of post-amnesty violations as well as those prior to 1978 but which are not covered by the amnesty law, such as the case involving General Manuel Contreras, the former head of the DINA, the military government's feared secret service. Despite UDI's complicity in the violation of human rights, the *gremialista* movement admits that unjustifiable excesses were committed. Guzmán himself stated that '*yo manifesté mi repudio a esos hechos, incluyendo el asesinato de Orlando Letelier, Tucapel Jiménez, de los jóvenes quemados y de los degollados'*.[15] Guzmán's role in attempting to limit the violation of human rights, and that of his *blando* collaborators, is worthy of some examination. Guzmán was clearly aware of the damage that General Contreras's bloody excesses could inflict on the military government and believed that Contreras was planning to assassinate him because of his repeated altercations with the DINA boss. Guzmán succeeded in convincing Pinochet to remove Contreras and disband the DINA in 1977, following US pressure to do so after the murder in Washington of Orlando Letelier, foreign minister and ambassador to Washington under the Allende government in 1976 (a crime for which Contreras is now serving a six-year prison sentence). Nevertheless, while Guzmán's contradictory position led him to become the protector of several communist activists, his unquestioning defence of the government's political role cannot distance the movement from responsibility.

The party has also criticized the UN's Universal Declaration of Human Rights. Although it recognizes that all states should adhere to it, UDI has stated that the declaration should not be *'visto como comprometido con los fundamentos filosóficos del derecho natural'*.[16] It has also criticized the document for not including concepts such as the right to private property, in an attempt to pacify what was then the Soviet Union, and for defining the election of authorities as inherent to human nature, because this does not take into account how this issue can be differently interpreted by various states. UDI continues by condemning the declaration for viewing all countries as 'photo images' of each other without taking into account particular national circumstances (such as post-1973 Chile). The party has also pronounced on other issues relating to the exercise of human rights. UDI has persistently condemned all human rights groups, accusing them of partiality owing to their examination of abuses committed by members of the armed forces while ignoring those of 'terrorists'. It has accused such bodies, principally the church-based *Vicaría de la Solidaridad*, of acting as a smokescreen to cover up acts of violence committed by left-wing groups and individuals. The party views terrorism as *'una de las peores violaciones de los derechos humanos'* because it threatens the fundamental human right of security and attempts against national sovereignty.[17] Virtually any actions designed to undermine and combat this threat are therefore justified.

Because of the composition of its leadership and the social sectors which it is seeking to represent, RN has found it particularly difficult to come to terms with the political legacy of the Pinochet regime. Foremost, its definition of human rights coincides more closely with that adopted by democratic parties in the industrialized world, than with UDI's authoritarian and qualified stance. According to RN, the UN Universal Declaration of Human Rights represents the best possible framework for limiting the excesses of state power and abuse. Moreover, the party rejects UDI's justification of human rights violations asserting that, in Allamand's words, they *'empañan las realizaciones efectuadas por este gobierno en los campos económico, social y político'*.[18] Although at first he believed such violations were inevitable, Allamand modified his position as events became clearer. He has repeatedly expressed sympathy with the families of the disappeared and has suggested that some solution *'entre la impunidad y la venganza'* is necessary. If abuses are not clarified and responsibility not meted out, then the military as an institution will be compromised. This position, although personal, can be perceived as a criticism of the amnesty law, which RN has officially supported.

Other RN leaders, primarily those belonging to the modernizing tendency, have been just as forthright in their criticism. After the discovery in 1990 of a mass grave in the northern port of Pisagua, Alberto Espina admitted that the 1973–90 period had been the country's 'darkest'. Evelyn Matthei stated that *'estamos empezando a enfrentar la verdad de lo que ha ocurrido durante todos estos años'*, while Gustavo Alessandri even asserted that Pinochet was indirectly responsible for the actions of his officers. In an unprecedented move from the right, several RN parliamentarians visited the relatives of those whose bodies were found in Pisagua to express their solidarity.[19] Moreover, modernizers in the party have rejected the notion of an amnesty law, in that it would have been preferential to have had such violations investigated by the courts. However, as such a law was decreed, they argue, RN must now support it, or risk undermining the democratic transition process. Nevertheless, RN supports the view that all Chileans must recognize their joint responsibility for creating a situation which led to the breakdown of the democratic system. Although the party also accepts that terrorism is one of the most serious threats to democracy, its approach is less authoritarian than that adopted by UDI. The party has stated that the threat of terrorism cannot be used as an excuse to declare a state of war in the country, since *'cuando el terrorismo logra equipar el Estado con su agresión, obtiene una victoria; el Estado abandona la ventaja ética que tiene para enfrentar esta agresión interna'*.[20]

In conjunction with this conciliatory approach, RN has also employed hardline rhetoric in an attempt not to alienate its natural constituency nor the party's conservative component. It has not only criticized the civilian government's stance *vis-à-vis* human rights, but has sought to justify, often in contradiction with earlier claims, these violations on the part of the armed forces. RN still asserts that the 1973 military coup and the subsequent violations of human rights did not occur in a vacuum. They took place in an atmosphere of political polarization and violence. RN places particular blame on the Marxist left. These events, according to the party, led to a regrettable repressive response from the armed forces, although criminal responsibility must always be personal, never institutional nor collective. The events which occurred in the post-1973 period, therefore, do not reflect negatively on the work of the armed forces nor in any way reflect the achievements of the military regime. Moreover, RN criticized the Truth and Reconciliation Commission on several grounds, including its limited remit in investigating abuses committed during the military government only, while excluding similar abuses carried out under the *Unidad Popular*, as well as its failure to include the armed forces in its deliberations. As such, RN rejected an invitation to participate in the creation of the commission.

This tension between public justification and private condemnation has plagued the party throughout. The party modernizers are concerned not to alienate the more conservative elements of the party nor its *pinochetista* support base. However, too intransigent an approach will invariably deter RN's potentially vital moderate electorate. This 'double discourse' is highlighted by the party's parliamentary group, which best reflects the unbridgeable gap between apologists of the military regime (mainly in the Senate) and its detractors (a majority in the Chamber of Deputies).

However, the right in Chile has progressed in terms of its attitudes to human rights. At least there is no one on the right who would now question the intrinsic value of human rights, irrespective of how it is defined. This does represent a step forward. Moreover, most on the right, both in RN as well as UDI, now accept that violations did occur during the military regime, although many, principally in UDI, persist in justifying these events. As time progresses and memory of the atrocities perpetrated by the military regime begins to fade, the human rights issue has progressively metamorphosed into a *querella histórica*. Until the Chilean right exorcizes this historical legacy, which may prove easier as time progresses, the spectre of the past will continue to haunt it. Although this is unlikely to perturb the *pinochetista* right, potential democrats within the right, most notably in RN, may find it difficult to penetrate those electoral sectors which seek a vision based on the future rather than the past.

Reforming the Authoritarian 1980 Constitution

The 1980 constitution is perceived by the right as the legislative embodiment of the military regime and as the principal mechanism for defending Pinochet's political, economic and social legacy. It is the fundamental 'sacred cow', the ultimate and defining benchmark by which loyalty to the *ancien régime* is gauged. Nevertheless, because of the reasons outlined in detail in chapter 4, the right, the military and the then opposition reached an agreement in 1989 to modify several of the more contentious elements of the constitution: an increase in the number of civilian members of the COSENA which ended the armed forces' majority in that institution, an increase in the number of directly elected senators, lowering the quorate necessary for reforming the constitution, repealing the draconian Article 8 and removing the president's power to dissolve the lower house. Although both RN and UDI are fervent disciples of the constitution's essential principles, they differ in several other important respects. This differentiation is clearly evident as a consequence of the varying degree of the parties' involvement in its elaboration. While UDI, through Jaime Guzmán, played an instrumental ideological and political role in its creation, the participation of figures now associated with RN was relatively non existent, bar some notable exceptions. As such, the constitution was essentially a *gremialista* creation and symbolizes the movement's fundamental principles and values. UDI's position *vis-à-vis* the constitution is therefore both emotional and uncompromising perceiving its as '*la gran y verdadera reforma constitucional que Chile necesitaba para favorecer una futura democracia eficiente y estable*'.[21] Moreover, the party has categorically rejected the possibility of further fundamental reform. It was an unwilling contributor to the 1989 constitutional reforms and has dogmatically refused to discuss the prospect of any future modifications.

During the early 1990s, RN also expressed, at least in public, its unwillingness to support substantial constitutional reform, although it consistently expressed its readiness to discuss the issue. This seemingly contradictory approach was again intrinsically related to its strategy of moving towards the centre without risking alienating the party's natural supporters. However, RN was willing to support reform of some of the less controversial aspects of the constitution. Consequently, several modifications were agreed in the early 1990s, principally owing to RN's wish to present itself as a 'constructive and loyal' opposition. Even UDI, due to its own strategic calculations, supported a number of these reforms. For example, agreement on lowering the presidential term of office from eight years to six was reached in 1993. UDI persistently vacillated on whether it actually supported such a reduction. A lengthy presidential term was considered an intrinsic part of the presidential system. However, with little medium-term prospect of a right-wing president winning office, UDI finally agreed to the reduction. RN's support for this measure was unequivocal. Its analysis, which was cognisant of the fact that a right-wing presidential option was not viable, concluded that excessively long presidential terms were likely to lead to political corruption, polarization and social instability.

RN also supported reform of Article 9 of the constitution which stipulated that no amnesty could be granted for 'terrorist' offences. The *Concertación* government believed that presidential powers to amnesty left-wing 'terrorists' were essential if there was to be more general acceptance of the military's 1978 amnesty law. Although UDI rejected this possibility, RN proved willing to support the legislation, known as the *Leyes Cumplido*, which gave the president the power to amnesty offenders convicted of 'political' violence. This controversial legislation led to increased tensions between RN and UDI, but was perceived as essential by the former in its quest to support political 'reconciliation'.

Reform of the municipal law was also successful, although it proved a more complicated piece of legislation. The constitution essentially left in place the authoritarian and non-elected local government structure existent throughout the military regime and no provision for the democratization of municipal bodies was thus included. The principal issues revolved around the question of whether to have directly elected mayors, what voting system to adopt and when elections would take place. Initially, UDI rejected the concept of reforming the constitution to allow for the democratization of local government and defended the right of the designated mayors to remain in office until their term expired in 1994. It would thus be willing to support reform thereafter. RN, on the other hand, favoured the concept of municipal elections but at first insisted that any constitutional reform to that effect would have to be conditional on a wider reform of regional government. Following 15 months of intense negotiations with both UDI and RN, who both vied at various times to become the principal opposition interlocutor, an agreement was finally hammered out in August 1991.[22] The process was marked by broken agreements, mainly due to the conservative RN senators vetoing an earlier settlement between the party and the government.

In recent years, RN has considerably softened its stance towards reforming some of the more fundamental aspects of the constitution, such as the designated senators and the powerful role of the armed forces in the country's political system, and a majority of its deputies have supported a number of government-sponsored initiatives to reform these aspects of the constitution. However, opposition from RN's conservative and anti-modernizing senators, assisted by the right-wing designated and UDI senators, which together form a majority in the upper chamber, have thus far blocked any attempt to reform the more authoritarian elements of the constitution.

Clearly, the military legacy continues to undermine the democratic transition process. Extensive political power remains in the hands of the armed forces and unelected state institutions dominated by appointees from General Pinochet, while the issue of human rights violations continues periodically to sour civil–military relations. As stated above, the Aylwin and Frei administrations have over the years proposed a series of reforms to correct this imbalance, principally in January 1993, April 1996 and June 1997, but as yet to no avail. It seems evident that the present institutional framework has stifled the full development of a democratic system. The COSENA, the *Tribunal Constitucional*, the binominal electoral system (which is weighted in favour of the right and is discussed in chapter 9) and the designated senators have provided the right-wing opposition with a high degree of political manoeuvrability.[23] This is why the issue of constitutional reform is so fundamental. For the authoritarian right, it is fundamental to maintain these institutional controls. Their existence provides them with powers which far exceed their electoral representation. However, it has to defend these institutions without undermining its democratic image. RN, more so than UDI, thus faces an intractable dilemma in its attempts to reassert the democratic credentials of the Chilean right. The issues of civil–military relations, reform of the authoritarian 1980 constitution and the vexed question of human rights violations represent a serious test of its success in this direction. Nevertheless, the persistent need to satisfy two seemingly incompatible constituencies is likely to continue to weaken the party.

Its failure to present a united front in these key areas may go some way in placating its *pinochetista* base, but it could alienate potential centre voters. Although the *pinochetista* vote is split between two competing right-wing parties, UDI will always emerge the victor in any struggle to win over the loyal adherents of the military regime. RN has yet to take the final plunge to liberate itself from the past. Until it is successful in abandoning its military legacy, with all the risks to party unity which this would entail, it seems likely to remain in opposition. UDI faces no such dilemmas, yet its identity as the civilian inheritors of the Pinochet regime will place limits on its electoral growth, although it is becoming an increasingly important parliamentary force, despite scant increases in its share of the vote.[24] Clearly, its fundamental electoral base is *pinochetista*, and as such the party may find it difficult to increase significantly its support base. The challenge it faces is, therefore, how to maximize its political influence while recognizing its electoral limits. These issues represent the fundamental concerns affecting the party right in democratic Chile.

STRATEGY AND TACTICS

The historical constitution of a democratic right-wing party and its internal structure are of paramount importance for a successful process of democratization. Such a process will, at least, require the neutrality of the right. For example, labour protests, on the whole, do not pose a real threat to democracy, while in contrast the belligerence of the business class can certainly undermine it. Therefore, agreements and pacts between former authoritarian rulers and their constituents and the rising democratic coalition are inevitable in political transitions. What is crucial here is the extent to which the democratizing alliance has the will and the ability to impose on the heirs of the authoritarian regime a set of policies which would curtail their privileges. The nature of the relationship between the right-wing parties and the democratic government is therefore of paramount importance, and begs the question as to whether or not these parties fall into the category of 'loyal' opposition.[25]

The right's strategy and tactics reflects in part its organizational structure, electoral base and policies, all areas covered earlier in this study. As such, an examination of such facets serves as a benchmark through which to assess the degree to which RN and UDI have inserted themselves into the democratic framework; in essence, to what extent they have assumed the classic roles which opposition parties adopt in a democracy: supervision, criticism and negotiation.

Renovación Nacional

As chapter 7 has outlined, the party's main strategic focus has centred on strengthening the role of political parties. Under Andrés Allamand's leadership, RN attempted to reinsert the party system back into the central arena. It sought to re-evaluate the right's historic hostility to Chile's dominant political system, based around a dynamic party framework. RN realized that the right could not win presidential elections without the dominant participation of parties. Consequently, the leadership sought to renovate the party's structures and tactics. With this in mind, RN has undergone a modernization process with the aim of becoming a western-style, mass, public-opinion based party. Another central element of the party's strategy was its attempt to shift RN towards the political centre. The party leadership understood the need to compete for the same votes as the *Partido Demócrata Cristiano* (PDC), Chile's largest party. This obsession with replacing the PDC as the natural party of the political centre led some of its detractors to coin the term *Renócratas Cristianos*. The modernizing wing of the party held the view that the only way forward was to capture that centre and attempt to win over this mass of potentially floating voters. This explains its efforts to distance the party from the legacy of the military regime.

This desire to adopt a centrist position led Allamand to claim in 1991 that *'una derrota catastrófica de la gestión del actual gobierno sería muy perjudicial para RN'*.[26] RN's strategy, therefore, stressed the party's positive and moderating role in the democratic transition process, as evidenced by its willingness to negotiate the 1989 reforms, and that a collapse of this process would have impacted negatively on RN. Consequently, the party supported a number of important reforms implemented by the Aylwin administration covering a range of policy areas: reform of the regressive tax system, redressing the balance away from employers in the military-inspired labour law, reform of Article 9 of the constitution and legislating for municipal elections and regional government. In this way, RN hoped to deflect many of the criticism levelled against it. On the issue of human rights it recognized, once and for all, the right's responsibility and agreed to carry out a process of self-examination, but demanded that the left and the centre do the same. In relation to its democratic credentials, it supported what it defined as 'good' constitutional reforms and refused unequivocally to defend a constitution that might have imperfections. On the issue of 'social sensibility' it agreed to support tax increases on the better-off.

This modernizing project was premised on the notion that the participation of parties close to authoritarian regimes in a post-authoritarian framework is essential. Historically, the role of such parties in a nascent democratic system has tended to be minimal and low key thus weakening their future political role in the state. Furthermore, RN strategists concluded that Chile not only experienced a process of democratic 'restoration' but one of democratic 'renewal' based on *'un equilibrio inteligente entre la estabilidad, proveniente de la solidez de acuerdos básicos y la vitalidad originada en su pluralismo y la coexistencia de enfoques y visiones diferentes'*.[27] As such, this process of democratic transition and consolidation should include a 'triple accord' encompassing political–institutional, economic–social and civil–military issues. These elements represent the sources of greatest possible conflict in democratic transitions and reaching agreements on these issues was, therefore, essential. The parliamentarians represented an integral part of this strategy, since prior to the transition, the relative strength of the parties could only be judged by the quality of its leadership, its historical trajectory, the number of rank-and-file members and the quality of its organization. The 1989 elections thus marked the first real test for the right and will be examined in detail in chapter 9. However, RN, aware that prospects for a right-wing presidential successor were severely limited, opted to stress the work of its parliamentarians to help determine the party's political image. Yet RN's overall strategy has faced serious setbacks precisely because it has sought to place parliament at the centre of political activity, where division between modernizers and traditionalists is most stark. The former dominate the right in the lower chamber and the latter, the Senate. This conservative group has persistently opposed the modernizers' strategy. Its former unofficial spokesperson, Sergio Onofre Jarpa, made no secret of his desire to become the great leader of the right and promote RN as the strong party of the opposition, which would confront the government and reject the possibility of agreements with his adversaries. As a consequence of this intractable hostility, RN senators sought to block the modernizers' attempts to reach a compromise solution on the municipal reform issue and have succeeded in impeding reform of the more authoritarian aspects of the constitution.

Despite RN's relatively strong electoral position, Allamand's stewardship of RN was plagued by difficulties in carrying through this modernizing strategy, constantly facing opposition from his conservative associates in the party. Nevertheless, by the time of the December 1997 mid-term congressional elections, Allamand felt sufficiently confident to launch what many regarded as a highly risky political strategy, which could not only threaten the future of his political career but that of the right's modernizing project: to resign from the party leadership and step down from his seat in the lower house in order to run for the Senate, as a springboard for the presidency in 1999. This strategy failed spectacularly. Not only was Allamand comprehensively defeated by the UDI candidate, Carlos Bombal, but RN's electoral performance at the national level *vis-à-vis* UDI was the poorest in the party's history, despite a slight increase in its share of the vote and remaining as the largest right-wing party in the lower house. This may have serious consequences for RN's project for modernizing and democratizing the right, and will be discussed in greater detail below.

Allamand announced his decision to resign in late 1996, following seven years as leader of RN, and expressed unequivocal support for his chosen successor, Alberto Espina, his closest collaborator since the early days of the party. Allamand's reasons for resigning from RN, and accepting a leading role in the party's *Instituto Libertad*, were clearly electoral.[28] Following RN's strong showing in both the 1989 and 1993 general elections, in which the party maintained its leadership role as the principal opposition interlocutor and second largest party in the country, Allamand, after four successful years as a parliamentary deputy, calculated that the next logical step towards his, and the modernizing right's, road to power, would be to stand for senator in the December elections.[29] His decision to join the *Instituto Libertad* was particularly calculated. The institute, a highly respected party political think-tank dominated by the former president's closest associates, was set to become Allamand's election headquarters. The institute would not only elaborate his election manifesto, but would provide the intellectual platform from which Allamand would proclaim on the great issues of the day, without involving himself in the day-to-day inter- and intra-party warfare which had so often threatened to damage not only his personal reputation but that of the party as a whole. He would now, in essence, be beyond the fray, free from the taint of association. Moreover, the institute's strength was based in municipal consultancy, enabling Allamand to prepare a future presidential strategy best suited to confront the authoritarian right's strongest possible candidate for the year 2000 presidential race, the UDI mayor of Las Condes, Joaquín Lavín, whose unprecedented popularity has been based on what many electors believe is his revolutionary and technical management of Chile's wealthiest municipality. This is the model Allamand hoped to replicate in his quest for the Senate, and ultimately the presidency.

His first task was to convince the hardliners on Espina's succession as party president, a task that was unlikely to prove easy. During a meeting with RN conservatives soon after his resignation announcement, Allamand expressed support for Espina's wish to set up a consensus party leadership, which would seek to reflect all shades of opinion. Although no agreement was reached, Espina's intense lobbying, in which he adopted a greater conciliatory tone, finally paid off and he was elected president at the general council in April 1997, as was his consensus leadership directorate. In common with UDI, RN once again failed to present competitive lists in either the election for party president or the leadership. Although the *duros* were too weak to oppose his candidacy, Espina's skills as a politician tipped the balance in his favour. He not only cultivated good relations with Jarpa, established more cordial ties with the senators and had the overwhelming support of the party's deputies, but won the backing of the party's councillors, a critical success given their powerful voting role in the general council, the party's highest decision-making body.

As party president, Allamand had been the prime example of a politician with *poder sin poder*, who was persistently attacked by his own senators, who formed the bulwark of conservative opposition to his modernizing programme, and was subsequently forced to devote most of his time to defending his position. Ironically, he found it politically easier to win support outside the party than within it, and is largely credited with having been a key player in the process of reforming the more authoritarian elements of the 1980 constitution, which enmeshed the then centre-left opposition and the parties of the right during the democratic transition in the late 1980s. His victories within and outside the party enabled him to consolidate his leadership and make substantial progress towards his ultimate objective, to become Chile's first democratically elected right-wing president since Alessandri in 1958.

Allamand had clearly chosen a successor, who although less charismatic and less confrontational than himself, clearly reflected the former president's aspirations for the future of a modern centre-right in Chile. However, Espina's success as RN president, and the future of RN's modernizing tendency within the party, rested firmly on Allamand's senatorial candidacy. Although the conservatives had lost influence within RN by the time of Espina's succession, they still maintain strong pockets of influence which could sour his presidency. His difficulties will now be exacerbated by Allamand's spectacular defeat, which has not only strengthened the position of RN hard-liners, who will now seek further to undermine the liberal wing of the party, but that of UDI, despite the party's continued electoral status as the smaller of the two.[30]

Espina's tenuous hold on the party was further complicated in July 1997 when Sergio Onofre Jarpa finally resigned from RN, the movement he helped launch a decade earlier. Jarpa represented one of the fundamental pillars guaranteeing the unity of the party leadership, and especially Espina as its president. However, unreconcilable and long-standing differences with the reformist leadership, the closeness of the party to the ruling centre-left *Concertación*, with which it was increasingly seeking to reach a definitive compromise on reforming some of the remaining authoritarian vestiges of the constitution, and Allamand's presidential ambitions, which Jarpa described as 'personalist', proved the breaking point for a politician who until then had sought to defend his conservative project from within. Subsequently, Jarpa not only established a new political movement, *Chilefuturo*, with the participation of former *Avanzada Nacional* activists, nationalists and retired military officers, but committed himself to supporting any right-wing candidate in the 1997 elections prepared to reject future constitutional reform. Jarpa's aim was clear: to destroy the electoral prospects of the party's modernizing sector, and more particularly to obtain a parliamentary bloc which would enable the conservative right to maintain their veto over the constitutional reform programme supported by the government and RN's modernizing leadership.

RN's failure to consolidate its former leader's modernizing project in the 1997 elections will make it more than likely that the party will, once again, fail to present a presidential candidate in 1999 who emanates from its ranks. RN's negotiating position in Congress, a central element in Allamand's strategy of placing the parties of the right in the centre of the political arena, will be further hampered by the existence of a strengthened hardline right-wing sector in the Senate. RN now faces a central dilemma, which in truth has always plagued the party: either to abandon its project to modernize and democratize the right, and adopt a more hardline position on issues such as constitutional reform and civil–military relations, or to seek further accommodation with the political centre. Although the former position would ease tensions with both the party's conservatives and UDI, it would entail the abandonment of the modernizing project, and thus the future of a fully fledged democratic right. RN's political and electoral future under this scenario would be uncertain, since UDI will always emerge the victor in any battle to prove their respective hardline right-wing credentials. It would also prevent the right from expanding towards the centre, and as such, its electoral viability will remain limited. If instead the party continues to pursue the centre ground, tensions within it will increase. It will prove difficult to maintain the party together under such circumstances, especially following Allamand's defeat and his decision to abandon party politics, at least for the time being. One possible scenario being considered by some in the modernizing wing of the party entails closer links, and a possible future electoral pact, with the Christian Democrats. This would serve a double function. First, it would at last free RN from UDI, one of the principal barriers to the party's wish to move towards the centre, although this would invariably lead to its disintegration. Second, it would liberate the ruling Christian Democrats, the largest partner in the *Concertación*, from its left-wing allies. This scenario would thus marginalize both the hard right and the left from Chilean politics. Right-wing elements in the Christian Democrats have also examined such a possibility, although it would equally result in serious fissures in the party.

Unión Demócrata Independiente

UDI's opposition strategy was devised virtually single-handed by Guzmán, the party's ideological and political leader. As a senator, he applied Riker's concept of game theory: that a small player can be more effective than a big player if he knows how to make the most of his possibilities of handing over or denying his vote to the majority group. He was the opposition's most effective senator and allowed his party to exceed all expectations as to what such a small party could achieve. Apart from his personal skills as a politician, Guzmán's strength could be explained by three factors. First, his close relationship to key government players such as the then Senate president Gabriel Valdés. Second, his presidency of the crucial senate constitution, legislation and justice commission. The government's programme of political and legislative reforms would not succeed unless it was approved by the commission, which Guzmán chaired, thus explaining his political importance. Moreover, the relative weakness of the commission's remaining opposition members, the designated senator Carlos Letelier and RN senator Sergio Diez, only helped to amplify Guzmán's role.[31] Third, the internal strife which plagued RN, in contrast to UDI's unity in Congress, reinforced the latter's negotiating position.

Guzmán created a made-to-measure party of ex-colleagues and ex-students. UDI organized itself around its master. He created the doctrine, the strategic changes and the tactical shifts. Guzmán did everything, including fund-raising and the designation of important posts. In this way, he created a homogeneous machine, capable of standing up to the many radical twists of the transition without faltering. This enabled UDI to become a kind of German Liberal Party, a small player among two big fish, RN and the *Concertación*. However, Guzmán's omnipotent role also led to serious inefficiencies not visible outside the party. As such, UDI organizers, such as Joaquin Lavín and Miguel Urquiza, faced serious difficulties in their attempts to project the party as a professional entity and to ensure that it *'produjera artesanía de exportación y no de consumo interno'*.[32]

Guzmán's assassination by left-wing terrorists outside the Catholic University campus in April 1991 thus caused shock waves in the party and forced a radical rethink in terms of its organization and strategy. UDI consequently experienced a mass increase in its membership, principally owing to a wave of public sympathy. Indeed, in the three weeks following Guzmán's death there was an increase of 10,000 members, including 2,000 converts from RN itself. The number of new members increased by a further 15,000 over the following months. The party capitalized on the subsequent publicity by organizing 84 public events over a 20-day period shortly after Guzmán's death. Several important independent right-wing personalities, not previously associated either with UDI or the *gremialista* movement, joined the party in solidarity, including former Pinochet minister José Piñera and the former right-wing presidential candidate, Hernán Büchi. Its rising membership and sudden popularity infused the party with a newfound sense of confidence which enabled it to fine tune its intransigent opposition strategy. With the incorporation of personalities such as Büchi and Piñera, the party could claim to include the principal architects of the military regime's political, social and economic revolution symbolized by the 1980 constitution, the socio-economic modernizations and the neo-liberal economy. For it is these projects, carried out under the tutelage of Guzmán, Piñera and Büchi, which are perceived by the right as the golden age of the military regime. However, it led to an important internal debate over whether UDI wished to remain an influential elite-based movement or become a mass-based party, which such growth implied. Guzmán had always favoured the latter and hoped to transform UDI into a twenty-first-century PDC: multi-class and popular, inspired by Christian principles and based around support for a social market economy. Some within UDI, such as Julio Dittborn, privately welcomed the expansion in party membership, and especially the incorporation of liberal figures such as Piñera and Büchi. Dittborn had opposed the party's definition as a 'Christian and popular' organization and wished it to adopt a more liberal and secular line. However, many within UDI felt uneasy with the party's sudden numerical expansion, principally because most of these new members were not from the *gremialista* tradition. This strategy was indeed risky, and still poses certain dangers for the party, since many of those joining UDI were, and still are, liberals. Such new members may prove impossible to control and could thus radically change the nature of the party. Although Joaquín Lavín insisted that strict controls to prevent nationalist leaders from entering the party were in place at the time of Guzmán's death, he recognized that no such controls existed to control rank-and-file membership. The expansion of its membership also puts at risk the party's generational element, which for so long has acted as an ideological adhesive. Despite these concerns, Guzmán's legacy still remains virtually intact. His influence could not be weakened despite the inconvenience of death, and those in charge of the party prior to Guzmán's assassination are mostly still in place. As such, the new liberal members of the party, such as Piñera and Büchi, joined an environment which was more stable than many commentators had believed. This meant that they would be unable to take up important and pivotal posts within the party organization.

As a response to these new circumstances, UDI organized a *congreso doctrinal* in September 1991 to mark out the future ideological and political orientations of the party.[33] Its aim was to ratify Guzmán's vision of UDI as a popular party inspired by Christian principles and to correct some of the problems now facing it. Two of the most important issues focused on the increase in membership and the lack of a successor. UDI realized that the growth in support experienced by the party in the aftermath of Guzmán's death did not correspond to the capture of the traditional right-wing vote. It was on the whole a *pinochetista* vote which in itself generates a certain fragile dependence on the attitudes of the General. They are Pinochet's people rather than UDI's and could easily abandon the party. Despite these realities, the congress consolidated the party's ideology by reaffirming UDI as a popular party inspired by Christian principles and economic freedom, albeit with some subtle changes.[34]

On the question of Guzman's successor, Julio Dittborn's role following his mentor's death seemed limited, despite being the party's 'symbolic' party president and Guzmán's heir-apparent. His liberal views, as well as his divorce, alienated a significant number of high-ranking party officials. Although accepted while Guzmán was alive, because the latter was viewed as the real leader, the role of president would now inevitably become a pivotal position. To this end, Jovino Novoa appeared as the consensus candidate. Novoa, a subsecretary-general in the military government, acted as the principal *albacea* (provisional administrator) of Guzmán's legacy. Although not the heir-apparent nor the most important public figure in UDI, he seemed perfectly fitted to act as arbiter of the party directorate. Elected to the Senate in the 1997 congressional elections, Novoa had acted as Guzmán's strategic adviser, and despite being more of a backroom man and not a natural charismatic leader, as Guzmán's personal friend, university colleague and principal founder of the *gremialista* movement together with the deceased leader, he remains the undisputed leader, despite stepping down as party president in April 1998.

Despite representing the smaller of the two right-wing parties, UDI's political and electoral standing has increased dramatically over the last few years. This is for several reasons: it has exploited the persistent internal difficulties facing RN, which appear all the more divisive when contrasted with UDI's homogeneity; the party has maintained a high profile in Congress despite its relatively small presence by maintaining Guzmán's strategy of either handing over or denying its support to its political opponents, although this has often exacerbated tensions with RN; and it has tapped into the popular psyche on issues such as corruption, drug trafficking, social inequality and law and order more successfully than RN given its highly populist and intransigent rhetoric, more popular with the right-wing electorate than RN's often contradictory and confusing stance.

The successful municipal administration of UDI's mayor of the wealthy Santiago suburb of Las Condes, Joaquín Lavín, has raised UDI's profile even further. Lavín, a fervent Catholic with links to the conservative *Opus Dei*, a disciple of the *gremialista* sympathizer, Miguel Kast, and a former employee with the state planning office ODEPLAN during the military regime, is a *gremialista* creation *par excellence*. Since being elected mayor in 1992 and again in 1996, when he won an outstanding 77 per cent of the vote, Lavín has been at the forefront of the *gremialista*/UDI populist project of using the municipal sector as a laboratory for the party's political, economic and social project, and ultimately as the springboard for national power.[35] Lavín has emerged as the right's strongest card for the 1999 presidential elections, a position reinforced following Andrés Allamand defeat in the 1997 Senate election. However, reflecting the right's weakness at the presidential level, and UDI's distaste for political parties and its preference for independent candidates, Lavín has over the years sought to distance himself from UDI.

The party's increasing electoral strength, largely at the expense of RN, has, however, led many in UDI to reappraise the party's strategic priorities, since its *pinochetista* trajectory is unlikely to prove sufficient to secure either a majority in Congress or the presidency. One sector, represented by UDI politicians such as Joaquín Lavín, and other younger party leaders such as Pablo Longueira and Andrés Chadwick, recognize that UDI will find it difficult significantly to increase its electoral profile unless the party modernizes its message. This would involve distancing the party from its *pinochetista* past, without abandoning its defence of the military regime's legacy. Joaquín Lavín's administration of the municipality of Las Condes represents the schema through which this sector hopes to forge its future electoral success, a model based on technocracy rather than ideology, and on efficient administrators rather than politicians. The second sector, represented by older individuals intrinsically linked to Jaime Guzmán, such as Hernán Larraín, Sergio Fernández and Jovino Novoa, are more closely associated with the military regime, although they share much of the younger group's modernizing agenda.[36] As such, they are likely to resist any attempt to dilute the party's commitment to the military. Although Allamand's modernizing project suffered a serious defeat in the 1997 elections, UDI's alternative is unlikely to garner the necessary support to win power in the medium term, even if Lavín presents himself as an independent. The correlation of forces within the right has altered considerably over the years, yet its overall level of support has remained more or less static and it has yet to prove it can penetrate successfully those sectors which have so far evaded it.

While RN's long-term strategy has sought to focus on attracting the centre ground, despite the dangers to internal unity such a strategy will undoubtedly pose, UDI's strategy, in contrast, has centred on transforming itself into a twenty-first-century right-wing version of the PDC: a semi-confessional, populist organization. UDI will thus have to establish itself as a respectable, solidly based party and will need to avoid becoming an ideological ghetto and present a more flexible stance, without reneging on its hardline principles. Given that UDI is an opportunistic party it is likely to do what it can to achieve this end. Of course, both parties will fail to increase their electoral support if they persist in attracting only the *pinochetista* vote. This dichotomy has plagued the parties on the right in terms of their relationship with each other, as well as in the wider electoral arena, which is itself a fundamental source of conflict between RN and UDI.

9 Politics and Elections

Traditionally, the right in Chile has never felt at ease with electoral politics. The lack of party institutionalization and the informal power networks it nurtured and developed over decades, as well as its fear of fermenting mass mobilization, has left it unable and often unwilling to participate fully in the democratic process. This suspicion of western liberal democracy became evident in the immediate post-coup period when it readily abandoned even its formal adherence to Chile's party political system and to any semblance of democratic forms of representation. The economic crisis of 1981–3 and the political difficulties which subsequently engulfed the military regime demonstrated that the institutional status quo would not endure. Consequently, the right arrived at the conclusion that electoral politics would once again become a reality in Chilean politics.

A central preoccupation has therefore centred on the question of the degree to which the right has been able and willing to insert itself into this nascent democratic framework. Two general elections (in 1989 and 1993) and one mid-term congressional election (in 1997) have taken place since the return to democracy. The manner in which the right has chosen to confront these electoral processes reveal much about the nature of conservative politics in Chile. The elections also act as a central pointer to the differences between the two principal right-wing parties, *Renovación Nacional* (RN) and *Unión Demócrata Independiente* (UDI). These have tended to centre on cultural and strategic issues rather than more specific ideological or policy concerns. Nor have the electoral battlelines been drawn between the right as a whole and its natural political adversaries, the centre-left coalition parties.

The right's competitive arena, both politically and electorally, has been intra-sector in nature. Since the party right abandoned its machinery in the immediate aftermath of the coup (unlike the Christian Democrats and the left which succeeded in maintaining virtually intact their party organizations despite the military repression) its starting point today is far more fundamental: What is the right? How should it be organized? Who does it represent? How should the right insert itself in the party political system? What vision should the right adopt in relation to the political system? These are questions which no longer preoccupy the Chilean centre and left, where to varying degrees, these issues have been adequately resolved. For the right-wing parties, although ideologically similar, such issues have yet to be determined.

INTRA-SECTOR RELATIONS: THE QUEST FOR ELECTORAL UNITY

An essential element in an analysis of right-wing electoral politics in Chile must therefore include an examination of the degree to which the two principal parties of the right have learned to coexist. This reality is all the more important given the 'pacted' nature of post-authoritarian electoral politics which has ensured that RN and UDI's futures remain intrinsically linked. The system works against independent candidates and parties, making the old strategy of the *camino propio* virtually defunct. Although the current electoral system exaggerates the right's level of support it also complicates their ability to confront these processes alone. This is a particularly difficult reality for RN and UDI who have learned from bitter experience that they cannot live together harmoniously yet would invariably perish if apart. Unity thus becomes a central preoccupation, not only for the right but also for the left and centre. This dilemma, cooperation versus competition, not only forms an integral part of UDI and RN's attempts each to present a distinctive identity concurrent with their political aspirations and the make-up of their electoral support, but also represents a central preoccupation in terms of their electoral strategy.

After tortuous eleventh hour negotiations, RN and UDI succeeded in establishing electoral pacts for the two general elections and the one mid-term legislative poll they have so far fought. In the 1989 presidential and congressional elections the *Democracia y Progreso* electoral pact brought together both principal parties of the right. They agreed to present a single presidential candidate, the former finance minister Hernán Büchi, and a joint parliamentary list. In the 1993 elections, the *Unión por el Progreso de Chile* coalition incorporated RN, UDI, the *Partido Nacional* (PN), independents and the *Unión de Centro Centro* (UCC), an electoral vehicle for the populist centre-right supermarket tycoon and former presidential candidate, Francisco Javier Errázuriz. It also presented a single candidate to the presidency, Arturo Alessandri, and a joint electoral list in the congressional contest. In the 1997 mid-term elections, *Unión Por*

Chile, incorporated both RN and UDI, as well as the small, southern-based *Partido del Sur*, but not the UCC, now renamed the *Unión de Centro Centro Progresista* (UCCP), which presented its own list.

However, the right's fragile unity when faced with the prospect of electoral annihilation, has disguised several important defining traits, which have traditionally hindered the electoral activities of the right, and which have been in evidence throughout the post-authoritarian period under study. These fundamental issues lie at the heart of the right's continued difficulties in forging an established internal identity. It has also resulted in an inability to establish a solid and long-lasting inter-party relationship, and more specifically, has severely undermined the sector's electoral pact-making processes. The Chilean right is not only divided by its interpretation of the past, in terms of its position *vis-à-vis* the military, but also by its vision of the future, not in terms of its policy orientations or lofty ideological pretences, but at the most fundamental level: what role the political parties should play in the country's democratic system. As I have outlined in previous chapters, RN and UDI share diametrically opposed conceptions over what political parties represent. While the modernizing wing of RN has sought to revitalize Chile's dominant party system, UDI has persistently striven to undermine their competitor's position within the national polity. This inherent difference has plagued the right's attempt to unite at times of electoral competition and has seriously undermined its ability adequately to perform. The right's tactical differences, especially at election time, originate from this central paradox.

The issue of whether to present independent or party candidates, especially in presidential elections, continues to be one of the most salient themes in right-wing electoral politics. The right has a long trajectory of presenting independent candidates to the presidency; Jorge Alessandri in the 1970 elections was only the last example in pre-1973 Chile. Despite RN being the larger of the two right-wing parties and its incessant determination to institutionalize the party right, it proved unable in both 1989 and 1993 to break the sector's, and especially UDI's, obsession with candidates whose prominence lay outside the established party structures. The fiasco surrounding the selection processes in the run-up to the 1989 presidential elections, the first since 1970, and the 1993 presidential elections demonstrate this polarity. RN privately conceded in 1989 and 1993 that the right would be unable to win the presidential elections. Its strategy, therefore, concentrated on stressing its parliamentary activity and the role of parties in the political system. As such, its commitment to the right's presidential candidates, which were imposed on the party despite its resistance, was at best lukewarm.[1]

The role of the non-party right, most notably the economic conglomerates, entrepreneurs, the media and the military, in right-wing party politics has been a vexed issue for decades. The right's institutional weakness has forced it, rather willingly, to rely on forces outside the party structures. This has severely weakened the sector's attempts to strengthen the role of political parties. UDI has persistently supported the right of non-party sectors within the right to 'interfere' in party activity, not only because of ideological considerations, but more importantly because the party enjoys the overwhelming support of these individuals and groups. RN has suffered most from the involvement of what Allamand termed the *poderes fácticos*. These groups, centred in the media, the business sector and the military, are also hostile to parties *per se*, and have used their economic power to dictate and determine the future of right-wing party politics in Chile. They have systematically striven to undermine the modernizer's attempts to reinsert the sector fully into the democratic system.

The lack of a party political culture within the right becomes all too evident during election campaigns. The involvement of non-party activists, almost exclusively hostile to, and ignorant of, the rules of the democratic game, have resulted in the right adopting a relatively amateurish approach to politics. The 'nod and a wink' approach has been adopted to the detriment of modern and professional techniques. The institutionalization of the party right has been hampered as a result. Moreover, the absence of a historical democratic party trajectory has resulted in a right which is both politically immature and lacking in confidence. The public internecine warfare which often erupts between RN and UDI, especially at election time, and more often than not over insignificant minutiae, is a clear and tangible manifestation of this lack of a party culture. The right, in essence, remains untrained in the matter of how 'to do politics'. Although RN's liberal wing has attempted to correct this deficiency, hostility to this modernizing project from other right-wing sectors, most notably UDI and the non-party right, has been fierce.

Different perceptions over how to define the very essence of democratic politics, rather than ideology or specific policies, therefore represents the most important differentiating element within the right. As the political scientist Oscar Godoy remarked, '*la derecha está en un estado de naturaleza, estado previo al de las sociedades políticamente organizada, donde todos compiten contra todos'.*[2] This still nascent sector is, therefore, enmeshed in an ongoing and remarkably painful inward-looking process of self-discovery. RN and UDI represent these diametrically opposed visions of the future. In essence, both parties embody the conflict between two competing, and mutually exclusive, projects aimed at defining the quintessential and permanent identity of the Chilean right. This struggle, and its related manifestations, have remained a constant in every electoral contest to date, as an examination of the 1989, 1993 and 1997 elections will demonstrate.

The 1989 Presidential and Congressional Elections

The electoral campaign which began in mid-1988 in anticipation of the plebiscite continued into the presidential and congressional elections of December 1989. The first and dominant issue to preoccupy the right centred on who should represent the sector in the presidential contest. RN, in keeping with its strategy of reinserting the parties into the political system, sought to convince both the political and economic wings of the right of the need to present a presidential candidate from party ranks. Once it became clear that Pinochet would not stand, the right began the process of selecting its presidential candidate and devising their respective strategic plans to confront the electoral contest.

Two contrasting positions soon emerged. As a consequence of the 1988 plebiscite debacle, RN came to the conclusion that the right would not win the 1989 presidential election under any circumstances. It therefore sought to devise a medium-term strategy aimed an ensuring victory in 1993. This centred on creating a centre-right political force whose focus would be the party's parliamentary activity. As such, it aimed to concentrate almost exclusively on the parliamentary campaign. The party nevertheless sought to convince the right of the need to present a party candidate to the presidency. RN thus promoted its then president, Sergio Onofre Jarpa. Although an opponent of Allamand's modernizing strategy, Jarpa was at least a party figure, and as such, would contribute to the institutionalization of the party right. However, traditional politicians such as Jarpa were unacceptable to Pinochet. Moreover, the business sector, now fervent devotees of the neo-liberal system, mistrusted such political figures for fear they would give in to populist demands, and a figure too closely associated with the regime, the view held by RN, seemed to have little chance of success.[3]

UDI faced a difficult position in which they were dialectically trapped between the pro-regime *blandos* and the *duros* whose influence with the General had grown significantly following the plebiscite defeat. To have allied themselves with the *duros* would have entailed the party's isolation from the principal historical trunk of the right, thus forcing UDI simply to become the falange of an ageing general. Yet to associate itself with the *aperturistas* and their strategy of gentle disassociation from the regime (RN's position) would have resulted in the loss of their *raison d'être*. With its usual high degree of unrealism, which had characterized its activities during the plebiscite, UDI maintained that a right-wing presidential option was viable. It opted to support any candidate which met with Pinochet's approval. The vacillating candidacy of finance minister Hernán Büchi, viewed by the business sectors as a successful economic manager, soon emerged as the most viable option.

Pinochet favoured the choice as Büchi would safeguard the economic model, and as a technocrat with little political experience would be easy to manipulate behind the scenes. RN viewed Büchi's candidacy with extreme suspicion and hostility, principally because it believed it would undermine its attempts to institutionalize the right. Moreover, while acknowledging Büchi's technocratic credentials, RN doubted whether he had the necessary skills of a politician. The party was fearful that the military government would repeat the same mistakes of the plebiscite. What was needed was a candidate as far removed as possible from the Pinochet regime. However, despite RN's objections, Büchi was eventually adopted as the right's candidate. The aim was to transform him into the Adolfo Suárez of Chilean politics: a man born out of the authoritarian regime who benefited from his relative youth, who maintained his silence on political matters during the military administration and who was a vocal supporter of the market. He was seen as the technician, the government's favourite son, the helmsman of the economic model, Pinochet's brave prince, the outsider who did not belong to the traditional right.[4]

The role of the economic conglomerates and the entrepreneurial sector was instrumental in the decision to adopt Büchi. In the run up to the 1989 elections, former finance minister Sergio de Castro was responsible for coordinating a group of individuals, installed in the recently privatized state companies, who used the vast financial resources available to them to fund the election campaign. These funds were funnelled into a quasi-secret organization, *Siglo XXI*, run by a group of powerful entrepreneurs linked to the economic groups. Backed by the right-wing *El Mercurio* newspaper and with the encouragement of a technocratic intelligentsia, this group adopted a hostile position *vis-à-vis* the traditional party right. The fear that the political and economic system inherited from the Pinochet regime would collapse if the centre-left coalition emerged victorious led the economic right to support the hardest sector, UDI. They also vetoed Jarpa's candidacy at an early stage by withdrawing RN's funding until the party expressed its support for Büchi. As an RN statement declared:

> It was proper and legitimate for the centre-right's most important organization to aspire to take its leader to *La Moneda*. Yet with the realism which has characterized Jarpa, he realized that after decades of systematic attacks on politicians, the centre-right is still not ready for political parties. After 16 years of an authoritarian regime, there are whole generations who do not understand the need for stable organizations to channel the concerns of citizens.[5]

RN finally relented but only after Büchi was forced to accept three conditions laid down by the party in return for its support. First, he would have to distance himself from the military government, second, his programme would have to be consistent with RN's election manifesto, and third, Büchi would have to hand over the direction of the campaign to the party. Allamand's strategy adopted the premise that, given that a party candidate was no longer a viable option, every attempt would be made to ensure that RN would represent the hegemonic force in the presidential campaign, thus ensuring a dominant position for the party right. The notion that RN would adopt Büchi as 'its' candidate, raised serious concerns within the UDI camp as well as with the *poderes fácticos*. RN was initially successful in drawing in the candidate. Not only did Sebastián Piñera and Allamand become Büchi's campaign managers but he announced, to the consternation of UDI and the military government, a relatively radical programme of constitutional reform very similar to that adopted by RN. UDI's concern that Büchi was moving too close to the Allamand camp was exacerbated when the candidate visited RN's headquarters but refused an invitation to visit UDI's central office. Guzmán's party, with government support, sought to retake the initiative to '*levantar una fuerza pinochetista, que se pare frente a RN*'. According to RN sources, government officials in the provinces sought to put pressure on RN to tone down its anti-regime discourse. However, the right was thrown into disarray in May 1989 when Büchi announced he would no longer be willing to stand, citing his lack of political vocation. Büchi was a weak candidate, as he himself recognized. However, many commentators believe his resignation was temporary and had very specific intentions in mind. First, the manoeuvre may have sought to shorten the length of a possible campaign and to make the most of the publicity which would follow an announcement relating to his return. Second, by resigning he would avoid the demands of an election such as the need to engage in public debate. Third, by waiting until a parliamentary agreement had been reached between RN and UDI, Büchi would avoid the difficulties inherent in any attempt to bring the warring parties together.

Büchi's decision rekindled prospects for a Jarpa presidential candidacy, despite the hostility that such an option would face from the non-party right, as well as UDI. Regardless, RN's political commission declared on 23 May that *'a estas alturas no existe la posibilidad de una candidatura independiente'*. RN thus called on Jarpa to accept the party's nomination which he did on 6 June. This decision raised serious concerns among those sectors who viewed Jarpa as an autarkist, statist, nationalist. They once again refused to fund his campaign, an act which Allamand referred to as an *'intento de chantaje de ciertos grupos empresariales'*. Renewed calls were made for Büchi to reconsider his position. Not to everyone's surprise, Büchi returned from a foreign trip on 10 July and announced that he would be standing as a candidate. Jarpa quickly renounced his candidacy and RN grudgingly agreed to support Büchi in return for a further set of conditions. First, economic support for RN's parliamentary candidates. In this way RN sought to achieve a certain degree of autonomy. Second, assurances that the party would have a prominent role in Büchi's electoral campaign. However, the second Büchi candidacy was discernibly different from the first. Piñera and Allamand were replaced as campaign managers by a group closely associated with the regime and the economic right, led by former minister and Chicago Boy, Pablo Baraona. This was clearly an attempt to wrest control from RN and the party right. Baraona sought to 'harden' the right's electoral campaign by adopting the same plebiscite strategy of stigmatizing the opposition and highlighting the (non-existent) link between the Christian Democrats and the 'Marxists'. He also used the government apparatus as an efficient tool in the campaign, an approach rejected by RN since it believed such unethical use of public resources would damage the right's reputation. The party also raised concern over Baraona's close links with UDI. RN favoured a campaign run by *núcleos tripartidistas* made up of RN and UDI party activists as well as members of Büchi's campaign team. Baraona, however, concentrated power in the hands of the economic right and the 'independent' commandos.

Despite the presence of US and British marketing experts, such as Margaret Thatcher's former adviser, Tim Bell, the right's presidential campaign was improvised and disorganized. The campaign organizers found it difficult to recruit local experts, such as electoral specialists, intellectuals and artists, despite being offered remuneration four times the market rates. The right's television party political broadcasts used Argentine models as Chilean ones were unwilling to work for the campaign, while the film directors necessary to produce television and cinema publicity had to be brought in from overseas. The fact that Chilean culture is predominantly democratic, therefore, became evident during the 1989 elections. The right's presidential campaign was deemed a complete failure. According to Angell and Pollack, its programme had the appearance of a hastily produced and contradictory document, while that of the opposition was both serious and viable. Büchi himself was persistently inconsistent in his public statements, on many occasions undermining his reputation as a prudent technocrat by making wild promises, such as the construction of 100,000 homes a year and the creation of one million new jobs. He was unable to disassociate himself fully from the regime without undermining his position within the government. His response to the issue of human rights violations was both inconsistent and confused. As the election approached, and as it became clear that the strategy of linking the Christian Democrats to the Marxist left was failing, those close to Büchi began to disassociate themselves from the presidential campaign.

RN felt marginalized from the presidential campaign and conceded that Büchi stood no chance of winning the election. As a result, the party opted to concentrate on the parliamentary campaign in an attempt to maximize its representation in Congress. This was an important exercise given that these elections represented the first test of strength for the parties on the right. A good performance on the part of RN would guarantee it senior status in respect to UDI. Similarly, UDI, while aware that it would emerge as the second largest right-wing party, hoped to limit the quantitative differences with RN. The parliamentary contest between the two was therefore intense, and contrasted widely with the opposition *Concertación's* good-natured and unified stance, despite the fact that differences between its members were far greater than within the right. The process of coalition-building within the right was, therefore, an extremely long and arduous process, and exacerbated the already tense relations between the parties. If it was not for the electoral system RN and UDI would have run separately. In February 1989, Jarpa even stated that he would not support UDI parliamentary candidates and that he did not expect them to support RN.

The right chose individuals outside the parties to act as arbiters in its attempts to unite around a single presidential candidate and a common parliamentary list: Carlos Cáceres, Jorge Ballerino and Pablo Baraona. The principal points of contention centred on the number of seats (*cupos*) each party would receive and whether and how independent candidates were to be incorporated into the pact. This latter point of contention was particularly difficult to resolve, especially in relation to distributing the Senate seats. Many of the prospective candidates were independents, who demanded that multiple personal negotiations take place between themselves, the party leaders and Baraona. Despite several acrimonious false starts, an agreement to present a joint parliamentary list was reached in August, but did not cover the Senate elections. Moreover, other right-wing sectors chose not to participate in the RN–UDI pact and presented their own parliamentary lists. In some areas there were as many as five competing right-wing lists. This only helped to magnify the general perception that the right was both disunited and chaotic. In fact, right-wing candidates were often competing against each other rather than with the then centre-left opposition.

The economic right not only held the purse strings for the presidential campaign but also provided much of the resources for the parliamentary candidates. This meant that independent candidates were favoured to the detriment of those representing the political parties, especially RN, who were constantly asked to change elements of the campaign in return for 'donations'. Although UDI was relatively well financed throughout the campaign, RN suffered as a result of its ambiguous position *vis-à-vis* the economic model and the military regime. Moreover, the government used all its available resources to assist UDI candidates, mainly through the use of government and municipal offices, more often than not staffed by UDI members or sympathizers. Coupled with the pro-UDI stance adopted by both the state owned television station, TVN, and *El Mercurio*, it was evident where the sympathies lay of the non-party right.[6]

The 1993 Presidential and Congressional Elections

While RN wrote off the 1989 presidential election campaign, hopes were high that the right would adopt a party option in 1993. This was for two reasons. First, the veto capabilities of the military were now much reduced given their withdrawal from government positions of influence and the natural concentration of their professional role. Second, the entrepreneurial sector seemed to have undergone a process of de-ideologicalization. The apocalyptic concerns on the part of certain business groups of what an opposition victory in 1989 would entail led the right to adopt a candidate who it believed would best serve this continuist position. This did not appear to be the case in 1993. The entrepreneurial vote, although still predominantly right-wing, was now more fragmented, and its support even extended to moderate figures within the governing centre-left coalition, such as the then finance minister, Alejandro Foxley. Moreover, faced with both the need to work in pacts, and a desire not to repeat the internecine disputes of the last election campaign, the right, including to some extent UDI, sought to work towards improving the image of the political parties. Many on the right now believed that after several decades of hostility towards the party system, the sector was in a position to institutionalize its political and presidential leadership through the parties.[7]

Two candidacies emerged from within RN, the then senator Sebastián Piñera and deputy (now senator) Evelyn Matthei, both members of Allamand's *Patrulla Juvenil*. Their ability successfully to project the presidential option of the party right was crucial if Allamand's project to reinsert the party system into the psyche of the sector was ever to materialize. Piñera represents an enigma within the right and represents the most 'left-wing' element within it. He was the only prominent politician publicly to support the NO in the 1988 plebiscite campaign, voted with the governing coalition in favour of tax and labour reform, supported the designation of his Christian Democrat brother, Pablo, as a member of the Central Bank's council, resisted pressure from the right to support the death penalty, and refused to take part in a right-wing walkout of Congress during a visit by Germany's Chancellor Helmut Kohl. He is viewed with suspicion by his fellow RN senators, most of whom are arch conservatives. He is also unpopular with the party's deputies, who criticize his person-alist style. However, RN's conservative wing lacked a leader who could compete on equal terms with Piñera. Senator Miguel Otero was singled out as a possible challenger but he lacked outside appeal and was unpopular within the party. Thus Jarpa opted to throw his considerable weight behind Matthei. Although she came from the same ideological stable as Piñera, Matthei was perceived as less confrontational and more loyal to the party. Moreover, Jarpa's personal dislike of Piñera forced him to support the candidate best able to displace him. As a result, most of the conservative RN senators, such as Sergio Romero, Alberto Cooper, Enrique Larre and Bruno Siebert, chose to support Matthei. One cannot exclude the gender element in this equation. Many of the party *grandées* believed that Matthei could easily be manipulated. These two prospective candidacies thus highlighted the high degree of personalism within the party. Both Piñera and Matthei were essentially ideological mirror copies of each other. The contest, therefore, did not resolve around policies or competing right-wing projects but around individuals.

However, the hope that the right would break with tradition and propose a party rather than an independent candidate were dashed by the *Piñeragate* scandal, which revealed the involvement of Matthei in a telephone tapping operation and subsequent coverup. The object of the operation was Piñera. Both candidates were eventually forced to abandon their campaigns. Matthei resigned from the party and joined UDI, despite her centre-right views. This rather bizarre conversion helped to undermine the modernizers' political strategy and further highlighted the inability of the right to project a coherent project. Further inquiries into the *Piñeragate* scandal revealed the involvement of other leading party members as well as sections of the armed forces. Many have seen the operation as an attempt by independent conservative elements and the military to wreck Allamand's attempt to create a modern, centre-right party and destroy Piñera's presidential aspirations. RN emerged discredited and Allamand abandoned all hopes of presenting a party candidate in the 1993 presidential elections.[8]

The personalist nature of right-wing politics in Chile also affected UDI. José Piñera (Sebastián's brother) had joined the party following Guzmán's assassination, ostensibly in an attempt to rise to a position of influence within it and thus become the heir to the former *gremialista* warlord. As explained in chapter 8, non-*gremialista* party members found it extremely difficult to insert themselves into the upper echelons of the organization. Piñera's ultimate ambition, to become UDI's presidential candidate, was therefore frustrated. As a result, he resigned from the party to stand as an independent right-wing presidential candidate. His 'independent' position was strengthened as a result of the *Piñeragate* scandal, which helped discredit not only RN but all parties on the right, as well as party organizations in general. Although some within UDI supported Piñera's independent candidacy, such as Lavín and Chadwick, the party opted to deny him its endorsement. While UDI is fiercely anti-party, Piñera's apparent disregard for the organization, as well as his calculating nature in utilizing his brother's misfortune for his own advantage, made him many enemies. Rather incredulously, UDI launched Büchi, the discredited right-wing candidate in 1989, who had also joined the party following Guzmán's death, as its presidential pre-candidate. This option was doomed from the start as it would prove, for obvious reasons, unacceptable to RN. Büchi had joined UDI because he knew RN would not adopt him as its presidential candidate. RN concluded that no matter what superficial changes were made, Büchi simply did not have what it took to be a successful politician. Although in typically idiosyncratic style UDI subsequently announced the candidacy of its then president, Jovino Novoa (who was never viewed as a serious candidate), the failure of the right to name a credible presidential candidate from within the party ranks, once again raised the spectre of its historic reliance on the *mal menor*: the adoption of an independent presidential candidate. However, RN wished to avoid the repetition of 1989 when Büchi was named as the right's candidate against the party's wishes. The aim was now to present an independent candidate who not only shared RN's support for a strong party system but who was politically distant and sufficiently critical of the military regime. As a result, the party chose the centre-right entrepreneur Manuel Feliú as its presidential pre-candidate. The electoral picture was further complicated by the non-party sponsored independent candidacy of Arturo Alessandri, who apart from his distinguished family lineage, had little to offer in terms of political pedigree.[9]

Attention now centred on developing the best possible mechanism for choosing the single candidate out of these three contenders. The negotiations, as could have been expected, were again tortuous to the extreme and took several months to conclude, by which time the governing coalition had already chosen its presidential candidate, the Christian Democrat Eduardo Frei, who, by the time the right's negotiations were complete, had been on the campaign trail for several months. The mechanism eventually adopted was similar to a US-style presidential primary: the *Gran Convención Presidencial Unión por*

Chile. The right lacks efficient mechanisms to facilitate and resolve its internal conflicts. Moreover, the existence of an amalgam of independents with excessive influence within the parties has made it more difficult to establish such mechanisms which would limit public polemic. As such, the convention seemed the best available option to redress these inefficiencies. The convention, held on 9 August 1993, brought together 1,847 electors, representing RN (with 29.6 per cent of the vote) and UDI (24.4 per cent), as well as Errázuriz's UCC (21.2 per cent), the PN (2.4 per cent) and the *Partido del Sur* (2.5 per cent). Independents, chosen by the three candidates themselves, accounted for 20.03 per cent of the vote. A candidate needed two-thirds of the total vote to be elected, thus each required cross-party support.[10] José Piñera refused to participate, despite calls on him to do so, for fear that his independent candidacy would split the right in December's presidential elections. Although his reasons seemed to emanate from a belief that the right's candidate should be chosen by rank-and-file members rather than by an elite-based convention, a more reasonable explanation centres on the recognition that, as a candidate who lacked the support of any of the parties, he had only limited prospects of success in the *Gran Convención*.

The convention proved a prime example of right-wing disloyalty. UDI, aware that Novoa was not a serious contender and fearful of a RN-dominated Feliú candidacy, chose to withdraw its candidate at the very last minute. In the morning of the convention, each of the three candidates presented their respective manifestos. However, Novoa ended his presentation with a declaration announcing that he was withdrawing from the contest and urged the audience to support Alessandri's candidacy. This announcement sent shockwaves in the RN camp as the two parties had agreed not to instruct party members on which way to vote. With UDI's endorsement, Alessandri emerged the victor with 885 votes (56.5 per cent) to Feliú's 607 (38.7 per cent). Although Alessandri did not obtain the necessary two-thirds, a second round did not take place. Feliú quickly conceded defeat and stepped down in favour of Alessandri.[11]

RN was thus left, as in 1988 and 1989, with no alternative but reluctantly to back a candidate supported by UDI which, furthermore, had very little prospect of success. The presidential campaign was even more lacklustre than in 1989. The two principal candidates, Frei and Alessandri, differed little on policy. Once again a broad consensus between all the major parties was at the core of the political agenda. Alessandri, like Büchi before him, gave the overriding impression that he was a reluctant candidate. The right's campaign was further hampered by the delay in nominating its presidential option. This damaged its chances of successfully securing the necessary financial and human resources, much of which had already been committed to the parliamentary campaign. This delay also postponed the critical debate over the sector's programme. Without a candidate it proved impossible to initiate a detailed discussion over the differing stances adopted by each party in the pact. Moreover, Alessandri's team faced hostility from RN and found it increasingly difficult to reach agreements on the various strategic options. This was compounded by the fact that the right had to face the governing coalition's huge electoral machine. The presidential campaign team was infused with a high degree of amateurism. Some of its star players took long holidays in mid-campaign while the parties opted to concentrate on the parliamentary campaign. This was the case not only with RN but with UDI too, who this time, unlike in 1989, chose to abandon Alessandri to the independents, who became solely responsible for his campaign.[12] Much to the consternation of the Alessandri campaign team, Sebastián Piñera publicly declared that Frei would win in the first round. Such was the apathy of the party right *vis-à-vis* the presidential contest.

Although the role of the economic right in the selection of the presidential candidate had not been as overbearing as in previous occasions, not only for the reasons described above, but also because none of the options presented to the convention were deemed to be unacceptable, their interference in the right's parliamentary campaign was as assiduous as ever. Tensions between RN and the non-party right had intensified as a result of what the party claimed was unwarranted interference in the party right's pact making process. The entrepreneurial sector had pressurized RN both through informal contacts and the media into accepting UDI's position in the negotiations. Consequently, in May 1993, Allamand described the economic right, the military and *El Mercurio* as a '*poder en las sombras*'. This spat between Allamand and the right's financial backers led the entrepreneur Eugenio Heiremans to abandon his efforts to raise entrepreneurial funds for the right. Moreover, Hernán Briones, founder of *Siglo XXI*, announced he would not be reactivating the organization for the 1993 elections. Allamand's position was further undermined by conservative elements within the party, particularly Senator Francisco Prat, who defended the existence of powers outside the political parties, claiming they provided a high degree of 'equilibrium'.

The RN–UDI parliamentary campaign was again a show of strength between the two parties, rather than a contest to defeat the 'real' opposition. The dispute between Allamand and UDI's Carlos Bombal, deputy for Santiago and a former mayor, for the lower house seat representing the prosperous Santiago suburb of Las Condes was particularly bitter and represented a microcosm of the wider conflict within the right. This contest was made all the more symbolic given that Las Condes and the neighbouring wealthy residential areas of Vitacura and Lo Barnachea are the spiritual as well as the physical home of the so called *poderes fácticos*. Many of the country's large economic groups are based there, as is *El Mercurio*. Moreover, the army academy is situated in the area, as is Pinochet's private residence. Las Condes is a critical seat for the right given that it is one of the country's wealthiest suburbs, and political home for the *gremialista* Joaquín Lavín's municipal administration. UDI hoped to increase the right's 61.7 per cent support it obtained in 1989 and thus provide the sector with two deputies rather than the one it gained in the last election (to do so the right-wing coalition would need to secure some two-thirds of the vote). However, RN claimed this would be difficult to achieve given that the Christian Democrat candidate, who obtained 26.6 per cent in 1989, was likely to secure at least the same level of support. It claimed that, as the party's candidate had more than doubled UDI's representative, UDI had promised to 'give' RN the seat *en forma cerrada* in order to ensure Allamand's selection. UDI denied the claim and said it had asked RN for exclusive rights to the district. Regardless of which version is correct, what is important here is that this was not a contest between individuals but between competing long-term projects. As such, it would have been surprising if either party had given way to the other, especially since UDI's strategy entailed using Las Condes, with Lavín as mayor, as a testing ground for its policies, combining the party's municipal and parliamentary work. The political objective of both parties was clearly to annihilate the other. Allamand's difficulties were exacerbated by the position of a large part of the business sector, which opposed Allamand's election as did most of the right-wing media. *El Mercurio* and the pro-UDI television station *Megavisión* adopted partisan positions, the former through pro-Bombal editorials and the latter by excluding Allamand's election activities in its news reports. Despite the ferocity of the Las Condes contest, the right-wing pact obtained the two-thirds necessary to double the *Concertación* and thus elected both Allamand and Bombal, although the latter emerged with the greatest number of votes. However, Allamand's victory was partly due to the *Concertación's* unofficial decision to back the RN president at the expense of its own candidate, a decision based on the premise that a strong moderate sector within the right was necessary to consolidate the democratic transition process.

The 1997 Mid-term Congressional Elections

As in 1989 and 1993, the 1997 congressional elections, to replace the whole of the Chamber of Deputies and half the elected senators, were marked by acrimonious negotiations over the distribution of seats (*cupos*) between the right-wing parties in the coalition. However, the 1997 contest was further complicated by the need for RN and UDI to define their relative electoral strengths with a view to nominating the sector's presidential candidate for the 1999 general election, since this was the first poll since the return to democracy in 1990 in which the legislative and presidential contests were not to be held simultaneously. Alberto Espina was elected as Andrés Allamand's successor as RN leader in April 1997, partly because he was perceived as less confrontational and would thus not only help placate the party's conservative factions, but would also facilitate the parliamentary negotiations with UDI in time for the 1997 elections, despite sharing Allamand's centre-right and modernizing tendencies. However, relations between RN and UDI deteriorated soon after Espina's election, following the unanimous decision by the party's deputies to support abolishing the designated senators, a decision which not only led to a rift with RN senators, but with UDI only months before the July deadline for presenting to the electoral authorities the list of candidates for the congressional contest.

Despite RN and UDI reaching an agreement to formalize a pact between the two parties at the eleventh hour (minutes before the legal deadline), they failed to introduce a mechanism to maximize their respective strengths, by distributing the *cupos* according to the strength of each party in a particular area. This would have prevented strong candidates from competing with each other. However, despite intense entrepreneurial pressure on the right-wing parties to distribute the seats according to their particular strengths, since the business sector was reluctant to finance what would have invariably become very fractured campaigns, both RN and UDI finally presented candidates to most of the 60 two-member lower house constituencies, while for the Senate RN presented candidates in all ten seats up for renewal and UDI in nine. What was significant about this decision, apart from reflecting the continued and intractable animosity between the main right-wing parties, was that both would, for the first time, be in a position clearly to measure their relative strengths. In all previous elections, RN, as the larger of the two, had presented more candidates within the pact.

Despite attempts by both parties to find common ground on less controversial issues, such as on economic policy, in time for the start of the election campaign, the generalized animosity between the two continued throughout, as in both previous elections. Moreover, as a change of government was not at play, as in 1989 and 1993, the campaign focused, albeit unofficially, on measuring each party's respective strength, with a view to the future nomination of the right's presidential candidate. This invariably resulted in a campaign in which RN and UDI, even more so than before, competed against each other rather than against their natural opponents in the *Concertación*. However, the electoral playing field was further complicated by Jarpa's decision, following his resignation from the party, to support non-RN candidates if these pledged to oppose constitutional reform, while one of RN's conservative senators expressed explicit support for UDI candidates. Thus throughout the campaign the right struggled to contain both inter- as well as intra-party conflict.

This internal competition, also evident for the first time among the government parties, as the centre and left fought to increase their respective positions in order to strengthen their claim to nominate the sector's presidential candidate, was especially fierce, as in 1993, between former RN leader, deputy Andrés Allamand, and UDI deputy Carlos Bombal, although this time at stake was the Senate seat for Santiago West. This contest, referred to by one newspaper at the time as 'the mother of all battles', and which the entrepreneurial sector had sought to avoid but to no avail, marked above all others the struggle between two competing and incompatible projects, that of the RN modernizers and UDI. Allamand sought not only to strengthen his personal ambition of representing the right in the 1999 presidential election, but to boost the viability of his modernizing project. Bombal's candidacy was seen as a litmus test for the self-professed aspiration of UDI's mayor of Las Condes and currently Chile's second most popular politician, Joaquín Lavín, to become the sole presidential candidate of the right in 1999. The contest for Santiago West was thus critical in that it marked the confrontation between the architect and leading figure of the right's modernizing project against the candidate of a party which not only sought to destroy the modernizers' project but at the same time promote its strongest card, Lavín, in a constituency which included the suburb of Santiago most associated with the UDI municipal and free market project, Las Condes. As expected, the right-wing campaign for Santiago West was fierce and highly acrimonious, especially since the electoral makeup of the seat meant only one would emerge victorious.

While Bombal's campaign was highly disciplined and had the full support of his party, as well as many in the entrepreneurial sector, Allamand faced an unruly mob of detractors, even among those assumed to be loyal supporters of his modernizing project. Only two weeks prior to the elections, Allamand launched a bitter attack on his erstwhile friend and political ally, Senator Sebastián Piñera, over the latter's business dealings in the controversial takeover of a Chilean electricity company.[13] Tensions between Allamand and Piñera, who also had presidential ambitions, had been on the boil for several years, but erupted just prior to the election, partly owing to resentment in the Allamand camp over Piñera's alleged lukewarm support for the former leader during the campaign. The crisis was particularly damaging since Piñera was the party's national campaign organizer and because RN's new leader, Alberto Espina, publicly defended Piñera against Allamand's accusations. Allamand's position was further undermined following the decision of Jarpa's new movement, *Chilefuturo*, to support Bombal.[14] Allamand's high-risk strategy of abandoning the lower house and the presidency of the party ultimately failed. Not only was he defeated by Bombal and the two *Concertación* candidates, but RN's position at national level suffered serious reversals at the expense of UDI.

Allamand failed for a number of reasons, most of which also explain RN's overall poor performance and the problems faced by the proponents of the right's modernizing project, although RN still remains the largest opposition party in the lower house, by far the more representative of the two chambers of Congress. First, Bombal was more successful than Allamand in focusing on the main concerns of the electorate (illicit drugs and corruption). Prior to the election, Bombal and UDI had spearheaded a campaign against judicial corruption, and in particular against alleged malpractice by Supreme Court judge Servando Jordan. Allamand and RN, on the other hand, sought to defend Jordan in Congress despite public opinion expressing support for the UDI position. Also, accusations against Allamand's alleged vacillation on the drugs issue following accusations by the former Pinochet minister, Fransisco Javier Cuadra, over alleged drug use by congressmen, enabled Bombal to adopt the moral high ground during the campaign on an issue of increasing public concern. Second, the persistent in-fighting within the RN camp, in contrast to the unified UDI campaign, increased the impression of an unorganized and disunited party which could not be trusted. It also appeared to confirm the view that Allamand had lost control over RN's modernizing project, thus undermining the very *raison d'être* for voting for the party. Third, RN's seemingly contradictory position on a number of fundamental issues, especially over the degree to which the party should collaborate with the government in areas such as constitutional reform and its vacillation over whether to support or condemn the *Concertación's* economic agenda, simply helped to confuse the electorate. Fourth, RN was unable to penetrate those areas in the constituency in which UDI was traditionally strong: the wealthy suburbs, such as Las Condes, where UDI's support had strengthened because of Joaquín Lavín's successful municipal administration, and the more working-class and marginal suburbs, where UDI's popular rhetoric has always reaped considerable electoral rewards.

The two general elections and one mid-term congressional election to have taken place in the post-Pinochet period have thus revealed the existence of two competing, and mutually exclusive, right-wing projects. The first, represented by RN, has attempted to reinsert the parties of the right into the democratic party political system, and a second, represented by UDI, has sought to use the power of external non-party right-wing forces to undermine such a project and promote its own particular brand of authoritarianism. This mutually hostile, yet dependent, relationship continues to undermine its ability to propel to a wider audience a coherent, independent and electorally viable long-term political project.

ELECTORAL EFFECTIVENESS

Although the right failed to elect a president from the sector in both 1989 and 1993 and remains in opposition at the parliamentary level, its electoral performance has far outweighed the expectations of not only its many critics, but of the right itself. Its electoral effectiveness has generally been underestimated for three principal reasons. First, the political right represents the civilian legacy of a military regime rejected, although not overwhelmingly, by the civilian population. Although its association with the Pinochet administration has acted as a break to any potential growth, this intrinsic link has not relegated the sector to the fringes of the political system. Second, the lack of strong and well-established party political organizations has in the past hindered the right's prospects for electoral growth, most notably at the parliamentary level. In 1989, 1993 and 1997 this deficiency did not prevent it from obtaining levels of parliamentary support far higher than one would have expected. Third, opinion poll data had persistently underestimated the right's level of support, especially at election time. This helped boost the impression that the sector had performed better than anticipated. This phenomenon can be explained by the general reticence of right-wing supporters, especially in the Chilean context with its laden symbolism, the military regime, publicly to admit their political preferences.

The Election Results

In the 1989 presidential elections, the candidate of the *Concertación*, Patricio Aylwin, won in the first round with 55.2 per cent of the vote. The candidate of the right, Hernán Büchi trailed on 29.4 per cent, while the independent centre-right populist candidate, Francisco Javier Errázuriz, obtained 15.4 per cent of the popular vote. The results in 1993 followed a similar trend, with the candidate of the *Concertación*, Eduardo Frei, obtaining an even clearer majority with 58.1 per cent. The right's candidate, Arturo Alessandri, obtained only 24.4 per cent, while the maverick right-wing former minister and former UDI activist, José Piñera, trailed on 6.2 per cent. Other candidates, mainly from the left, obtained only a few percentage points, although some, such as the independent Maximiliano Max-Neef and the Communist-sponsored Eugenio Pizarro, performed better than expected, with 5.5 per cent and 4.7 per cent of the vote respectively. The right's parliamentary performance proved more successful in 1989, 1993 and 1997. In the 1989 congressional elections, the right-wing pact *Democracia y Progreso* obtained 34.2 per cent of the vote in the lower house elections, while the *Concertación* won 51.5 per cent of the vote. RN emerged as the larger of the two principal right-wing parties with 17.4 per cent of the vote to UDI's 9.3 per cent. In terms of seat distribution, the Christian Democrats emerged by far as the largest party in the Chamber of Deputies with 38 representatives. RN became the second largest with 29, followed by the centre-left *Partido por la Democracia* (PPD) on 17, UDI with 11 and the Socialists with four. In the Senate, the Christian Democrats obtained 13 seats, RN six, the PPD four, and UDI two.

The 1993 congressional results were very similar to those in the previous election. Support for the *Unión por el Progreso de Chile* pact increased slightly to 33.6 per cent to the *Concertación's* 55.5 per cent (the separate radical left coalition won 6.4 per cent and the New Left 1.9 per cent). Within the pact itself (not including independents), RN's vote fell to 14.9 per cent, while UDI's increased to 11.0 per cent. There were only slight changes in the parliamentary representation with the Christian Democrats again emerging as the largest party in the Chamber of Deputies with 37 seats. RN maintained its position as the second largest political force with 29 seats, with UDI, the PPD and Socialists with 15 seats each. In the Senate, where only nine of the seats were being contested, the Christian Democrats ended up with 13 seats, RN with 11, the Socialists with five, UDI with three and the PPD with two.[15]

In the 1997 mid-term congressional elections, the vote of the right-wing *Unión por Chile* coalition fell to 29.9 per cent, with RN emerging as the largest of the two main coalition parties with 13.8 per cent and UDI with 11.9 per cent. RN's number of seats fell from 29 to 23, while UDI's increased from 15 to 17, maintaining its position as the third largest party in the lower house. The *Concertación's* share of the vote fell to 41.6 per cent (the Communist-led coalition's share increased to 6.2 per cent). Although the Christian Democrats vote fell to 18.9 per cent, they increased their number of seats to 38, compared to 16 for the PPD and 11 for the Socialists. Although the parties' relative strength cannot be gauged from an examination of the senatorial election, since only half the elected seats in the Senate were up for re-election, it is worth noting that RN won in only two of the eight seats it contested, while UDI won seven of its nine seats (although this figure includes four independent candidates sponsored by the party). If the independents are included, and by and large they are likely to support the party's line, UDI has emerged as the larger of the two parties in the upper chamber, with 11 senators (three in 1993) to RN's seven (11 in 1993).[16] This result may have important consequences for Chile's democratic transition process, since this strengthened hard right bloc, in conjunction with the designated senators (most of whom are hardline *pinochetistas)* and

General Pinochet (who became a senator for life in March 1998) will have even greater control over the upper chamber, making the 1980 constitution all the more difficult to reform.

The Results: an Examination

A superficial examination of the post-1989 results reveals that although a breakdown of the electoral figures points to the revitalization of the traditional *tres tercios* of Chilean politics, whereby left, right and centre poll approximately one-third of the popular vote, the electoral system has in practical terms created a bipolar political system. Placing voting habits and parties in terms of a left-right spectrum has always been very important in Chile, unlike in many other Latin American countries. Voters identified more with their political position on the spectrum rather than specific parties. The military regime, once it realized that it would be unable to exclude the political parties from the institutional framework, strove to end the concept of the *tres tercios*, which it blamed for the breakdown of democracy in 1973, by attempting to create a bipolar political system. The existence of two large electoral and political blocs, the *Concertación* and the right, both in terms of presidential and to a lesser extent in congressional elections, bears this out. This has severely restricted the electorate's choice. Chilean politics has now become a simple confrontation between two coalitions and two principal candidates. This is very different from the traditional multiparty system in existence prior to 1973.

At the most fundamental level, the right's presidential performance in both 1989 and 1993 was down on the results achieved in the pre-1973 period, although this is partly distorted by the existence of other competing independent right-wing candidates. However, the combined total of all right-wing presidential candidates, especially in 1989, compares favourably with the historical trend. Moreover, its level of support at the parliamentary level in the 1989, 1993 and 1997 has surpassed its 1937–73 historical average of 30 per cent. However, a more exhaustive analysis of the right's electoral results is more complicated given the existence of a series of distortions: the electoral system, coalition-building and the role of independents.

The Electoral System
Although the electoral system adopted for the presidential elections is straightforward in that a winning candidate has to obtain 50 per

cent plus one of the votes to be elected in the first round, the binominal system adopted by the military regime for the congressional elections is considerably more complicated. Each constituency, whether for the Senate, consisting of 38 elected members, or the 120-seat Chamber of Deputies, returns two members, although the electorate has only one vote. Parties are allowed to form coalitions to present lists of two candidates per constituency. If a coalition's list wins more than twice the votes of the next most voted list, it takes both seats. If it obtains less, then it returns only one member and the next most voted list takes the other. Therefore, if there are only two lists competing in a given constituency a list with a 66 per cent majority would return two members. In this way, a list would have to obtain only one-third of votes to control one-half of parliament. The system was thus designed to ensure that the right, a minority political force, would secure a level of representation in excess of its share of the vote. An examination of one of the two hotly contested 1989 senatorial elections for Santiago provides a fitting example of the effectiveness of this strategy. The race included four political heavyweights: the *Concertación* candidates, the Christian Democrat Andrés Zaldivar who obtained 29.8 per cent of the vote and Ricardo Lagos of the PPD who won 29.2 per cent, against UDI's Jaime Guzmán with 16.4 per cent and RN's Miguel Otero with 14.6 per cent. The *Concertación* candidates, with a total vote of 58.9 per cent, were unable to reach the required 66 per cent necessary for electing two candidates. Therefore, with only 30.9 per cent of the vote, the right was able to obtain the second representative, the list's most voted candidate, Jaime Guzmán, although Lagos with 399,000 votes polled more votes than Guzman (223,302).

The electoral system had a negative impact on the centre-left coalition. In eight senatorial contests in 1989 where the total vote for the *Concertación* was below 66 per cent, the second Senate seat went to the right-wing coalition, of which RN was the senior partner, and thus the principal beneficiary. Moreover, from a total of 63 deputies elected by the *Concertación* list, the centre-left coalition elected both deputies in only 12 out of the 60 constituencies. The right-wing coalition elected 46 deputies but was unable to secure two representatives in any seat. In 12 contests, one of the two lower house seats went to the right, although the *Concertación* or independent candidates obtained more votes than the successful right-wing candidate. In 1993, there were 14 lower house seats in which the second representative elected was not the second most voted candidate; of these, nine went to the right and only five to the *Concertación*. This anomaly occurred in only one instance in the nine senatorial seats contested and the beneficiary in this case was again the right.[17] In the 1997 election lower house elections the *Concertación* lost seven seats for identical reasons, while the right lost only four. In the Senate, the governing coalition lost three seats to right-wing candidates with fewer votes, while the right lost none.

Coalition-building

Although in terms of number of votes, RN and UDI are not that different, the former, as the senior partner in the coalition, obtained more than double the number of deputies in the 1989 elections. UDI was at a disadvantage in the electoral pact: it presented only 30 candidates in the 60 districts, while RN presented 66 (including party-sponsored independents, which enabled RN to bypass the maximum two candidates per district). As such, there were only a few areas in which an UDI candidate competed with a representative from RN. Comparing their electoral performance *vis-à-vis* each other is therefore difficult. In most of the cases in which both competed, the results were virtually equal, RN elected 11 deputies and UDI nine. In the 1993 lower house elections, RN and UDI competed in 16 districts, of which RN came ahead in ten and UDI in six. The fact that UDI increased its number of deputies, at RN's expense, in the 1993 lower house elections can be explained by the nature of the 1993 electoral pact, which this time worked to RN's disadvantage: while in 1989 it presented candidates in all 60 districts, in 1989 it had representation in only 43. The electoral map was further complicated by the inclusion of the UCC in the right-wing coalition. It obtained a number of *cupos* which otherwise would have gone to the traditional parties of the right. The UCC, a personalist vehicle for the populist entrepreneur Francisco Javier Errázuriz, is not a right-wing party in the strictest sense of the word. In fact, it is not strictly speaking a traditional political party *per se*, lacking an organizational structure and a coherent set of policies. Although it attracted right-wing votes on the whole, its appeal in many cases crossed the political spectrum. Errázuriz would have allied himself with the *Concertación* had he believed it would provide him with a greater number of electoral spoils. However, in the 1997 elections, RN and UDI presented candidates in most of the 60 constituencies, while the UCCP (the former UCC) was excluded from the coalition. This will make it somewhat easier to examine the parties' respective strengths, unlike in previous elections.

The Role of Independents

The seemingly high percentage figures obtained by the party right in certain areas is explained by the high number of independents who formed part of the right-wing pact. In the 1989 senatorial elections, eight of the 16 candidates elected on a right-wing ticket were independents, while in the lower house elections, a further eight of the 48 right-wing deputies elected were also from outside the parties. In the 1993 lower house elections, right-wing independents stood in 23 of the 60 districts, and in 1997 in ten, most of them representing the UDI sub-pact. Moreover, given the lack of a highly organized national structure and a lack of resources, the parties on the right rely on independents, many of whom finance their own campaigns, to fill the organizational gap. Many of these independents are local or regional figures whose personal prestige, rather than ideological identification, was the main reason for their electoral success.

Regardless of the difficulties inherent in an analysis of the right's electoral performance, several trends are evident from an examination of the 1997 results which help to differentiate between RN and UDI's electoral constituencies. RN has a greater level of representation in the regions, which, owing to the large size of the country, reflects its greater organizational capacity. This is particularly the case in the north of the country, where in 1997 it won most votes of any right-wing party in Vallenar (with 37.8 per cent of the vote, in contrast to UDI's 1.3 per cent), Arica (21.2 per cent to 3.1 per cent), Iquique (27.2 per cent to 2.8 per cent) and in Copiapó (21.5 per cent to 7.4 per cent). Although in the 18 seats at stake in the four most northern provinces, RN and UDI won a similar number (three to two respectively), with the centre-left coalition taking 12 (reflecting its dominant position in what is a strong mining area) and an independent the remaining one, in most of the constituencies in which RN emerged as the larger of the two it did so by a very high margin. In contrast, in those few areas where UDI outvoted RN, it did so only narrowly. Moreover, the four most northern regions account for a greater share of RN's total national vote than UDI's (11.7 per cent to 9.1 per cent). RN's performance in the two most southern regions of the country was also stronger than UDI's, winning five seats to the latter's two (including an independent standing on the party ticket). RN's vote held up especially well in the agricultural areas of the south, where it emerged as the most voted party as a whole in Constitución (31.7 per cent), Chillán (45.9 per cent), Villarrica (45.3 per cent), Puerto Montt (30.9 per cent) and La Unión (28.9 per cent).

It also won seats in Linares, Cauquenes, Victoria and Temuco. In fact, the country's three most southern regions accounted for 9.1 per cent of the party's total national vote, higher than that for the *Concertación* (8.96 per cent) and UDI (3.9 per cent), thus reinforcing RN's position as heir to the traditional, rural-based, clientelistic and squire-dominated pre-1973 PN. RN, like UDI, did well in the central core regions, where the largest and wealthiest urban conurbations are situated, including Santiago, with 40 per cent of the total voting population. RN generally performed well in lower-middle class, lower-middle income and middle-class, middle-income urban areas, polling the highest votes overall in areas such Santiago's Providencia/Nuñoa (41.6 per cent), La Reina (50.7 per cent), La Florida (30.8 per cent) and central Santiago (31.4). This vote corresponds to that of the traditional pre-1973 right-wing electorate which views UDI's hardline support for neo-liberalism and support for authoritarian forms of political control with hostility and fear.

UDI's strength, on the other hand, lies in the industrialized central core region and the major provincial cities, such as Antofagasta (21.1 per cent), Viña del Mar (28.2 per cent), Valparaíso (31.6 per cent) and Concepción (25.5 per cent). It also performed spectacularly well in both the wealthiest and poorest urban districts, especially in the capital. It polled more than any other party in Santiago's wealthiest suburb, Las Condes (34.1 per cent), and in very poor urban areas, with high concentrations of *poblaciones*, where it relegated RN's vote to single percentage figures, such as in the Santiago district of San Bernardo (40.3 per cent to RN's 5.1 per cent). UDI also elected deputies to the Greater Santiago working-class districts of Pudahuel (30.2 per cent), Recoleta (29.6 per cent), Macul (28.9 per cent), La Cisterna (37.2 per cent) and San Miguel (22.9 per cent). Although the Santiago metropolitan area is electorally critical for all political sectors (since it includes more than one-third of the total population), it accounted for a far greater proportion of UDI's national vote (53.9 per cent) than for either RN (42.7 per cent) or the *Concertación* (29.3 per cent).

UDI performed especially well in the upper class suburbs of Santiago because its political rhetoric and style, its total commitment to the free market model and the reputation of its candidates as faithful and capable civil servants under the Pinochet administration echoed well with the most privileged sectors of Chilean society. Moreover, although the *poblaciones* continue to represent fertile ground for the Christian Democrats and the left, UDI's electoral penetration in these areas has been remarkable. While its general level of support continues to be lower than that achieved by its ideological opponents, the party has succeeded in obtaining parliamentary representation in areas previously regarded as anathema to the right. This demonstrates the existence of a 'popular right', unafraid and knowledgeable about utilizing political techniques more commonly associated with the radical left, and particularly with the Communists. It reflects the ideologically inspired work carried out by *gremialista* administrators in these working-class areas during the military regime and marks the development of clientelistic networks and relationships which have delivered to UDI a significant portion of the urban working-class.[18]

It would have proved very easy to hypothesize that because of the post-1989 development of a bipolar system consisting of generally moderate positions, such a system could maintain certain social affinities, in the sense of providing more popular support to centre-left positions and more middle and upper-class support for the right. Although this hypothesis holds at one level, it disguises the fact that these electoral coalitions are not monolithic groupings. In fact, the differences within coalitions, particularly on the right, are more often than not greater than those between competing coalitions. This reality is reflected in RN and UDI's electoral constituencies. Although the bulk of right-wing support has come from urban areas with relatively high standards of living, and that the right is rooted in the financial, industrial and agricultural elites of the country (the core constituency: those who benefited most from the Pinochet regime), the sector has actively sought, and to some extent succeeded, in attracting sectors not normally associated with the right (non-core constituencies). The problematic for RN and UDI, however, is that it has had to hand-tailor its political rhetoric and style to suit its respective and more often than not mutually exclusive, non-core constituencies. This has invariably led to the development of two quite distinctive right-wing parties which are both responsive to very different audiences. This may inevitably make coexistence very difficult, but because of the political and electoral legacy of the military regime, of which they were a part to varying degrees, this accommodation, if not often peaceful, may prove the only viable and realistic electoral option for the right. Despite these problems, the right's electoral performance has been both relatively strong and stable, especially given the difficulties inherent in competing with such a solid political grouping as the centre-left *Concertación*. Moreover, the fact that the sector is divided into two very different parties may have even helped boost its electoral representation. Each represents very distinct social and political sectors and ideological positions which may have been lost to other political groupings if the party right were to be represented by a single monolithic movement.

Why was RN and even UDI's performance so impressive considering the circumstances? Part of this, of course, can be explained by the Pinochet-inspired electoral system which exaggerated the right's electoral support while underestimating that of the centre-left coalition. With a fairer system it seems unlikely that the right would have obtained as many seats in the various elections. The right's clientelistic approach is also an important factor. While a significant proportion of the Chilean population has traditionally supported right-wing candidates this cannot account for the scale of their 1989, 1993 and 1997 vote. It is, therefore, reasonable to suppose that the regime's process of decentralization, at the municipal level, of public services such as education, health, housing and subsidies for the poorest, combined with a structure of limited participation, would have provided the right with a powerful clientelistic network among the country's popular and lower-middle classes. It is no coincidence that many of the regime's young former mayors obtained good electoral results in popular urban areas. Finally, in the 1989 election at least, many still feared the consequences of an opposition government. The government's electoral campaign attempted to maximize these fears and in some respects it seems to have been successful. Pinochet's strategy was made all the easier by the economic boom that Chile experienced after 1985, which appeared all the more spectacular when set against the 1981–3 recession. The subsequent economic growth after 1990 does not seem to have had much effect on the electoral core of the right, at least at the congressional and municipal level. This suggests that there is in Chile a solid bloc of the electorate loyal to the right: a political 'sub-culture' of the right, historically rooted, and not susceptible to the attractions of the other political parties.

Conclusion

The military coup in September 1973 offered an ailing and uncertain right an opportunity which had never before presented itself and was unlikely to do so again. After decades of relative electoral failure, ideological stagnation and a lack of definition, and political defensiveness, the Chilean right recognized the possibilities of influencing, without dominating, the country's new political masters, the military. Lacking both a long-term project and the experience to carry one out, the armed forces were seen as the *inocentes vis-à-vis* the *grandiosos* of the traditional right-wing parties. Having failed under democracy, the right now hoped to succeed under an authoritarian system of government. This was the challenge which it accepted all too readily. What emerged after 1973, however, was a 'new right'. The old, traditional conservatives and liberals, under the guise of the now disbanded *Partido Nacional*, were unable, or unwilling, or simply too passive, to adapt to the new reality facing the country. As a consequence, they were quickly and ruthlessly overshadowed and marginalized by groups which themselves had, prior to the insurrection, been on the sidelines of Chilean political and cultural life.

This study has revealed the existence of two groups which performed this function and which were to become the principal political and ideological actors throughout the military regime (1973–90): the Chicago-trained economists and the *gremialistas*. While both shared common roots at the Catholic University, a tendency towards authoritarianism and a distaste for Marxism and the state, their ideological heritage could not have been more dissimilar. Yet they formed an impenetrable dominant axis within the regime, in which their ideas and abstract notions were readily put into practice. Together with General Pinochet they constructed, developed and nurtured a unique and solid triangular relationship in which each used or supported each other to maximize their influence. The technocrats used the military as a source of power and control without which the political and economic model could not have succeeded. They manipulated and finally 'converted' the *gremialistas* into becoming the 'political wing' of the regime, providing it with the necessary expertise and connections, together with a possible political power base from which to grow and expand. The *gremialistas* utilized the Chicago Boys as an ideological lifeline, to compensate for serious deficiencies in their growingly archaic philosophy, especially within the economic sphere. They seemed ready and willing to embrace the notions of neo-liberalism which promised them authoritarian forms of control, anti-statism and the exclusion of Marxists, all indispensable prerequisites for the *gremialistas*. Watering down and restructuring the foundations of their ideology became acceptable in return for political power and influence. Pinochet, in a classic case of divide-and-rule, used everybody. While initially lacking a political and economic project, he was readily convinced of the merits of the Chicago Boy/*gremialista* model. Throughout the dictatorship the general played the role of 'puppet-master', giving a little here and a little there, seeming to favour one side and then another. His role in determining the course of Chile's political, economic and social development must not be underestimated. The hegemonic position of the Chicago Boys–*gremialista* alliance was only possible through Pinochet's unequivocal support.

These two dominant ideologies themselves experienced a process of development and renewal during the regime's formative years. As the old traditional and nationalist right continued on its route to nowhere, the Chicago Boys and *gremialistas* underwent a process of ideological expansion and modernization. As the economic successes of the model became increasingly apparent, saturating them with greater levels of confidence, this initial group of technocrats became a political and ideological *tour de force* more willing to espouse the all-embracing philosophy of Hayek rather than the relatively limited ideas of Friedman. The once corporatist and 'medievalesque' *gremialistas* rapidly recognized the advantages such a model could provide, despite the apparent philosophical contradictions. As both groups gradually began to adopt the notions of neo-liberalism as social theory, the initial distinctions between them became increasingly blurred. By 1981, this merging process seemed so complete that it became more difficult to distinguish between them. Despite this, a clear division of labour had developed in relation to government activity. The Chicago Boys, being economists, had concentrated within this sphere, clustering around the state planning office ODEPLAN and the finance and economy ministries while also shouldering responsibility for debt negotiations and foreign loan agreements. In this respect their involvement with the modernizations becomes all the more apparent. The *gremialistas*, on the other hand, were from a mostly legal tradition, and had thus centred on the justice and interior ministries and in the *alcaldías*. They were in a unique position to influence the lengthy institutional process and the actual drafting of the 1980 constitution.

The implementation of the modernizations and the constitutional plebiscite marked the high point for the right-wing alliance and for the regime itself. After 1981, as the economy began to collapse, the model was placed under serious scrutiny for the first time since its inception. The 'myth' of *criollo* neo-liberalism began to shatter and never really recovered. The regime, despite its authoritarian nature, still sought to generate popularity to enable it to legitimize itself both internally and in the eyes of the international community. In this respect, the drafting of a constitution was intended to fulfil this purpose. The government was well aware that in such a legalistically minded country, as Chile had historically been, the notion of constitutionally defining the regime and future institutional processes would be positively received. Following the cessation of the boycott by the US trade union federation, the AFL-CIO, following implementation of the labour laws, the government also believed that the international community could be placated through the introduction of more defined political norms. Government propaganda also became an important tool of legitimacy. Television, radio, magazines and newspapers, especially *El Mercurio*, were all used to great effect. During the Pinochet years *El Mercurio* became the principal instrument of information and ideological direction of the different factions which constituted the ruling social and political bloc. While television and radio, which reached over 80 per cent of the population, functioned as a means of communication for the popular sectors, *El Mercurio* performed the function of orienting and ideologizing the classes which adhered to it. While television tended to act as an instrument of cultural indoctrination over the masses, the written character of this long-established daily validated it as an 'oracle', all-knowing and all-powerful, like the Bible.

The support of both the economic groups and the entrepreneurial sector was critical for the survival of the regime, and of its civilian coalition, primarily the Chicago Boys and *gremialistas*. These conglomerates had provided the financial resources necessary for the functioning of the ideological dissemination strategies and the overseas training of the Chicago Boys. The economic groups had been the first national organizations to show an active interest in the ideas of the market, and were responsible for the many trips to Chile incurred by internationally renown neo-liberals such as Friedman, Hayek Nozick and Buchanan. They provided employment possibilities for

the many government technocrats either prior to official appoint-
ments or soon after. This gave them an invaluable connection with the
sources of political and economic power. The rewards for such
unbending loyalty to the model and the military regime were vast.
Without a doubt, the very creators of the economic system, the
economic groups and their faithful side-kicks, the Chicago Boy minis-
ters/managing directors were its greatest beneficiaries. The position
with the entrepreneurial sector is somewhat more complicated. After
1973, the *gremios* had attempted to maintain the structures of their
organizations, but had failed. Despite this, they continued to assume
that their needs would be satisfied and that the government would
continue with a *gradualista* approach to the economy. With the 1975
economic 'shock' this optimistic evaluation was shattered. Yet dissent
was still contained with promises of 'future' benefit, or kept in check
by memories of the Allende government. With the intensification of
the model after 1977 a dualization of the economic structure developed, between a successful and modernizing sector and one which
became increasingly depressed. Those sectors historically orientated
towards the internal market were badly hit, in the face of an unre-
stricted market. Despite increasing protests over the management of
the economy the depressed *gremios* continued to support and identify
with the authoritarian political model. This led to a segmented and
defensive approach from a sector rapidly in decline, and its opposition could thus easily be ignored. Out of the ashes of the old, a new
breed of entrepreneur evolved. Linked to the financial markets,
exports, and high technology it matured into the natural base of
support for the neo-liberal orientated military regime. These entrepreneurs boomed during 1977–81 and provided the administration
with the *raison d'être* for their *triunfalismo*.

The regime's control at municipal level, through the *alcaldías*, was
a further attempt to generate popularity and thus legitimize itself.
The first stages of the military government were marked by a relatively high degree of defensiveness in which the armed forces,
working with civilian collaboration, had an exclusive role in the political decision-making process. This was a period when most mayors
had been elected prior to 1973 and which were now been ratified by
the military government. Many tended to be acting or retired military
personnel. After Chacarillas, the *fundacional* dimension of the regime
brought to the fore the problem of legitimacy, of a need to create a
new democracy, a new political system which would replace the old.
The new *alcáldes* conformed to the necessities of this second phase.

Despite having lost the 1988 plebiscite these attempts to generate popularity had been relatively successful. Securing over 43 per cent of the vote is, after 15 years in power, and despite the inevitable obstacles to a true and fair election, a formidable achievement for a regime which had caused so much bitterness and division. The Chicago Boys/*gremialista* neo-liberal attempts at socialization and ideological persuasion had been relatively successful in winning over a highly significant minority of the population. The level of support received by Pinochet in 1988 trounced the highest votes ever achieved by the right since the 1950s and was the best result since the 1930s.

One aspect we cannot ignore is the international dimension. Throughout the predominance of the Chilean new right, the links with the outside world were intrinsic and far-reaching. Its success mirrored that of its Southern Cone, European and US counterparts. Ronald Reagan in Washington, Margaret Thatcher in London, Helmut Kohl in Bonn were all strongly influenced by neo-liberalism throughout the late 1970s and early 1980s. The high point of the Chilean dominant 'triumvirate' echoed the rise of similar phenomena in the whole of the western world. It was a period when even social democratic governments, such as Felipe Gonzáles in Madrid, began to adopt the mechanisms of the free market. Just as the model became apparently dominant in Chile, so it was in the developed world. Since the immediate postwar period, certain sectors within the United States had attempted to disseminate into Latin America the 'logic' of the free market. These private actors, involved in autonomous and technical concerns, maintained the pressure to create a permanent ideology destined to reorder the integration of the Latin American economies to the international market. It was in the 1960s when the initial group of Chicago Boys first became the beneficiaries of this new policy. This was a period when both left and right possessed a desire to wipe out anything that had come before. It is within this context that the Chilean new right and the new right as a whole adopted the monetarist model. It was directly linked to the antagonism felt by those sectors towards the Chilean model of *estatización social* which mirrored the increasing welfarism of the European postwar governments. What evolved in the developed world also evolved in Chile, in similar ways and in corresponding periods. The link between the formation of the Chilean new right, as expressed by the *criollo* neo-liberals, and the new right as an international phenomenon was intrinsic. But nowhere was the new economic and political model applied so vigorously as in Chile. In many respects it remains a dependent country and not least economically. If the ideas of the Chilean right were not new, the rigour of their application was, and in this sense, the Chilean experiment became internationally as well as nationally significant.

However, the conjuncture of 1981–3 changed the very nature of Chilean politics: recession, government intransigence on the political front, the development of an effective opposition, and the growth of social mobilization led to a crisis within the Pinochet regime. In the face of growing popular unrest, supporters of the military recognized that the days of unbridled political power were possibly at an end and thus attempted to form a united right-wing movement to confront this new and uncertain reality. But fragmentation, which had usually been a feature of the left, plagued this nascent process. Nevertheless, by 1987 two main parties had developed. First, the *Unión Demócrata Independiente* (UDI), heirs and loyal supporters of the Pinochet regime, made up of the ideologically fused *gremialistas* and Chicago-trained economists; in essence, the bureaucratic technocracy of the military government. The party emerged as politically and socially conservative, but economically very liberal, representing an urban, predominantly metropolitan right, economically modern, but at the same time paternalistic and authoritarian with a strong presence in the marginalized underclass of Chile's principal cities. Second, *Renovación Nacional* (RN), which consisted of traditional right-wing personalities, most of whom had played no part in the military regime. The party, strong with the urban middle-class and the rural sector, represents the legacy of the traditional pre-1973 conservative/liberal right. With RN one can perceive a certain economic ambivalence, especially among its parliamentarians. In the political sphere, the party has a more democratic and liberal emphasis. It has attempted to distance itself from the Pinochet regime and thus move towards the political centre in an effort to widen its appeal beyond the confines of the traditional right-wing electorate. By the time of the 1988 plebiscite what had occurred within the right, therefore, was its division into those who wished to continue with the essentials of the political and socio-economic model of the last 15 years, represented by UDI, and those who saw the emergence of a democratic regime as inevitable and recognized the need to occupy the traditional space of the political right, a view symbolized by RN.

Although the right has made a relatively successful adaptation to democratic politics and behaviour, this has been overshadowed by the success of the parties belonging to the governing centre-left coalition which have reinserted themselves into the democratic process in a spectacular way, especially given their absence from democratic politics for over 17 years. This is principally because, although the left in particular had also suffered decades of damaging internecine warfare which led to its fragmentation, its strong and well-established party political culture has enabled it to adapt more successfully to the needs of unity, especially important given the limitations of the current democratic system. Moreover, the Aylwin and Frei administrations have been very successful in terms of economic policy. GDP growth had been maintained at a sustainable 6 per cent throughout most of the 1990s, while inflation remains in single figures. Higher social spending, which has reduced overall poverty levels, although these remain relatively high, has been achieved without undermining investor confidence in the economy. The right, therefore, has found it difficult to wave the banner of the Pinochet economic model, as its principal orientations have been maintained virtually intact. This is not to say that the right has been an electoral failure. It clearly has not and has, in general, succeeded in maintaining its traditional share of the vote in the 1989, 1993 and 1997 congressional elections. However, many factors continue to work against the sector. Until these issues are addressed the right may be unable to expand its current levels of support and the democratizing project of some of its representatives, primarily that espoused by the modernizing sector of RN, may as a result suffer some serious reverses. Their project is conditional on reaping good results, especially in electoral terms. If these are not forthcoming, authoritarian and conservative elements within the right, as in the mid-1960s, may seek to find alternative organizational and strategic models in an attempt to reassert their power.

Despite its successes, the right still lacks a well-established and fully democratic party political culture. This has led it to adopt various positions which have contributed to its ineffectiveness as a political and electoral force. At the most fundamental level, the sector has still not shed its traditional strategy of *mal menor*. This not only resulted in its support for the Christian Democrat presidential candidacy of Eduardo Frei in 1964, rather than its own option, but in its unconditional support for Pinochet, despite the right's historic dislike of the armed forces, which it described as *capataces de fundo*. This fear of being *desplazada* by competing electoral forces may continue to force it to rely on seemingly attractive, quick-fix, independent personalities to rescue it from possible electoral oblivion. The *Piñeragate* scandal was a symbolic example of the right's self-destructive nature brought on by this high degree of personalism. Clearly, the so-called 'death of ideologies' did not free the sector from intolerant forms of behaviour but replaced the *ceguera* of the ideologies with the *desolada obstinación de los ególatras*. This lack of a party political tradition has prevented the right from uncovering a natural party leader capable of representing the sector at a national level and to unite it around a single programmatic banner. In the last few decades, the right has thus failed to find an institutional leader from party ranks who has been successful in developing a project from within and been able to articulate it with sufficient conviction and vigour. Moreover, only two personalities have succeeded in disciplining the right: Jorge Alessandri and Pinochet himself. Both are authoritarian leaders, whose political origins lie outside the formal party structures, who are respected and admired, but loved by only a few, principally UDI. Since the return to democracy in 1990, the right, as in the past, has sought out 'providential' leaders who can wave a magic wand but who invariably fail to deliver. The right has thus for too long relied on figures whose importance lie outside the political parties, the *poderes fácticos*, referred to by Allamand, who have played a dominant role in virtually every aspect of right-wing political and electoral activity. The entrepreneurial sector, the large economic and financial conglomerates and the right-wing media have been unwilling to respect the political autonomy of the parties to which they adhere. This intervention, which has plagued the right since its inception, has had serious repercussions in terms of stalling the right-wing modernizers' attempts to reinsert the parties into democracy's central arena.

The absence of a well-defined and stable democratic political culture has had serious organizational and strategic repercussions for the party right, not only in terms of its parliamentary oppositional activities but within the parties themselves and in relations with each other. RN and UDI have not overcome their long-standing differences, which in many respects, have proven significantly more fundamental than those which affected the 'unrenovated' left until the mid-1980s. The post-Cold War socialist parties at least share a common political agenda. They are also not divided in terms of the past (the legacy of the military regime). The parties on the right are ideologically similar. However, their political and strategic differences are enormous. They do not possess a common history, nor do they share a common perception about the fundamental nature of democratic institutions, most notably what role the parties should play in the new democratic order. Moreover, their animosity is rooted at the most personal level: they simply do not like each other. They are also divided by their vision of the past, most importantly by disagreements over the level of loyalty which both should express towards the political and economic legacy of the military regime. This has severely weakened its capacity to become an effective oppositional force. The right has thus been unable to create a consistent oppositional model. In Congress, it has failed to develop an efficient and solid scheme while the Aylwin and Frei governments have been successful in weakening the parliamentary right through a strategy of 'divide and rule'. The performance of its parliamentarians, especially those from RN, has been divisive and ineffective. RN senators in particular, most of whom are conservatives of the old type, have persistently used their positions of influence to undermine the modernizing project espoused by Allamand and his successor Alberto Espina. In general, right-wing legislators, in both parties, have sought to undermine each other rather than their logical adversaries. RN and UDI parliamentarians are all too ready to hammer out deals with the centre-left coalition in an attempt to undermine their sectoral opponents. This has not only facilitated the government's divide and rule strategy but has highlighted the immature nature of right-wing parliamentary politics. The right has also failed to establish a cultural dialogue since the collapse of the Berlin Wall. The right has always acted reactively when threatened. This is how its various tendencies kept together and remained dynamic. With the collapse of the East European communist model, the right has no overriding ideological preoccupation, and its components are left squabbling with each other over the minutiae of party politics. This has resulted in a failure in its strategy. Both RN and UDI have adopted, as main themes, support for the economic model, personal liberty, security and efficiency. However, the governing *Concertación* has also taken up these issues and made them their own. The right does not have an alternative project and is relying on being portrayed as the most efficient political sector to carry out these generally accepted ideals.

Pinochet's legacy has, therefore, been contradictory for the liberal-conservative bloc. On the one hand, the military regime initiated a radical political and socio-economic modernizing project, while on the other, it opted to lead by itself in the political arena, thus making the parties redundant. Moreover, Pinochet abandoned power at the precise moment when Chilean and world socialism ceased to be the dangerous bogeyman of the past. However, he left the civilian supporters of the regime without an all-encompassing project and a coherent set of ideals which could propel it towards the future. This has left the right with a sterilizing contradiction which it has been unable to resolve. This is why two competing models now coexist uneasily within the right: a conservative, nationalist, traditional and moralist right and one which perceives itself as liberal, democratic and modern. The tensions between RN and UDI, both internally and externally, are the manifestation of this legacy. Moreover, neither project is sufficiently dominant to prevail over the other. This dichotomy, exacerbated by the present need to present large electoral pacts, will continue to act as a double-edged sword for the sector. On the one hand, its electoral representation may well be boosted by the existence of two competing right-wing parties, each able to attract support which the other would find difficult to capture, but on the other, the ensuing debilitating struggles which both have experienced will weaken its prospects of expanding into previously marginal electoral constituencies. Most on the right privately conceded that the sector would not win either in 1989 or in 1993. Its underlying strategy has, therefore, been to close the possibility of any kind of substantial constitutional reform. The present institutional formula has prevented the full adoption of a democratic system. It includes a series of power instruments which the right needs to maintain: the Supreme Court, the greater autonomy of the armed forces, and several institutions which do not emanate from popular sovereignty which can veto the actions of the legislature and the executive – the designated senators, the *Tribunal Constitucional* and the *Consejo de Seguridad Nacional*. These institutions have given the opposition a level of power far superior to that delegated to it by the electorate. For the right it is fundamental to maintain these institutional controls. But it has to defend them without weakening its already fragile democratic credentials. This has been the implicit function of the non-party right. RN and UDI have ensured that the most hardline elements of their political and electoral strategy come from the sectors of civil society which the right controls so as to leave its purely political agents to stress their democratic credentials. This process of mutual collaboration has compensated for the right's continued inability to function effectively within the party political system and is a further example of the weakness of the right's party structures. Until this is corrected both UDI and RN will continue to be dominated and undermined by forces outside the parties' structures. This can do nothing to help either the right expand its current level of electoral support or Chile's process of democratic consolidation. Moreover, the serious setback suffered by the moderate wing of RN following its poor performance in the 1997 elections, and the important gains made by UDI, will make it more difficult to consolidate a fully democratic right-wing sector in Chile. Nevertheless, elements within the right have made a concerted effort fully to reinsert the sector into the country's democratic processes. Even semi-authoritarian parties, such as UDI, have until now chosen to function within the fundamental confines of the democratic game. This is a relatively pragmatic new right which bears little resemblance to the insurrectionist right which existed prior to 1973. It recognizes that authoritarian systems of government are no longer a viable option and that its interests will best be served under a democratic system, although residual sectors may still be inclined to prefer authoritarian solutions.

Postscript

General Pinochet was arrested in London on 16 October 1998 on a warrant issued on behalf of Spanish judge, Baltasar Garzón. The general is wanted in Spain over his alleged involvement in the murder, torture and kidnapping of Chilean and foreign citizens during his period in office. Regardless of whether Pinochet is extradited to Spain or is allowed to return to Chile, his arrest has proved to be a defining moment for Chile's main right-wing parties, *Renovación Nacional* (RN) and *Unión Demócrata Independiente* (UDI). Although RN and UDI have in the past been bitterly divided over the Pinochet legacy – with the modernizing wing of RN seeking to distance the party from the general in order to attract the centre ground, while UDI has sought to maintain its close links to the former military ruler – his arrest has, paradoxically, drawn the two parties closer together in defence of the general. However, it remains to be seen how long this cooperation will last, especially in the run-up to the December 1999 general election.

RN has once again, therefore, been forced to confront its central historical dilemma – whether it should continue efforts to move to the centre, with the accompanying risk of losing its *pinochetista* base, or reaffirm its identify as a right-wing party, which would help ease the conflict in the party between moderates and hardliners. For the time being at least, the party has chosen this second option. Its defence of the general during his detention in England has dramatically reversed its long-term strategy of seeking to distance itself from the figure of Pinochet. The party modernizers are clearly in retreat, with efforts to democratize the right severely weakened. Even high-ranking modernizers, such as party leader Alberto Espina, have been placed on the defensive. Espina has, since Pinochet's arrest, mounted a vociferous campaign in favour of the general.

RN's rightward shift and its closer identification with UDI on this issue could also undermine government efforts to reform the authoritarian 1980 constitution. Although RN had over the last few years shifted considerably in favour of an accommodation with the centre-left *Concertación* government on a number of reform proposals, especially over abolishing the designated senators and reducing the autonomy of the armed forces, the Pinochet case will make a compromise solution to the issue of constitutional reform more difficult to achieve. Moreover, RN may pay a heavy electoral price for its decision to ally itself with the *pinochetistas* by alienating its more moderate supporters. In a development which further demonstrates the modernizers' increasingly weak position within the right, RN's presidential pre-candidate for the December 1999 elections, the moderate Sebastián Piñera, was forced to step down in January 1999 owing to his consistently low opinion poll ratings. Once again, RN has been left without a presidential candidate of its own, and may be forced, as in the 1989 and 1993 presidential elections, to accept a UDI-linked candidate. This will further strengthen the hands of conservatives within the party.

The Pinochet case has also affected the more hardline UDI. Efforts by its presidential pre-candidate for the December 1999 elections, Joaquín Lavín, the mayor of the wealthy Santiago suburb of Las Condes, to distance himself from the military regime, in order to widen his appeal, have been thwarted. However, rather than risk losing the moderate vote he is seeking to attract, Lavín has opted to remain largely silent on the issue, although this could lead to tensions within the party, which has maintained its vociferous and belligerent pro-Pinochet stance.

Ironically, both RN and UDI, albeit to varying degrees, had over the last few years sought to limit the impact of the country's military legacy on their political campaigning. However, Pinochet's arrest has brought the vexed issue of civil-military relations (and related issues such as human rights) back to the top of the political agenda, an area which is unlikely to win the right many new voters, although it might shore up the *pinochetista* vote. The biggest losers, however, are those within the right seeking to modernize and democratize the sector. The vitriolic language by RN and UDI politicians – who have blamed an 'international socialist conspiracy' for Pinochet's arrest – is reminiscent of the rhetoric employed by the sector in the months prior to the 1973 coup, although there is no suggestion that the right today is seeking to overthrew Chile's elected government, despite support for military action by more extremist right-wing elements.

Notes

INTRODUCTION

1. In this period the non-party right dominated the pro-regime civilian coalition. Aside from the Chicago Boys economists and *gremialistas*, both of which will be analysed in greater detail at a later stage, the right consisted of the domestic entrepreneurial sector and the powerful economic groups. Both the *gremialistas* and the Chicago Boys played an important role in the process which culminated in 1973 with the fall of the *Unidad Popular* coalition and in the development of the regime's political and economic ideas. It was the fusion of Chicago Boys and *gremialistas* with the business sector which gave the right a solid base in Pinochet's Chile.
2. This figure reflects the historical 'three thirds' of Chilean politics. Over the last few decades, and despite Pinochet's attempts to break up the traditional makeup of national political life, voters still tend to split their vote evenly between left, right and centre.
3. See Douglas A. Chalmers et al. (1992).
4. See Guillermo Camper (1984) for a detailed analysis of the entrepreneurial sector.
5. With the possible exception of the agricultural sector which still clamours for state subsidies, especially in the runup to Chile's membership of the North American Free Trade Area (NAFTA), the trade bloc currently made up of the United States, Canada and Mexico.

1 THEORIES OF THE RIGHT

1. On a similar vein the *Petit Larousse* defines the right as the 'least advanced parties which sit on the extreme right of the chamber'. Conversely, the *Larousse* asserts that 'the most advanced parties sit on the extreme left'. See Hans Rogger and Eugene Weber (1965), p. 34.
2. Roger Eatwell and Nöel O'Sullivan (1992), p. 34.
3. Roger Eatwell (1992), p. 20.
4. Ibid.
5. Robert A. Nisbet (1967), p. 6.
6. Roger Eatwell (1989), pp. 47–8.
7. The arguments around 'positive' and 'negative' freedom, developed by Isaiah Berlin, have been of particular interest to western scholars and politicians on both left and right.
8. See Roger Eatwell (1989) for a more detailed analysis of this approach.
9. When I refer to *liberalism* I am specifically dealing with the European interpretation of the word and not its American counterpart. While American liberalism includes the jurisprudence of Ronald Dworkin

and the writings of economists such as J. K. Galbraith, European liberalism, or 'classical liberalism' as it is more commonly termed, is an eighteenth-century phenomenon and includes such thinkers as Jeremy Bentham and John Stuart Mill.

10. Norman Barry (1991), pp. 45–6.
11. Robert Nisbet (1967), p. 10.
12. Norman Barry (1991), pp. 45–6.
13. Dunleavy and O'Leary (1987), p. 73.
14. Stephen Davies (1991), p. 187.
15. By 'left-wing' governments I am referring to the post-1945 social democratic consensus.
16. Chantal Mouffe (1982), pp. 22–36.
17. Desmond King (1987), p. 7.
18. In Chile, the *compromise state* also implied the redefinition of the crucial dimension of the coalition-building process: the creation of a coalition consisting of urban wage earners, public sector enterprise and manufacturing business. The evolution of these new compromises was, in part, the result of different types of state–society relations which began to develop in the early twentieth century: economic and demographic expansion and a growth in social mobilization. New elites assumed power with reformist agendas. These new elites opposed the prevailing models of development and concentrated on resolving 'social questions'.
19. Hector Schamis (1992), pp. 63–88.
20. Nugent and King (1977), p. 7.
21. Civil Association is the notion of limited politics based on hostility to arbitrary power and the rule of law. Social politics is the concept of integration through the adoption of a shared purpose to which everyone within the state is subordinated.
22. Nöel O'Sullivan, pp. 167–9.
23. See chapter 2 for an analysis of the Chilean nationalist right.
24. Sofía Correa and Sol Serrano (1984), pp. 5–11.
25. See M. and R. Friedman (1980).
26. Nick Bosanquet (1986), pp. 17–22.
27. Alan Ryan, pp. 23–31.
28. See chapter 2 for an analysis of the *Gremialistas*.
29. The classic goal of the IMF-inspired structural adjustment programmes, imposed on most Latin American countries in recent years.
30. Desmond King (1987), pp. 7–27.

2 THE ORIGINS OF THE CHILEAN NEW RIGHT

1. See Brian Loveman (1979) for an analysis of the Chilean political system.
2. While the right's electoral support had always been sustained at a level above 40 per cent, from 1937 to 1949 it averaged 31.4 per cent. In 1952

it was reduced to 27.8 per cent and in 1953 to 21.1 per cent. See Cruz-Coke (1984).

3. The process of electoral enfranchisement was gradual. Women were first included for congressional and presidential elections in 1949. In 1962, electoral registration was made compulsory and in 1969 18 year olds and illiterates were enfranchised.

4. Pilar Vergara (1985), p. 24.

5. See Brian Loveman (1979).

6. Since the 1930s the concept of economic liberalism had penetrated most of Chile's mainstream political parties. Conservatism had many points of conflict with liberalism. They belonged to different cultural universes. This contradiction was based on their different conception of man and society. The *Partido Conservador* based itself on the social doctrine of the Catholic Church: the philosophy of the common good and social justice. This questioned the liberal notion of a basic relationship between economy and society which expressed itself in terms of the market. Yet the *Partido Conservador* adopted this typically bourgeois ideology whose central tenets were individualism and the primacy of the market. This radical change occurred as a consequence of Chile's insertion into the world economic system. Both conservative leaders and its supporters were members of an elite whose interests lay in maintaining both the primary exporting order and a *latifundist* agricultural system and a minimalist state in economic matters. Conservatives also feared the rising tide in Marxist and other revolutionary ideologies which threatened the natural order. It was simply a case of adhering to the tide of change or drowning under it.

7. See *Declaración de Principios del Partido Nacional* (1966).

8. The PDC policy of *camino propio* had made it hostile to any form of political alliance. The intention was to secure a hegemonic Christian Democrat government.

9. *Qué Pasa*, No. 555, 27 November 1983.

10. *Apsí*, No. 133, 27 December 1983.

11. This was a complicated political manoeuvre by which the right asked the Christian Democrats to drop its support for Allende in Congress thus allowing a 'stalking horse' candidate, Alessandri, to be elected president. He would then immediately resign forcing a new election. In this new election the right would pledge its support to the PDC candidate, Eduardo Frei. This plan collapsed as the PDC refused to cooperate.

12. The PDC had the contradictory role of simultaneously 'supporting' the government in order to satisfy the left wing of the party and of 'neutralizing' government policy through negotiation and pressure in order not to lose its status as opposition leaders.

13. See Moulian and Torres (1988) for a more detailed analysis of the 1970–3 Chilean right.

14. See Cristi and Ruiz (1992) for an analysis of Chilean conservatism.

15. See Brunner (1985), pp. 177–260.

16. Carlos Ruíz (1992), pp. 67–102.

17. Quoted in Carlos Ruíz (1992), pp. 67–192.

18. The defeat of European fascism after World War II and the consolidation of democracy as the only legitimate political model made the corporatist vision untenable.
19. As one supporter declared to *Apsi*, No. 248, 18 April 1988: '*el lo imaginó, él lo pensó, él lo creó, él era todo el movimiento*'.
20. Augusto Lecaros Zegers (1984), p. 24.
21. For an examination of the *gremialistas* at the Catholic University, see Catalan (1985).
22. Chilean society has had an enduring love affair with its intellectuals (and the universities they inhabit) that stretches far beyond their natural sphere of influence. Where else in Latin America would you find university-run national TV and radio stations, internationally renowned football teams and professional theatre companies? Intellectuals are regularly asked to comment on sport, the arts and other issues which seem far removed from their traditional ivory towers existence. They act, in essence, as an 'oracle' for Chilean society.
23. Declaration of Principles, *gremialista* movement.
24. See Jaime Guzmán (1992).
25. See Ibid.
26. Ibid., pp. 46–53.
27. Jaime Guzmán (June 1979), pp. 33–44.
28. *Qué Pasa*, No. 652, 6 October 1983.
29. Ibid.
30. Jaime Guzmán (1992), p. 63.
31. *Qué Pasa*, No. 652, 6 October 1983.
32. See below for an analysis of the role of *El Mercurio*.
33. For an analysis of Prat and *Estanquero*, see Cristi and Ruiz (1992).
34. Pilar Vergara (1985), pp. 60–1.
35. Juan Luis Ossa (1970), pp. 38–40.
36. Yet many PN documents still had a marked corporatist slant.
37. Pilar Vergara (1985), p. 61.
38. *Apsí*, 236, 1 August 1988.
39. The *gremialista* leader, Jaime Guzmán, was even rumoured to have been a student leader of *Patria y Libertad* despite his activism within the *gremialista* movement.
40. Julio Faúndez (1988), p. 181.
41. For an analysis of the development debate, see Patricio Silva (1991).
42. *Qué Pasa*, 8 October 1981.
43. Patricio Silva (1991).
44. See chapter 2 for an examination of the Chicago model.
45. J.G. Valdés (1989) examines the Chicago influence on Chilean right-wing economics.
46. They were disgusted that the university was going to introduce a course in the social principles of the Church which they felt was ideological indoctrination.
47. J.G. Valdés (1989), pp. 303–4.
48. This was the notorious *Ladrillo* document which became the *documento fundacional* of the post-1973 regime.
49. The navy link can be explained by the pivotal figure of Roberto Kelly. An

ex-navy officer and Chicago enthusiast, Kelly was also a high-ranking employee of the Edwards economic conglomerate. He thus had a close relationship with high-ranking navy officers. He was the key figure in the negotiations between the economists and the armed forces.
50. Pilar Vergara (1985), p. 57.
51. Guillermo Campero (1984), pp. 290–1.
52. *Cauce*, No. 29, 29 October 1984.
53. According to Fernando Dahse, an economic group is defined as a person or family which controls a significant number of companies of various kinds or sectors of the national economy, with the aim of diversifying their investments to reduce risks and maximize profits.
54. For an examination of the link between the Chicago Boys and the economic conglomerates, see Fontaine (1988).
55. J. G. Valdés (1989), p. 307.
56. See ibid. for an examination of the CESEC.
57. Ibid., pp. 307–10.
58. See Ruiz (1992) for an examination of Eyzaguirre.
59. Renato Cristi (1992), pp. 124–39.
60. Carlos Ruiz (1992), pp. 103–23.
61. Ibid., pp. 103–23.
62. Guillermo Sunkel (1986), pp. 99–111.
63. It states that in the modern world many political parties have divided into various factions, each one which assumes the name of a party. As a result, the intellectual element of the organic party will, in many cases, belong to none of these factions, but will act as if it were an independent force, superior to all parties. It will usually adopt the guise of a newspaper editorial.

3 THE RIGHT UNFETTERED

1. A characteristic strain of military mentality was its pretensions of neutrality, of being *por encima de los conflictos e intereses* and of playing a tutelary role in relation to all classes in society. The armed forces, who were thrown onto the political stage after years of subordination to civilian authority, refused to appear as mediators for one particular group or as representing the interests of one particular class.
2. Excluding the left which was not seen as a legitimate part of the country's political tradition.
3. Manuel Antonio Garretón first identified these two positions. See Garretón (1984).
4. D.L No. 77, quoted in Pilar Vergara (1985), p. 20.
5. *Ercilla*, 1999, 21 November 1973.
6. The best example of this new emphasis was the *Declaración de Principios del Gobierno de Chile* published in March 1974. This document outlined the main tenets of the regime during this phase and is dealt with in the second part of this chapter.
7. This consisted of an attempt to reconcile economic liberalism with

advanced social policies.

8. Moulian and Torres (1986), pp. 63–118.
9. Andrés Benavente (1982), p. 24.
10. Manuel Antonio Garretón (1978), pp. 1259–82.
11. For more on Kast, see Fontaine (1988).
12. The *secretarías* were government-sanctioned *gremialista* attempts at social mobilization. This was directly related to the concept of *poder social* analysed below.
13. *Ercilla*, No. 2135, 30 June 1976.
14. *Declaración de Principios* (1974).
15. In accordance with the principle of decentralization the *gremialistas* defined *poder político* as the *'facultad de decidir en los asuntos de interés general para la nación, constituye propiamente la función de gobernar el país'*, and was seen as separate to the *poder social*.
16. Guillermo Campero (1984), pp. 294–5.
17. See Fontaine (1988) for an examination of the relationship between the Chicago Boys and the initial post-1973 government economic team.
18. Economic figures in this section are quoted from Stefan de Vylder (1985), pp. 5–49.
19. See Pilar Vargara (1985) for an analysis of the internal struggles.
20. Arturo Fontaine Aldunate (1988), p. 42.
21. Ibid., p. 54.
22. Interview with Rolf Lüders.
23. One possible explanation for Pinochet's reluctance could lie in his distrust of mass political mobilization. The regime was of an essentially authoritarian, rather than totalitarian, nature in which political de-mobilization was favoured as a form of social control, rather than indoctrination, more common in regime's of the latter type.
24. As Arturo Fontaine Aldunate had commented, *'el presidente no deja actuar solos a los economistas. Los comandos no constituyen la totalidad de la fuerza y han de encuadrarse en una disciplina general'*. Arturo Fontaine A. (1988), p. 105.
25. For example, Mario Zañartu, Eduardo García, Patricio Meller, Oscar Muñoz and Andrés Uthoff. All had doctorates in economics from US universities.
26. *Apsi*, No. 101, 16 June 1981.
27. *Analisis*, January 1981.
28. Interview with Rolf Lüders.
29. *Qué Pasa*, no. 250, 5 February 1976.
30. Pilar Vergara (1985), pp. 104–6.
31. *El Mercurio*, 11 July 1977.
32. For an elaboration of this argument, see Garretón (1986).
33. *Ercilla*, 10 May 1978.
34. Pilar Vergara (1985), p. 125.
35. *Qué Pasa*, 19 June 1980.
36. The *comisión constituyente* was set up by the regime to elaborate a future constitutional framework. Guzmán and other *gremialistas* domi-nated this body, although a semblance of ideological plurality was at first introduced.

37. For an elaboration of this thesis, see Pilar Vergara (1985).
38. Interviews with Manuel Antonio Garretón, Tomás Moulian and Isabel Torres.
39. In a conversation with M.A. Garretón, Guzmán admitted in a conversation to his lack of economic understanding: '*Yo de economía no entiendo nada*' (interview with M.A. Garretón).
40. Pilar Vergara (1985), p. 161.

4 THE RIGHT'S INSTITUTIONAL AND POLITICAL LEGACY

1. At the same time, the conservative historian Gonzalo Vial, admired by the gremialistas, was appointed education minister. Education was an area of particular interest to the gremialistas, better understood by them than the 'alien' discipline of economics.
2. The extent to which the *gremialistas* had been neo-liberalized by the end of the 1970s is borne out by their support for the modernizations. As Guzmán wrote, '*Aparte de perjudicar el desarollo económico, ese estatismo exagerado menoscabó fuertemente la libertad de los chilenos para decidir en aquellas materias que dicen más directa relación con su destino personal o familiar, como la libertad de trabajo, de sindicación, de escoger la educacion de los hijos, de elegir entre diversas prestaciones de salud, de resolver sobre la administración de los propios fondos previsionales, y en fin, de emprender una actividad económica sujeta en su éxito sólo a las reglas objetivas e impersonales*' (December 1979).
3. See Pilar Vergara (1985).
4. Ibid.
5. Ibid., pp. 224–7.
6. Nigel Haworth and Jackie Roddick (1981), pp. 49–62.
7. *Qué Pasa*, No. 454, 27 December 1979.
8. Non-union workers could also negotiate with the management under the same conditions as those of union members. This was an attempt to remove the bargaining privileges of organized labour by removing any benefits an employee could receive as a member.
9. Alejandro Foxley (1983), p. 105.
10. Ibid., pp. 106–7.
11. The Chacarillas plan had envisaged an *Estatuto Constitucional Provisorio* which would limit itself to consolidating the regime's *Actas Constitucionales* rather than the adoption of a separate constitution. Opting for the second choice was a clear break from the commitments made by Pinochet in 1977.
12. Jaime Guzmán (December 1979).
13. Jaime Guzmán (June 1979).
14. In allying themselves with the Chicago Boys, the *gremialistas* relinquished any possibility of publicly supporting their traditional concepts of corporatism and communitarianism. The extent of their neo-liberalization was such that it seemed highly unlikely that they maintained a belief in such obviously archaic concepts.

15. *Qué Pasa*, 24 August 1978.
16. Bascuñan and Evans both resigned after the constitutional banning of political parties, while Ovalle was sacked for supposedly criticizing the regime while abroad. Many believe the real reason was his close relationship with the 'maverick' junta leader, Gustavo Leigh.
17. Ascanio Cavallo *et al.* (1988), p. 239.
18. *Ercilla*, 13 September 1978.
19. See Angell and Pollack (1989).
20. The proportion of those not having to pay income tax was increased from one-third to two-thirds. By raising the income tax threshold from US$125 to US$250 a month, approximately one million people were removed from the direct tax-paying bracket. There were also sweeteners for the remaining top third. With income tax reductions ranging from 6 per cent to 23 per cent the government was prepared to lose US$150 million a year in revenue to boost its electoral chances. The reduction of indirect taxes on vehicle and estate sales, as well as the elimination of duties, and a 15 per cent reduction in taxes on electricity and gas consumption, were a blatant attempt to attract any remaining middle-class waverers.
21. *Latin America: Weekly Report*, No. 37, 19 September 1980, p. 6.
22. Eugenio Hojman (1990), p. 137.
23. Hernán Pozo (1987), p. 4.
24. *Constitución de 1980*, Article 8.
25. *Constitución de 1980*, Article 45.
26. Keith Rosen (1987), pp. 23–39.
27. *Constitución de 1980*, Article 95.
28. *Constitución de 1980*, Articles 81 and 82.
29. Pilar Vergara (1985), pp. 203–4.
30. Manuel Antonio Garretón (1983).

5 THE RE-EMERGENCE OF PARTY POLITICS

1. External credits obtained by Chilean private banks more than tripled in 1980.
2. In 1979 the Chicago Boy Finance Minister, Sergio de Castro, fixed the nominal exchange rate at 39 pesos to the dollar.
3. The CRAV financial group collapsed in mid-1981.
4. Real annual short-term interest rates rose from 12 per cent in 1980 to 35 per cent in 1982.
5. Manuel Antonio Garretón (1989), p. 151.
6. Pilar Vergara (1985), pp. 237–8.
7. See Campero (1984) for an analysis of the role of the entrepreneur during this period.
8. Manuel Antonio Garretón (1989), p. 152.
9. The AD, set up in 1983, was made up of the republican right, moderate socialists, Christian Democrats, Radicals and Social Democrats. The MDP consisted of the Communists, radical socialists and the

Movimiento de Izquierda Revolucionario.

10. See Garretón (1989) for an examination of the role of the protests.
11. For the effect of Jarpa's failure successfully to carry out his plan see Garretón (1989).
12. Moulian and Torres (1988), p. 34.
13. *Analisis*, No. 165, 10 March 1987.
14. *Apsi*, No. 127, 4 October 1983.
15. *Apsi*, No. 191, 26 January 1987.
16. The plebiscite would consist of a YES (to the continuation of the regime) and a NO (support for open elections) vote.
17. See chapter 7 for an examination of internal party structures.
18. *Qué Pasa*, No. 883, 10 March 1988.
19. Liberalization of the capital markets, opening up of the economy to the exterior and privatization of the economy.
20. Quoted in Karina Berrier (1989), p. 23.
21. *Apsi*, No. 241, 29 February 1988.
22. The crisis in RN must be seen in the context of events within the military itself. Junta members Rodolfo Stange and Fernando Matthei supported the notion of a consensus candidate. This potential split within the armed forces caused anxiety in the Pinochet camp. Jaime Guzmán shared these concerns. This goes some way to explain his turn-around *vis-à-vis* the plebiscite versus election issue. To have continued supporting the notion of competitive elections would have generated uncontrollable tensions within the pro-government coalition.
23. *Apsi*, No. 244, 21 March 1988.
24. RN internal document (1991), p. 26.
25. Document from RN's first general council held on 16–17 July 1988.
26. Despite Jarpa being re-elected as president in the July 1988 general council, the sector closest to Allamand became the majority, thus displacing the *jarpistas*. Out of the 20 members of the political commission, 13 were supporters of Allamand, three were *jarpistas* and four were independents.
27. See Karina Berrier (1989).
28. *Renovación*, No. 28, October-November 1988.
29. A few days after the result, Fernández appeared on television in an attempt to portray Pinochet's 43 per cent as a victory compared to the whole of the opposition's 54 per cent. He called on the YES parties to defend that victory. This provoked serious incidents in the wealthy districts of Santiago where young UDI supporters and other far right groups caused havoc in the streets.
30. Interview with Carlos Cáceres.
31. The government had delayed the announcement of the result. Even after midnight nothing much was known. The government had only released a limited number of results which showed the YES to be victorious. The NO computers though showed the reverse to be the case. On a television programme, however, Jarpa recognized the NO victory. It was clear that RN was forcing the government to accept the result. General Fernando Matthei's recognition that the votes were not going their way, meant the chances of fraud had greatly diminished. RN's

role in preventing a possible fraud had been crucial and this was recognized by all the opposition political parties. In the morning of 6 October, Allamand made a public declaration calling on the government to release the real results. RN thus consolidated its position as a party independent of the regime and succeeded in becoming, in the eyes of the public, the 'democratic right'. UDI, on the other hand, kept silent. Only on 7 October did it make its first official declarations in which it feebly recognized its failure.

32. RN's *Plan de Organización y Acción Política* (1991).

6 NEW IDENTITIES AND FACES

1. Guillermo O'Donnell (1992), pp. 56–62.
2. Political parties are generally accepted as positive agents for long term democratic stability and consolidation.
3. Among these are RN luminaries such as Andrés Allamand (former party president and ex-deputy who lost the race to be elected senator for Santiago in the December 1997 mid-term congressional election), former Senator Sebastián Piñera (who became a virtual outcast in the right for his support of the NO in the 1988 plebiscite), Deputy Alberto Espina (party leader since April 1997) and Senator Evelyn Matthei (who resigned from RN and joined UDI).
4. The *Patrulla Juvenil* consisted mainly of young politicians, most of whom were under 40. The old guard consisted of much older men, most of whom were already well-established politicians in pre-1973 Chile.
5. See Boylen (1994).
6. Figures such as Miguel Otero, Gonzalo Eguiguren, Enrique Larre, Sergio Romero and Julio Lagos.
7. *Qué Pasa*, No. 1009, 9 August 1990.
8. See chapter 8 for a detailed analysis of these issues.
9. For an analysis of the party's organizational structure, see chapter 7.
10. *Hoy*, No. 666, April 1990.
11. *Hoy*, No. 666, April 1990.
12. *Qué Pasa*, No. 1006, 19 July 1990.
13. In the party directorate, Allamand had the support of Alberto Espina, Carlos Reymond, Félix Viveros and Cristián Correa. In the political commission he could count on the support of Juan Luis Ossa, Francisco Bulnes, Pedro Ibáñez, Miguel Luis Amunátegui, Roberto Palumbo, Fernando Otero, Evelyn Matthei and Sebastián Piñera. In the directorate, Jarpa had the support of Miguel Otero, Gonzalo Eguiguren, Enrique Larre and Marina Prochelle. In the political commission, he could count on Alberto Cardemil (who came first in the elections), Gustavo Alessandri, Catalina Parot, Gustavo Lorca, Francisco Bayo, Sergio Romero and Julio Lagos.
14. *Hoy*, No. 703, 7 January 1991.
15. Interview with Oscar Godoy.
16. See chapter 2 for an analysis of the historical origins of UDI and its

precursor, the *gremialista* movement.

17. Most of the party's most prominent figures were law students at the Catholic University, such as Javier Leturia, Andrés Chadwick, Juan Antonio Coloma and Hernán Chadwick.
18. See Sofía Correa (1993), pp. 164–74.
19. *Apsi*, No. 417, 23 March 1992.
20. *Opus Dei* was also influential in the business world and had links at the time with Juan Antonio Guzmán, president of the *Confederación de la Producción y del Comercio*, and Fernando Agüro, president of Sofofa; in the military with the then commander-in-chief of the navy Admiral Martinéz Bush; in education, especially in the Catholic University's law, philosophy and literature faculties, and now has its own university, Los Andes, and several schools including Los Andes, Huelén, Tabancura and Apoquindo. It is also represented in other newspapers apart from *El Mercurio*, among which are *La Segunda*, *Qué Pasa* and *Ercilla*. The television station *Megavisión* also has links with *Opus Dei*, as have the radio stations Portales and Minería.
21. This 'sameness' is so extreme that in visiting an UDI parliamentarian's office you are confronted with the same room time and time again. For example, three photographs adorn nearly all UDI congressmen's rooms: that of Pinochet, the Pope and Jaime Guzmán.
22. Interview with Miguel Flores.

7 PARTY ORGANIZATION, FINANCE AND SUPPORT

1. See Boron (1992), pp. 89–124.
2. See Ibid. for a more detailed examination of the subject.
3. *Ley Orgánica Constitucional de Partidos Políticos* (1987).
4. RN, *Plan de Organización y Acción Política* (1991).
5. RN, *Evaluación Gestión Organizativa* (1990).
6. RN, *Informe Político y de Prensa*.
7. Before the creation of RN, the magazine represented the views of the *Movimiento de Unión Nacional* (MUN), the party's previous incarnation.
8. Interview with Malcolm Coad.
9. Interview with Eugenio Cantuarias.
10. Interview with Carlos Recondo.
11. Interview with Pablo Longueira.
12. See chapter 8 for an analysis of the party's growth following Guzmán's assassination.
13. Interview with Oscar Godoy.
14. *Hoy*, No. 751, 8 December 1991.
15. All political parties must present their annual accounts to the Electoral Service which makes the information available to the public. However, only limited information has to be made available. According to Electoral Service statistics, UDI's income for 1989 amounted to around US$107,000, which had climbed to around US$222,000 by 1992.

According to the entry all this originated from membership affiliations. There are no entries for donations. RN apparently had an income of about US$564,000 in 1989 and US$401,000 in 1990. Of this total, donations accounted for only around US$25,000 in both years. However, party documents suggest the figure for 1990 could have been as high as US$650,000, most of that originating from large donors. The Christian Democrats, by far the largest and wealthiest Chilean political party, made only US$261,000 in 1989, US$420,000 in 1990 and US$628,000 in 1991. It did not specify what proportion came from affiliations or donations. Only the bare minimum of information is thus provided, and the exceptions are many, for example, how much is donated to the respective parties' research institutes and how much is spent on campaigning. The figures are thus meaningless.

16. See chapter 9 for an examination of the 1989 and 1993 general elections and the 1997 mid-term congressional elections.
17. Interview with Hernán Larraín.
18. Interview with Oscar Godoy.
19. See chapter 3 for an examination of the relationship between the Chicago Boys and the economic groups.
20. Funding by foreign organizations directly into the parties is illegal. Most resources are therefore channelled into the research institutes, many of which are set up with the sole purpose of becoming conduits for foreign funds.
21. See Gibson (1992).
22. For an analysis of RN's policies and strategy, see chapter 8.
23. Interview with Andrés Chadwick.
24. A February 1992 study by the *Centro de Estudios Públicos* presented the following results: only 11.8 per cent of those polled identified themselves as on the right of the political spectrum, while 8.6 per cent identified themselves as on the left. On the other hand, 10 per cent perceived themselves as belonging to the centre-right, 14.6 per cent as centre-left, 38.8 per cent as centre, 8.9 per cent as independents, and 5.2 per cent did not know.
25. Interview with Arturo Fontaine.

8 THE RIGHT IN ACTION

1. See chapter 4 for an analysis of the 1980 constitution.
2. See chapter 4 for a description of the functions and composition of the COSENA.
3. Interview with Oscar Godoy.
4. UDI, *Declaración de Principios* (1983).
5. *Análisis*, No. 334, 4 June 1990.
6. Interview with Oscar Godoy.
7. RN, *Chile: Una Sociedad de Oportunidades, Una Democracia de las Libertades* (1989).
8. For an examination of RN's role as a support instrument for the

military government, see chapter 5.
9. Around 60 per cent of the most serious violations were committed during this period.
10. José Antonio Viera Gallo (1988), p. 35.
11. Since the Supreme Court ruling in 1995 upholding a six-year sentence on former DINA chief General Manuel Contreras for the assassination of Chile's former foreign minister and ambassador to Washington, human rights once again became a salient issue. Prior to the ruling, and in spite of periodic flare-ups, relations between the government and the military had been relatively cordial. The Contreras case led to a deterioration in civil-military relations.
12. UDI, *Declaración de Principios* (1983).
13. Ibid.
14. RN, *Realidad*, No. 6, 1979.
15. *Hoy*, No. 663, 2 April 1990.
16. See Viera Gallo (1988) for an examination of UDI's position on human rights.
17. Viera Gallo (1988).
18. *La Epoca*, 5 June 1988.
19. *Hoy*, No. 674, 18 June 1990.
20. RN, *Renovación*, No.17, May 1987.
21. UDI, *Sobre el Tema Constitucional* (1989).
22. The quest for opposition supremacy was a defining characteristic of both parties' political strategy during this period and will be examined below.
23. See chapter 9 for an examination of the electoral system.
24. This is principally because its support is concentrated in populated urban areas and owing to its ability to wrest from RN, as its coalition partner, a large share of winnable seats.
25. According to Linz, the role of the opposition in a democratic system is to *controlar, fiscalizar y denunciar*. A loyal opposition is one that has an unequivocal commitment to achieve power only through electoral means and a commitment to hand over power unconditionally to other participants with the same desire; a clear and unconditional rejection of the use of violence; a rejection of all unconstitutional appeals to the armed forces; a rejection of violent rhetoric to mobilize support in the quest for power; a commitment to participate in the political process, elections and parliamentary activity without placing conditions beyond those guaranteeing civil liberties necessary for the development of a reasonably just democratic political order; substantive rather than procedural support for democracy and a commitment to define the political role of the neutral powers within reduced limits to ensure the authenticity of the democratic political process (María de la Luz Benavente (1994), pp. 43–8).
26. *Hoy*, No. 703, 7 January 1991.
27. RN Working Paper, *The New Political Scene* (1990).
28. See chapter 7 for an examination of the role and position of the *Instituto Libertad*.
29. See chapter 9 for an examination of the 1989, 1993 and 1997 elections.

30. *Qué Pasa*, No. 1338, 29 November–5 December 1996.
31. Diez was plagued throughout by attempts to unite the RN senators around the party line, while Letelier lacked the will to challenge the government.
32. *Hoy*, No. 716, 8 April 1991.
33. *Antecedentes Para el Congreso Doctrinario 'Jaime Guzmán'* (1991) and *Bases Doctrinarias y Programáticas de la UDI: Resumen de las Conclusiones del Congreso Doctrinario 'Jaime Guzmán'* (1991).
34. The phrase 'inspiration' was changed to *sentido* while 'economic' was removed from the party's principles following a declaration from the Pope stating that economic freedom was but one single aspect of the general notion of freedom.
35. See chapter 3 for an examination of the role of the *gremialistas* in the municipalities during the military government.
36. *Qué Pasa*, No. 1395, 30 December–5 January 1998.

9 POLITICS AND ELECTIONS

1. For RN's position on the elections, see Angell and Pollack (1990 and 1995).
2. Interview with Oscar Godoy.
3. See below for an examination of the role played by the economic right in the presidential selection process.
4. *Cauce*, No. 204, 1 May 1989.
5. *Renovación*, No. 32, June 1989.
6. *Apsi*, No. 300, 13 November 1989.
7. *Hoy*, No. 750, 2 December 1991.
8. See Cristián Bofill (1992) for a detailed examination of the scandal.
9. Family names are very important in Chilean politics. As a result, the mere fact of being the relative of former presidents can provide enough kudos to mount a credible electoral challenge. President Eduardo Frei is a case in point. His political experience and interest were very limited, but he originated from an important political family which includes his father, former President Eduardo Frei (1964–70).
10. *El Mercurio*, 1 August 1993.
11. *El Mercurio*, 9 August 1993.
12. *El Mercurio*, 29 August 1993.
13. *Qué Pasa*, no. 1391, 9–15 December 1997.
14. *La Epoca*, 15 September 1997.
15. Angell and Pollack (1995).
16. Electoral data for the 1997 elections from *La Epoca*, 15 December 1997 and the National Electoral Service.
17. Data from *La Nación*, 13 December 1993.
18. See chapter 8 for an examination of UDI's strategy to penetrate the popular urban areas.

Bibliography

PRIMARY SOURCES

Government Documents

Constitución Política de la República de Chile (1980).
Declaración de Principios del Gobierno de Chile (1974).
Ley Orgánica Constitucional de Partidos Políticos (1987).

Gremialista and UDI Documents

Bases Fundamentales para un Programa de Gobierno (1989).
Declaración de Principios (1983).
Exposición del Presidente de Estudiantes de la Universidad Cátolica ante el Consejo Superior (1969).
El Gremialismo y su Postura Universitaria (1971).
Por La Paz: Propuesta de la UDI Destinada a Subsanar las Dificultades Surgidas Recientemente en las Relaciones Cívico-Militares (1993).
Sobre el Tema Constitucional (1989).
Discurso del Presidente de la UDI Jovino Novoa: Acto de Inauguración Consejo General Extraordinario (1992).
Antecedentes para el Congreso Doctrinario 'Jaime Guzmán' (1991).
Bases Doctrinaria y Programáticas de La UDI: Resumen de las Conclusiones del Congreso Doctrinario 'Jaime Guzmán' (1991).

RN Documents

First General Council document (1988).
Political Declaration of the Third General Council (1990).
Internal document of the Commission of Constitutional Studies (1991).
Evaluation of the General State of the Country: *Comites de Trabajo – RN/Instituto Libertad* (1990).
Renovación (April 1984–August 1990).
Evaluación Gestión Organizativa (1990).
Informe Político y de Prensa (March 1990–November 1993).
RN internal document: Resumé of Party's History (1991).
Plan de Organización y Acción Política (1991).
Chile: Una Sociedad de Oportunidades, Una Democracia de las Libertades (1989).
Definiciones y Objetivos Políticos (1991).
Proposición de Programa de Gobierno: Candidatura Presidencial – Manuel Feliú Justiniano (1993).
Centro de Tecnología Política y Comunicación (1991).

The New Political Scene: Working Paper on the post-1989 election situation (1990).

Plan de Acciones Comunicacionales Estratégico-Políticas Para Enfrentar las Tareas que el Partido Debe Asumir en los Próximos Tres Años (1989).

Instituto Libertad: Reflexiones en Torno a la Opocisión política más allá del Acuerdo Parlamenario y Presidencial, Perspectiva, Vol. 1, No. 11 (April 1993).

Opposition-Government Relations and RN–UDI Relations, *Boletín Semanal del Instituto Libertad* (1990).

Other Right-wing Documents

Declaración de Principios del Partido Nacional (1966).
Programa de Gobierno: Alessandri (1993).

Magazines and Newspapers

Analisis (January 1981–March 1987).
Apsi (December 1983–November 1992).
Cauce (June 1984–May 1986).
El Mercurio (occasionally).
Ercilla (November 1973–April 1980).
Hoy (April 1990–February 1998).
La Epoca (occasionally).
La Nación (occasionally).
Latin American: Weekly Report (occasionally).
Mensaje (October 1984).
Qué Pasa (February 1976–February 1998).

Interviews

Miguel Luis Amunátegui: member of RN political commission (13 August 1992 and 19 January 1994); Pablo Baraona: economy minister in the military government (31 August 1990 and 6 July 1992); Enrique Beltrán: RN metropolitan region executive secretary (29 October 1992); Carlos Cáceres: interior minister in the military government (7 August 1992); Eugenio Cantuarias: UDI senator (20 August 1992); Andrés Chadwick: UDI deputy (19 August 1992); Malcolm Coad: journalist (14 July 1992 and 13 January 1994); Fernando Cuevas: RN executive secretary (17 June 1992); Sergio de la Cuadra: Central Bank president in the military government (24 August 1990); Manuel Délano: journalist (15 September 1992); Sergio Diez: RN senator (20 August 1992); Julio Dittborn: UDI vice-president (22 July 1992); Tomás Duval: researcher at RN's *Instituto Libertad* (27 January 1994); Alberto Espina: RN deputy (20 August 1992); Miguel Flores: UDI central office worker (24 January 1994); Arturo Fontaine Aldunate: former director of *El Mercurio* (22 July 1992); Arturo Fontaine Talavera: political scientist (7 July 1992); Antonio Galilea: RN deputy (18 August 1992); Manuel Antonio Garretón: political scientist (14 August 1990 and 13 October 1992); Oscar Godoy: political scientist (22 July 1992 and 18 January 1994); Mark Klugman: assistant to presidential candidate and former labour minister in the military government, José Piñera (29 July 1992); Hernán Larraín: UDI vice-president (21 August 1992); Cristián Larroulet: researcher at the *Instituto Libertad y Desarrollo* (28 August 1992); Juan Jorge Lazo: adviser to UDI president Jovino Novoa (25 August 1992); Fernando Léniz: economy minister during the military government (3 July 1992); Arturo Longton: RN deputy (19 August 1992); Pablo Longueira: UDI deputy (26 August 1992); Rolf Lüders: finance and economy minister in the military government (16 August 1990); Federico Mekis: RN deputy (19 August 1992); Tomás Moulian: political scientist (13 August 1990 and 29 July 1992); Jaime Orpis: UDI deputy (18 August 1992); Hugo Ortiz: RN senator (20 August 1992); Víctor Pérez: UDI deputy (21 July 1992); Francisco Prat: RN senator (19 August 1992); Tomás Puig: subsecretary of defence (7 July 1992 and 15 July 1992); Carlos Recondo: UDI deputy (20 August 1992); Federico Ringeling: RN deputy (18 August 1992); Marco Riveros: secretary for RN deputies (18 August 1992 and 10 January 1994); Andrés Sanfuentes: president of the *Banco del Estado* (4 August 1992); Raul Sohr: journalist (20 July 1992); Esteban Tomic: PDC councillor (13 July 1992); Isabel Torres: government official (7 September 1990); Mario Varela: UDI metropolitan region president (29 October 1992).

SECONDARY SOURCES

Allamand, Andrés (1989) *Discursos, Entrevistas y Conferencias* (Santiago: Editorial Democracia).

Allamand, Andrés (1993) *La Centro-Derecha del Futuro* (Santiago: Editorial Los Andes).

Alvayay, Rodrigo (1988) 'Estrategia del Gobierno Militar y la Revalorización de la Democracia', *Opciones*, No. 13, January–April.

Angell, Alan (1989) 'Report by the International Commission of the Latin American Studies Association to Observe the Chilean Plebiscite', *Bulletin of Latin American Research*, Vol. 8, No. 2.

Angell, Alan and Benny Pollack (1990) 'The Chilean Elections of 1989 and the Politics of the Transition to Democracy', *Bulletin of Latin American Research*, Vol. 9, No. 1.

Angell, Alan and Benny Pollack (1995) 'The Chilean Elections of 1993: from Polarisation to Consensus', *Bulletin of Latin American Research*, Vol. 14, No. 2, May.

Ashford, Nigel and Stephen Davies (1991) *A Dictionary of Conservative and Libertarian Thought* (London: Routledge).

Baño, Rodrigo (1990) 'Tendencias Políticas y Resultados Electorales Despues de Veinte Años', in *Documentos de Trabajo*, No. 460, September (Santiago: Flacso).

Barry, Norman (1991) in Nigel Ashford and Stephen Davies, *A Dictionary of*

Conservative Thought (London: Routledge).

Benavente, Andrés (1893) *Consideraciones en Torno a la Derecha Política* (Santiago: ICHEH).

Benavente, María de la Luz (1994) *La Nueva Derecha* (Santiago: Instituto de Ciencia Política, Universidad de Chile).

Berrier, Karina (1989) *Derecha Regimental y Coyuntura Plebiscitaria: Los Casos de RN y la UDI* (Santiago: Programa de Investigadores Jóvenes del WUS).

Bofill, Cristián (1992) *Los Muchachos Impacientes* (Santiago: Editorial Copesa).

Boron, Atilio A. (1992) 'Becoming Democrats? Some Sceptical Considerations on the Right in Latin America' in Douglas A. Chalmers, María do Campo Campello de Souza and Atilio Boron (eds) *The Right and Democracy in Latin America* (New York: Praeger).

Bosanquet, Nick (1986) 'Hayek and Friedman', in Nicholas Deakin *et al.*, *The New Right: Image and Reality* (London: The Runnymede Trust).

Boylan, Delia M. (1994) 'Evelyn Matthei: The Rise and Fall of a Technopol', conference paper, *LASA* Conference, Atlanta, 10–12 March .

Brunner, J. J. (1985) 'Estudios' in J. J. Brunner and G. Catalan, *Cinco Estudios sobre Cultura y Sociedad* (Santiago: Flacso).

Cáceres, Carlos (1982) 'La Vía Chilena a la Economía de Mercado', *Estudios Públicos*, No. 6, Segundo Trimestre.

Campero, Guillermo (1984) *Los Gremios Empresariales en el Período 1970–1983* (Santiago: ILET).

Catalan, G (1985) 'UC Gremialismo' in J. J. Brunner and G. Catalan, *Cinco Estudios sobre la Cultura y Sociedad* (Santiago: Flacso).

Cavallo, Ascanio, Manuel Salazar and Oscar Sepulveda (1988) *La Historia Oculta del Régimen Militar* (Santiago).

Caviedes, César N. (1991) *Elections in Chile: The Road Toward Redemocratization* (Colorado: Lynne Rienner Publishers).

Chalmers, Douglas A., María do Carmo Campello de Souza and Atilio Boron (eds) (1992) *The Right and Democracy in Latin America* (New York: Praeger).

Cohen, Gerald (1986) 'The Ideas of Robert Nozick', in Nicholas Deakin *et al.*, *The New Right: Image and Reality* (London: The Runnymede Trust).

Correa, Sofía and Sol Serrano (1984) *Condicionantes Externos Para la Democracia en la Derecha Política* (Santiago: Material para Discusión del CED, No. 11, July).

Correa, Sofía (1985) 'Algunos Antecedentes Históricos del Proyecto Neoliberal en Chile, 1955–1958', *Opciones*, No. 6, May–August.

Correa, Sofía (1993) 'The Chilean Right after Pinochet' in Alan Angell and Benny Pollack (eds) *The Legacy of Dictatorship: Political, Economic and Social Change in Pinochet's Chile*, University of Liverpool Institute of Latin American Studies Monograph Series, No. 17.

Cristi, Renato and Carlos Ruiz (1992) *Pensamiento Conservador en Chile* (Santiago: Editorial Universitaria).

Cristi Renato (1992) 'La Síntesis Conservadora de los Años 70', in Renato Cristi and Carlos Ruiz, *El Pensamiento Conservador en Chile* (Santiago: Editorial Universitaria).

Cruz-Coke, Ricardo (1984) *Historia Electoral de Chile, 1925–1973* (Santiago: Editorial Jurídica de Chile).

Davies, Stephen (1991) in Nigel Ashford and Stephen Davies (eds) *A Dictionary of Conservative and Libertarian Thought* (London: Routledge).

Dooner, Patricio (1984) 'La Prensa Oficialista Escrita en el Período 1973–1983', *Estudios Sociales*, No. 40, Segundo Trimestre.

Drake, Paul W. and Iván Jaksic (eds) (1991) *The Struggle for Democracy in Chile, 1982–1990* (Lincoln: University of Nebraska Press).

Dunleavy, Patrick and Brendan O'Leary (1987) *Theories of the State* (London: Macmillan).

Eatwell, Roger (1989:1) 'Right or Rights? The Rise of the New Right', in Roger Eatwell and Nöel O'Sullivan (eds) *The Nature of the Right: European and American Politics and Political Thought since 1789* (London: Pinter).

Eatwell, Roger (1989:2) 'The Nature of the Right: Is There an Essentialist Philosophical Core?', in Roger Eatwell and Nöel O'Sullivan (eds) *The Nature of the Right: European and American Politics and Political Thought Since 1789* (London: Pinter).

Faúndez, Julio (1988) *Marxism and Democracy in Chile: From 1932 to the Fall of Allende* (London: Yale University Press).

Fontaine A, Arturo (1980) 'Más allá del Leviatán', *Estudios Públicos*, No. 1, December.

Fontaine A., Arturo (1988) *Los Economistas y el Presidente Pinochet* (Santiago: Zig-Zag).

Foxley, Alejandro (1983) *Latin American Experiments in Neo-Conservative Economics* (Los Angeles: University of California Press).

Friedman, M. and R. (1980) *Free to Choose* (London: Penguin).

García, Noel S. (1989) 'El Proyecto de la Nueva Derecha en Estados Unidos y sus Efectos en América Latina', *Política Internacional* (Bogotá), No. 13, January–March.

Garretón, Manuel Antonio (1978) 'De la Seguridad Nacional a la Nueva Institucionalidad: Notas Sobre la Trayectoria Ideológica del Nuevo Estado Autoritario', *Foro Internacional* (Ciudad de Mexico), No. 3.

Garretón, Manuel Antonio (1983) *Modelo y Proyecto del Régimen Militar Chileno* (Santiago: Revista Mexicana de Sociología/Flacso).

Garretón, Manuel Antonio (1984) *Dictadura y Redemocratización* (Santiago: Flacso).

Garretón, Manuel Antonio (1986) in Guillermo O'Donnell, Phillipe Schmitter and Laurence Whitehead, *Transitions from Authoritarian Rule* (Baltimore: Johns Hopkins University Press).

Garretón, Manuel Antonio (1989) 'Mobilization and the Military Régime in Chile: The Complexities of the Invisible Transition', in Susan Eckstein (ed.) *Power and Popular Protest: Latin American Social Movements* (London: University of California Press).

Geisse, Francisco and José Antonio Ramírez Arrayas (eds) (1989) *La Reforma Constitucional* (Santiago: CESOC).

Gibson, Edward L. (1992) 'Conservative Electoral Movements and Democratic Politics: Core Constituencies, Coalition-Building and the Latin American Electoral Right' in Chalmers, Douglas A., María do Carmo Campello de Souza and Atilio Boron (eds) *The Right and*

Democracy in Latin America (New York: Praeger).

Gress, Franz (1986) 'The New Right in France and the Federal Republic of Germany', in Nicholas Deakin *et al.*, *The New Right: Image and Reality* (London: The Runnymede Trust).

Guzmán, Jaime (1987) *Líderes Políticos de Cara Hacia el Futuro*, Interview by Juan Pablo Illanes (Santiago: Documento de Trabajo del CEP).

Guzmán, Jaime (1979) 'El Sufragio Universal y la Nueva Institucionalidad Política', *Realidad*, No. 1, June.

Guzmán, Jaime (1979) 'El Camino Político', *Realidad*, No. 7, December.

Guzmán, Jaime (1992) *Escritos Personales* (Santiago: Zig-Zag).

Haworth, N. and J. Roddick (1981) 'Labour and Monetarism in Chile, 1975–1980', *Bulletin of Latin American Research*, Vol. 1, No. 1, October.

Hojman, Eujenio (1990) *Memorial de la Dictadura* (Santiago: Editorial Emisión).

King, Desmond (1987) *The New Right: Politics, Markets and Citizenship* (London: Macmillan).

Klugman, Mark (1992) 'The Crisis within the Right', in *Puntos de Referencia, CEP*, No. 100, June.

Lecaros, Augusto (1984) 'El Gremialismo y la Unión Demócrata Independiente Frente a la Tradición Hispana' (Santiago: unpublished thesis).

Levine, Barry B. (ed.) (1992) *El Desafío Neoliberal: El Fin del Tercermundismo en América Latina* (Bogotá: Grupo Editorial Norma).

Levitas, Ruth (1986) 'Ideology and the New Right', in Ruth Levitas (ed.) *The Ideology of the New Right* (London: Blackwell and Polity Press).

Meller, Patricio (1984) 'Los Chicago Boys y el Modelo Económico Chileno, 1973–1983', *Apuntes CIEPLAN*, No. 43, January.

Mouffe, Chantal (1982) 'Democracia y Nueva Derecha', *Escritos de Teoría*, V, October.

Moulian, Tomás and Pilar Vergara (1980) 'Estado, Ideología y Políticas Económicas en Chile, 1973–1978', *Estudios CIEPLAN*, No. 3, June.

Moulian, Tomás and Isabel Torres (1986) 'La Derecha en Chile: Evolución Histórica y Proyecciones a Futuro', *Estudios Sociales*, No. 47, trimestre 1.

Moulian, Tomás and Isabel Torres (1988) *La Reorganización de los Partidos de la Derecha Entre 1983 y 1988* (Santiago: Documento de Trabajo de Flacso).

Nisbet, Robert A. (1967) *The Sociological Tradition* (London: Heinemann).

Nugent, Neill and Roger King (1977) *The British Right* (London: Saxon House).

O'Donnell, Guillermo (1986) in Guillermo O'Donnell, Phillipe Schmitter and Laurence Whitehead, *Transitions from Authoritarian Rule* (Baltimore: Johns Hopkins University Press).

O'Donnell, Guillermo (1992) 'Substantive or Procedural Consensus: Notes on the Latin American Bourgeoisie' in Douglas A. Chalmers, María do Carmo Campello de Souza and Atilio Boron (eds) *The Right and Democracy in Latin America* (New York: Praeger).

Oppenheim, Lois Hecht (1993) *Politics in Chile: Democracy, Authoritarianism and the Search for Development* (Boulder: Westview Press).

Ossa, Juan Luis (1970) *Nacionalismo Hoy* (Santiago: no publisher).

Ossandón, Fernando (1986) 'El Mercurio y la Represión, 1973–1978', in Fernando Reyes Matta, Carlos Ruíz and Guillermo Sunkel (eds) *Investigación Sobre la Prensa en Chile 1974–1984* (Santiago: CERC/ILET).

O'Sullivan, Nöel (1992) 'The Quest for a Civil Philosophy in Europe and America', in Roger Eatwell and Nöel O'Sullivan, *The Nature of the Right: European and American Politics and Political Thought since 1789* (London: Pinter).

Pollack, Marcelo (1995) 'The Right and the Transition to Democracy', in David Hojman (ed.) *Neo-Liberalism with a Human Face? The Politics and Economics of the Chilean Model*, University of Liverpool Institute of Latin American Studies, Monograph Series, No. 20.

Pozo, Hernán (1987) *1989? La Constitución de 1980* (Santiago: Materias de Difusión de Flacso).

Ryan, Alan (1986) 'Roger Scruton and Neo-Conservatism', in Nicholas Deakin *et al.*, *The New Right: Image and Reality* (London: The Runnymede Trust).

Rosen, Keith S. (1987) 'Soberanía y Participación Política en la Constitución de 1980', in Francisco Geisse and Rafael Gumucio (eds) *Elecciones Libres y Plebiscito: El Desafio Democrático* (Santiago: CESOC).

Rodríguez, Pablo (1977) *Democracia Liberal o Democracia Orgánica?* (Santiago: Cuadernos del Instituto de Ciencia Política de la Universidad Católica de Chile).

Ruiz, Carlos (1992) 'Corporativismo e Hispanismo en la Obra de Jaime Eyzaguirre', in Renato Cristi and Carlos Ruiz, *El Pensamiento Conservador en Chile* (Santiago: Editorial Universitaria).

Ruiz, Carlos (1992) 'El Conservativismo como Ideología: Corporativismo y Neo-Liberalismo en las Revistas Teóricas de la Derecha', in Renato Cristi and Carlos Ruiz, *El Pensamiento Conservador en Chile* (Santiago: Editorial Universitaria).

Schamis, Hector E. (1992) 'Conservative Political Economy in Latin America and Western Europe: The Political Sources of Privatisation' in Douglas A. Chalmers, María do Carmo Campello de Souza and Atilio Boron (eds) *The Right and Democracy in Latin America* (New York: Praeger).

Silva, Patricio (1991) 'Technocrats and Politics in Chile: From the Chicago Boys to the CIEPLAN Monks', *Journal of Latin American Studies* 23 (2).

Silva, Patricio (1993) 'Intellectuals, Technocrats and Social Change in Chile: Past, Present and Future Perspectives', in Alan Angell and Benny Pollack (eds) *The Legacy of Dictatorship: Political, Economic and Social Change in Pinochet's Chile*, University of Liverpool Institute of Latin American Studies Monograph Series, No. 17.

Solar, Julio Silva (1987) 'Constitución de 1980: Obstáculo Para la Transición a la Democracia', in Francisco Geisse and Rafael Gunicio (eds) *Elecciones Libres y Plebiscito: El Desafío Democrático* (Santiago: CESOC).

Subercaseaux, Julio (1983) *Estudio Sobre la Derecha Democrática* (Santiago: ICHEH).

Sunkel, Guillermo (1986) 'El Mercurio Como Medio de Educación Político-Ideológico, 1969–1979', in Fernando Reyes Matta, Carlos Ruíz and Guillermo Sunkel (eds) *Investigación Sobre la Prensa en Chile, 1974–1984* (Santiago: CERC/ILET).

Valdés, Juan Gabriel (1989) *La Escuela de Chicago: Operación Chile* (Buenos Aires: Editorial Zeta).

Valdés, Juan Gabriel (1995) *Pinochet's Economists: The Chicago School in Chile* (Cambridge: Cambridge University Press).

Valenzuela, Arturo (1987) *The Breakdown of Democratic Régimes: Chile* (London: Johns Hopkins University Press).

Valenzuela, Arturo (1989) 'Chile: Origins, Consolidation and Breakdown of a Democratic Régime', in Larry Diamond, Juan J. Linz and Seymour Martin Lipset (eds) *Democracy in Developing Countries: Latin America* (London: Adamantine Press).

Vergara, Pilar (1985) *Auge y Caída del Neoliberalismo en Chile* (Santiago: Flacso).

Viera Gallo, José Antonio and Teresa Rodríguez Allendes (1988) *Ideologías, Partidos Políticos y Derechos Humanos: La Derecha* (Santiago: Programa de Derechos Humanos, Cuadernos de Trabajo, No. 7).

Vylder, Stefan de (1985) 'Chile 1973–1984: Auge, Caída, Consolidación y Crisis del Modelo Neoliberal', *Ibero-Americana, Nordic Journal of Latin American*.

Index